CW00471952

Adaptive Project

Framework

Adaptive Project Framework

Managing Complexity in the Face of Uncertainty

Robert K. Wysocki, Ph.D.

✦✦Addison-Wesley

Upper Saddle River, NJ • Boston • Indianapolis • San Francisco
New York • Toronto • Montreal • London • Munich • Paris • Madrid
Capetown • Sydney • Tokyo • Singapore • Mexico City

Many of the designations used by manufacturers and sellers to distinguish their products are claimed as trademarks. Where those designations appear in this book, and the publisher was aware of a trademark claim, the designations have been printed with initial capital letters or in all capitals.

The author and publisher have taken care in the preparation of this book, but make no expressed or implied warranty of any kind and assume no responsibility for errors or omissions. No liability is assumed for incidental or consequential damages in connection with or arising out of the use of the information or programs contained herein.

The publisher offers excellent discounts on this book when ordered in quantity for bulk purchases or special sales, which may include electronic versions and/or custom covers and content particular to your business, training goals, marketing focus, and branding interests. For more information, please contact:

U.S. Corporate and Government Sales
(800) 382-3419
corpsales@pearsontechgroup.com

For sales outside the United States please contact:

International Sales
international@pearson.com

Visit us on the Web: informit.com/aw

Library of Congress Cataloging-in-Publication Data

Wysocki, Robert K.
  Adaptive project framework : managing complexity in the face of uncertainty / Robert K. Wysocki.
    p. cm.
  Includes index.
  ISBN 978-0-321-52561-1 (pbk. : alk. paper) 1. Project management. I. Title.
  HD69.P75W93 2010
  658.4'04—dc22

                                                        2009045216

ISBN-13: 978-0-321-52561-1
ISBN-10:   0-321-52561-2

Text printed in the United States on recycled paper at RR Donnelley in Crawfordsville, Indiana.
First printing, January 2010

Editor-in-Chief
Karen Gettman

Acquisitions Editor
Chris Guzikowski

Development Editor
Sheri Cain

Managing Editor
John Fuller

Project Editor
Anna Popick

Copy Editor
Steve Freedkin

Indexer
Jack Lewis

Proofreader
Linda Begley

Editorial Assistant
Raina Chrobak

Cover Designer
Chuti Prasertsith

Compositor
Molly Sharp

Contents

Preface

I feel a sense of relief and accomplishment in completing this book. The Adaptive Project Framework (APF) was born in two client engagements—one a product-development project, and the other a process-design project. It was not our intention to build another approach to project management. Our intention was to solve client problems. An unexpected deliverable was APF.

The projects had two things in common. For both projects, the goals were clearly known, but the solutions were not. These points of intersection between the two projects became the two variables that drove the definition of the project landscape used extensively in this book.

Since then, I have been all over the world speaking at conferences and professional society meetings about APF and how it differs from the myriad other agile approaches. Virtually all agile approaches are designed for software-development projects. Sometimes it is hard to tell the difference between the software-development life cycle and the project-management life cycle. Where does one start and the other leave off? APF was not built as a software-development project management methodology. It is robust in the sense that it applies to any type of project, including software development.

This book has been on my mind for almost ten years. As APF continues to gain in adoption, I will certainly incorporate learnings from those experiences into future editions. I welcome your sharing of experiences using APF. APF is a work-in-process, so this book is also a work-in-process. Please contact me at rkw@eiicorp.com.

Acknowledgments

So many of my colleagues and clients have offered comments on APF—both supportive and critical. To all of them I am indebted. Each in their own way has made a contribution to APF, and now to this book.

I owe a special thanks to the technical reviewers:

- Greg Githens, Partner at Catalyst Management Consulting
- Bob Tarne, Senior Program Manager at Lombardi Software
- Chuck Walrad, Managing Director at Davenport Consulting
- Kent McDonald, Program Manager at Wellmark Blue Cross and Blue Shield

All of these gentlemen spent considerable time reading the manuscript and offering their candid comments. I know the end product is much better because of their efforts.

About the Author

 **Robert K. Wysocki, Ph.D.,** has more than forty years of experience as a project-management consultant and trainer, information-systems manager, systems and management consultant, author, and training developer and provider. He has written sixteen books on project and information-systems management. One of his books, *Effective Project Management,* now in its fifth edition, has been a best seller and is recommended by the Project Management Institute for the library of every project manager. The book has been adopted by more than one hundred colleges and universities worldwide, as well as by training organizations, companies, and practicing professionals. Dr. Wysocki has published more than thirty articles and presentations in professional and trade journals, and has made more than one hundred presentations at professional and trade conferences and meetings. He has developed more than twenty project-management courses and trained more than ten thousand senior project managers.

In 1990, Dr. Wysocki founded Enterprise Information Insights (EII), Inc., a project-management consulting and training practice specializing in project-management methodology design and integration; project support office establishment; development of training curricula; and development of a portfolio of assessment tools focused on organizations, project teams, and individuals. His clients include AT&T, Aetna, Babbage Simmel, the British Computer Society, Boston University Corporate Education Center, Computerworld, Converse Shoes, the Czechoslovakian government, Data General, Digital, Eli Lilly, Harvard Community Health Plan, IBM, J. Walter Thompson, Novartis, Ohio State University, Peoples Bank, Sapient, the Limited, the State of Ohio, Travelers Insurance, the U.S. Army Signal Corps, Wal-Mart, Wells Fargo, ZTE, and several others.

Dr. Wysocki is Series Editor for Effective Project Management for Artech House, a publisher for the engineering profession. He is a member of the ProjectWorld Executive Advisory Board, the Project Management Institute, the American Society for Training & Development, and the Society for Human Resource Management. He is past Vice President of the Association of Information Technology Professionals (AITP, formerly the Data Processing Management Association). Dr. Wysocki earned a B.A. in mathematics from the University of Dallas, and an M.S. and a Ph.D. in mathematical statistics from Southern Methodist University.

Introduction

The traditional world of project management belongs to yesterday. There will continue to be applications for which the traditional linear models we grew up with are appropriate, but as our profession matures we have discovered a whole new set of applications for which traditional project management (TPM) models are totally inappropriate. The majority of contemporary projects do not meet the conditions needed for using TPM models. The primary reason is the difficulty in specifying complete requirements at the beginning of the project. That difficulty arises from constant change, unclear business objectives, actions of competitors, and other factors.

Not having a complete and defined set of requirements precludes generating a complete work breakdown structure (WBS), required by all TPM models. Most observers would agree that except for the simplest of projects, it is not possible to specify complete requirements at the start of a project. Even if you could, one could easily argue that the world doesn't stand still just because you are managing a project. Changes in business conditions, the competition, and technology all can and do render requirements incomplete or at least misguided. The contemporary business climate is one of unbridled change and speed. Requirements are never really established; they continue to change throughout the life of the project. Cyclical and recursive models are coming into vogue; yet, many organizations continue to try to fit square pegs into round holes. How foolish, and what a waste of time and money. The paradigm must shift, and any company that doesn't embrace that shift is sure to be lost in the rush. Alan Deutschman's axiom "change or die" was never truer than it is in today's project-management environment.[1]

---

[1] Alan Deutschman, *Change or Die: The Three Keys to Change at Work and in Life* (New York: HarperBusiness, 2007).

The Contemporary Project Landscape

Change is constant and unpredictable! That comes as no surprise to anyone. In fact, change itself is changing at an accelerating pace. That should come as no surprise to anyone either. Yesterday's practices belong to yesterday. Today is a new day with new challenges. All project managers, whether the most senior or simply the "wannabes," are challenged to think about how to effectively adapt their approaches to managing projects rather than routinely follow yesterday's recipe.

There is a great deal of uncertainty on the road to breakthrough performance. Success will not come unless accompanied by courage, creativity, and flexibility. If we simply rely on the routine application of an off-the-shelf methodology, failure is very likely. As you will see in the pages that follow, I am not afraid to step outside the box and perhaps take you outside of your comfort zone. I am going to stretch your thinking about how to deliver effective project management, and hence deliver expected business value.

Nowhere is there more need for change than in the approaches you take to managing the class of project whose solution is not clearly defined or whose goal is only vaguely defined. These projects occur often, and most often do not fit your current practices. Anecdotal data I have collected from my world travels suggest that at least 70 percent of all projects do not fit the traditional, linear project-management life cycle that we have grown up with. A challenge has been issued to all of us. That challenge is to align our project-management processes and techniques with the changing needs of the project, your business environment, and the markets you serve—or risk being dismissed as irrelevant. That means we must embrace change in our approaches and models, as well as develop models that embrace change. The goal of this book is to introduce a new approach to managing projects—one that rises to these challenges. I call this approach the Adaptive Project Framework (APF).

The initial version of APF was developed as part of two separate engagements with my clients. Neither of these was a software-development project. In one engagement, the client required development of a project-management life cycle (PMLC) that was fully integrated into a systems-development life cycle (SDLC). The other engagement was to design a kiosk application for a large supermarket chain. So, one project involved business process design, while the other involved new-product development. APF can be applied to both types. That sets APF apart from most of the Agile approaches, which are designed around software-development projects. I'll have more to say on both of these engagements as two of the four case studies used in this book.

Buried beneath the mysticism that surrounds the technology revolution, a problem has surfaced. Businesspersons have an insatiable appetite to have their wants met. Sounds good so far, and no one would deny them that right. Surely technology could come to their rescue and help them get what they wanted. However, I have learned that wants are often the clients' expression of what they think is a solution to some unstated or poorly defined problem they face. If we are lucky and their wants accurately reflect the solution to their problem, then the direction of the project is clear. But wants don't often align with needs. Therefore, if you focus on satisfying wants, you may be focusing your attention in the wrong place and courting possible failure. Behind those wants are the true needs, which are often not stated. The businessperson has not distinguished between wants and needs; in fact, the wants have gotten in the way of seeing the real needs. This is not a matter of prioritization. It is a lack of understanding of the problem. This situation has persisted from the beginning of the technology revolution to this day.

If you remember anything from this introduction, remember the message conveyed in Figure I.1: that what the client wants is probably not what the client needs. If you blindly accept what clients say they want and proceed with a project on that basis, both you and the clients may be in for a rude awakening. You will have built something the clients cannot use. Often

Figure I.1
Wants versus
Needs

What the client wants is probably not what the client needs.
The project manager's job is to make clients want what they need.

in the process of building the solution, the clients learn that what they need is not the same as what they say they wanted. Here we have the basis for rolling deadlines, scope creep, and an endless trail of changes, reworks, over-budget situations, and schedule slippages. TPM has to strain to keep up with the realities of projects such as these. A lot of time is wasted planning things that never happen. It's no wonder that more than 65 percent of projects fail. That has to stop.

We need two things. The first is a process for discovering the needs that underlie the wants. Continuously asking "why" questions can uncover needs. I use Root Cause Analysis almost exclusively to peel away the wants and get to the real needs. Second, we need an approach that is built around change—one that embraces learning and discovery throughout the project life cycle. The approach must recognize that change will occur regardless of our attempts to the contrary. Our approach must have built-in processes to accommodate the changes that result from the learning and discovery that will certainly take place during execution of the project.

This book introduces a model that was designed precisely to accommodate these requirements. APF is that model. The name APF was carefully chosen.

Adaptive

From its very beginning to its very end, APF is designed to continuously adapt to the changing situation of a project. A change in the understanding of the solution might prompt a change in the way the project is managed, or in the very approach being used. Learning and discovery in the early cycles may lead to a change in the approach taken. For example, starting with an APF approach, you quickly discover the complete solution from the first few cycles of the project plan. Should you continue to use APF? Maybe some other Agile Project Management (APM) model would now fit better, or you might consider switching to some form of TPM, say an incremental approach. The new characteristics of the project will be the basis for any change of approach.

Nothing in APF is fixed. Every part of it is variable, and it constantly adjusts to the characteristics of the project. The changes in APF are not taken from a predefined list of possible changes. The changes in approach are a creative response to the changing needs of the situation. Obviously, APF requires meaningful involvement of the client and the project team, acting in an open and trusting partnership. Anything short of that will invite failure. To be successful with APF, you have to think like a chef and not like a cook! The cook can only follow recipes, and if an ingredient is missing, may be at a loss as to how to continue. A chef, on the other hand, has the skills and experiences to adapt to the situation and create recipes that work within the constraints of available ingredients.

My girlfriend provides an excellent example of what I mean. She makes a cheesecake that is to die for. Late one Sunday evening, she asked whether I would like her to bake a cheesecake for us. That's a no-brainer for me, and so I said "you bet." A few minutes after she started, I heard some rummaging around in the cupboards, followed by a moan from the kitchen. There was no vanilla extract, and that was an essential ingredient of her recipe. It was too late to go to the market, so I suggested she put the batter in the fridge and we'd pick up the vanilla extract in the morning. A few minutes later, I could smell a cheesecake in the oven. Maybe she had found the vanilla extract? No she hadn't. Instead, she found a container of vanilla frosting, and vanilla extract was one of its main ingredients. She figured out how much vanilla frosting would equal the vanilla extract called for in the cheesecake recipe and used that instead. The cheesecake was awesome! So what does this have to do with project management? My point is that if all you can do is blindly follow someone else's recipe for managing a project, you won't have a chance. But if you can create a recipe adapted to the conditions of the moment, you will have planted the seeds of success.

Project

Projects are unique, and are never repeated under the same set of circumstances. So why isn't our approach to managing them unique as well? I'm not advocating a wholesale change in management approach, but rather a thought-out approach—one that takes into account and deals with the vagaries of the project. There are project, organizational, and environmental characteristics to account for in choosing the best-fit project management approach. Among the characteristics I have encountered, the following arise frequently, and their impacts must be considered in your final decision as to the best-fit approach:

- Risk
- Cost
- Duration
- Complexity
- Market Stability
- Business Value
- Technology Used
- Business Climate
- Client Involvement
- Goal and Solution Clarity
- Number of Departments Affected
- Organizational Environment
- Team Skills and Competencies
- Completeness of Requirements
- Project Manager and Team Member Availability

Any combination of these project characteristics can cause a change in how the project is approached. For example, if a project approach requires heavy client involvement and you know from experience with this client that that won't happen on this project, then you wouldn't choose that approach. That may mean you have to compromise and choose a less-than-ideal approach to work around lack of meaningful client involvement. (*Chaos Report 2007*[2] lists, for the very first time, lack of meaningful client involvement as the number-one reason why projects fail.) Alternatively, you might build in a workshop on client involvement, and based on the results of the workshop make your decision on which project-management approach to use.

---

[2] Standish Group, *Chaos Report 2007: The Laws of CHAOS* (Boston: Standish Group International, 2007).

As another example, suppose your organizational environment is characterized by frequent reorganization and realignment of roles and responsibilities. In such an environment, sponsorship and priorities of active projects will change. Your best-fit project management approach should be one in which deliverables are introduced in increments or short intervals rather than all-at-once at the end of a long project. Such a strategy will reduce the risk of wasted resources and loss of business value due to early termination of the project. I'll return to this discussion in Chapter 9: APF Frequently Asked Questions.

Framework

APF has several variations. I compare it to following a recipe versus creating a recipe. TPM follows recipes. APF follows a framework. The TPM project manager needs to know how to follow a step-by-step task list with little thought of why. The TPM project manager is, in a certain sense, captive to the accompanying project-management approach. APF, on the other hand, creates recipes. APF project managers need to understand the situation they face and adapt their toolkits to fit the situation. APF allows for that adaptation as the project situation changes. The APF project manager is in charge of the approach rather than the approach being in charge of the project manager, as is the case with TPM projects.

In order to place APF in the proper context, I like to envision the various project-management approaches as being mapped into a very simple project landscape. That is the topic of the next section.

The project-management environment is an ever-changing one. It is defined by no fewer than seven interdependent variables. They are:

1. The characteristics of the environment in which the project will be executed
2. The characteristics of the project itself
3. The business process life cycle
4. The project management life cycle
5. The profile of the project team
6. The profile of the client team
7. The hardware/software technology to support the whole endeavor

While this may seem overwhelming, it isn't. I'll explore the complexities of this multi-dimensional environment with you and show you how to obtain and sustain an effective project-management presence in this changing environment.

For years now, management gurus have preached that an effective organization is one where there is a balance among staff, process, and technology. Staff is smart. Of that there is no doubt. How many times have you heard an executive say, "Just put five of our smart people together in a room and they will solve any problem you can throw at them"? That may be true, but I don't think anyone would bet the future of the enterprise on the continuing heroic efforts of an anointed few. Technology is racing ahead faster than any organization can absorb, so that can't be the obstacle. Process is the only thing left, and it is to the business process that we turn our attention in this book. But it isn't just your normal everyday business process that interests us. We are going to look at a process that is really a process to define a process, rather than a staid and fixed approach—or recipe as I like to call it. Following the recipe analogy a bit further, I want to teach you how to create the recipe rather than just blindly follow some predefined recipe.

Balance between Staff, Process, and Technology

Several researchers have observed that successful organizations exhibit a balance among staff, process, and technology. As far as I know, no one has been able to build an assessment tool to measure the extent to which that balance exists. Several years ago, I undertook a project to develop an assessment instrument that measures the project-management balance in an organization with respect to the priority (and attention) it gives to staff, process, and technology. The assessment instrument is used to establish the current state and desired end state, and to suggest strategies for evolving from the current state to the desired end state. The underlying model that I developed is shown in Figure I.2.

The triangle represents the three dimensions that determine project management balance: staff, process, technology. For the purposes of this assessment tool, Staff refers to the project team. Process refers to the project-management strategy that has been selected for the project. (The same model applies to any business process.) Finally, Technology refers to

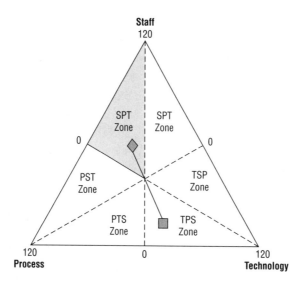

Figure I.2
The Balance
among Staff,
Process, and
Technology in
an Organization

the tools, templates, hardware, and software that support the chosen project-management process.

The triangle is divided into six non-overlapping zones. Each zone is named with a combination of the letters **S** (representing Staff), **P** (Process), and **T** (Technology). Their ordering in the sector name gives us the ordering of their distances from each vertex, with the closest vertex listed first. The closer to a vertex a data point lies, the more important is that vertex to the organization. So, the combination SPT would mean that Staff is most important, Process less important, and Technology of even lesser importance to the organization. The ordering in this example also means that Staff (the project team) drives the choice of Process (the PMLC model) and that Staff and Process drive the choice of Technology (supporting hardware and software to be used).

The scores for each of the three parameters are linearly constrained. For this model the sum of their scores is 200, but it could be any number. This means that there is a dependency among the three parameters, and that every data point is constrained to lie within the boundary of the triangle.

The assessment data is summarized along these three dimensions and represented in the form of a straight line with a square at one end (current state) and a diamond at the other (desired state). The distance of the end points of the line to the vertices of the triangle give us a comparative measure of the priority of the given dimension to the organization. The closer the end point is to the vertex, the higher is the priority of the variable associated with that vertex. In this example, the location of the square tells us that the organization currently places a high degree of importance on Technology, less on Process, and least on Staff. In other words, the technology infrastructure has been dictated. That infrastructure determines the project-management process to be used, and the project team is chosen to be compatible with the established technology and process infrastructure. The location of the diamond tells us that the desired project-management culture is to have more-or-less equal importance placed on Process and Technology (Process has a bit higher priority than Technology), with the highest priority given to Staff. In other words, members of the project team are chosen first. They then determine the best project-management strategy to be used for the project they are to be assigned to, and finally they choose from among all available technologies those that best support their choice of project-management strategy. The SPT zone is the zone that should be preferred by most organizations, although not every organization will have the same desired end state. There will be variations depending on industry. For example, financial institutions will depend more heavily on Process and Technology, whereas the retailing industry might depend more heavily on Staff and Process.

The length of the line is directly proportional to the degree of organizational change that will be needed for the organization to reach its desired support environment. As part of my research, I expect to develop strategies to help the organization move from its current state to its desired state. If you are interested in more information about the SPT assessment tool, please contact me at rkw@eiicorp.com.

In this book, I take the position that the characteristics of a project are the entry point into this model, and those characteristics drive our choice as to the team skills and competencies needed; then the team will determine the project-management tools, templates, and processes that should be used; and finally, the team and the tools, templates, and processes chosen will determine the best-fit technology to support it all. Obviously, this is not a recipe book to be blindly followed. Rather, it is a framework that teaches you how to create a recipe. Figure I.3 tells my story clearly. In other words, one of my objectives is to help you think like a great project manager and become a great project manager.

Figure I.3
Would You
Rather Be a
Chef Than a
Cook?

Would you rather follow a recipe
or know how to create a recipe?

Characteristics of the Project

When I think of the project-management landscape, I think of it at a higher level of abstraction than the seven variables discussed earlier. In keeping with my penchant for the simple and intuitive, I visualize it as a simple two-dimensional grid like the one shown in Figure I.4. The first dimension relates to the goal of the project. It has two values. The goal is either clearly specified (therefore completely known) or not clearly specified (therefore not completely known). The second dimension relates to the solution, or how you expect to reach the goal. That also has two values. The solution is either clearly specified (therefore completely known) or not clearly specified (therefore not completely known). If we intersect these two dimensions as shown in the figure, we have defined a four-category classification of projects. It is important to note that the boundary between clear and not-clear is a conceptual boundary. It is not quantitatively defined, but is only conceptually defined. This classification is simple, but it is inclusive of every project that ever was or ever will be. That is, every project must fall into one and only one of these four quadrants:

- TPM: Traditional Project Management (linear and incremental PMLC models)
- APM: Agile Project Management (iterative and adaptive PMLC models)
- xPM: Extreme Project Management (extreme PMLC models)
- MPx: Emertxe Project Management (extreme PMLC models)

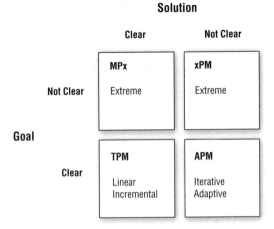

Figure I.4
The Project-management Landscape

The projects in the TPM quadrant are those for which the goal and the solution are clearly defined. These will be simple projects that have been repeated a number of times in the past. There will be well-developed templates for all, or significant parts, of these projects. Because these projects are very familiar to the organization, the requirements will be known as well. Having complete requirements means that the solution will be clearly defined and the complete work breakdown structure (WBS) can be generated. TPM models will work quite well for these projects.

Next in order of increasing uncertainty are projects in the APM quadrant. The range of projects will be from those where the goal is clearly defined and most of the solution is known (perhaps with the exception of choosing how to render some features) to those where very little of the solution is known, and it must be discovered as part of the PMLC model chosen for managing the project. Because some of the solution is unknown, the risk associated with these projects is much higher than the risk associated with projects in the TPM quadrant. The successful completion of such projects will be critical to the organization. The business value must therefore be high enough to warrant taking on these higher-risk projects. Obviously, the requirements can't be clearly and completely defined because that would imply knowing the complete solution. Therefore a complete WBS cannot be generated, and TPM Models cannot be used. What's needed instead are PMLC models that incorporate solution-learning and -discovery features so that the complete solution can be found as part of executing the project.

Our focus in this book will be on APF approaches which fall in the APM quadrant.

Next in the order of increasing uncertainty are projects in the xPM quadrant. For these projects, neither the goal nor the solution is clearly known; they must be concurrently learned and discovered as part of executing the project. These are usually R&D projects for which the risk of failure is very high. For these projects, the best-fit PMLC model must embrace a great deal of uncertainty and include investigative cycles that are designed to converge on a goal and a solution to support that goal. Even when that may be done successfully, there remains the question of business value. Does the solution to the now clearly defined goal offer sufficient business value to be useful to the organization? A good example of this situation is the project that eventually led 3M to the Post-it Note product. The glue produced from the original project did not deliver a product that had business value as originally defined, and sat on the shelf for about seven years until someone found an application with business value.

The discovery of that business value came from a project from the MPx quadrant. Projects in the MPx quadrant may seem like nonsense projects at first glance. Are there meaningful projects that consist of a solution looking for a problem? In fact there are. Wal-Mart's initial investigation of the newly introduced RFID technology provides a good example. The question Wal-Mart was asked in this MPx project was: "Can you find an application (the project goal) of RFID technology (the solution) that has business value?" This sounds like an xPM quadrant project, but with the sequence reversed. That is why I call these projects **Emertxe** projects. If you haven't already observed, Emertxe is Extreme spelled backwards. Both the xPM and MPx quadrants are heavily populated by R&D projects. The xPM-quadrant projects are projects looking for a solution to a fuzzily defined goal. The MPx-quadrant projects are projects looking for an application (the goal) of a technology (the solution or some variant of it) that has business value. xPM and MPx projects use the same PMLC model. An MPx project can be very simple or very complex. Refer to Chapter 8: APF in the Extreme for more details.

The best-fit quadrant can change as the project progresses. For example, early in a project's life cycle, the goal may be clearly defined but the solution not clearly defined. That places the project in the APM quadrant, and the best-fit project management process for that quadrant can be chosen. As the project progresses, the solution may be discovered and become clearly defined. The project then moves to the TPM quadrant. The best-fit PMLC model approach may be changed from one in the APM quadrant to one in the TPM quadrant. There are a number of considerations when one is faced with this decision. They are discussed in Chapter 9: APF Frequently Asked Questions.

I contend that APM represents a class of projects that is continuously growing. I have traveled throughout the U.S., Europe, and Asia and have asked project managers what percentage of their projects falls into each of the quadrants. With very little variance in the estimates, they believe that 20 percent of their projects fall in the TPM quadrant, with 70 percent in the APM quadrant and 10 percent split between the xPM and MPx quadrants. I believe that the industry a company is in will have an impact on these percentages, but I don't have any data to support that view. For example, in the building-construction industry, there should be a higher percentage of projects in the TPM quadrant than there would be for the financial-services industry.

My colleagues have confirmed these percentages from their own client experiences. There is a lot of consistent anecdotal evidence to support that distribution. I just haven't come to a firm conclusion yet, since much of the APM quadrant is new. After we have gained more experience with APM projects and I hear more from my colleagues, we'll have a better understanding of this landscape.

If we try to fit projects into the TPM quadrant when they really belong in the APM quadrant, then we are heading for trouble. This is what many have been doing even though they know that their approach is rigged. Many are not ready to embrace the alternatives. The results of a rigged approach range from mediocre success to outright failure. For years I have advocated that the approach to the project must ultimately be driven by the seven variables listed earlier. Once we have decided that the project is a TPM or APM or xPM project, then we can take these seven variables into account as we choose the specific best-fit PMLC model aligned with the chosen quadrant.

The APM quadrant is the focus of this book. The other quadrants will be referred to as needed to complete the discussion.

Even at this early stage in the discussion of the APM quadrant, you should be able to list some of the characteristics you would expect to see an APF PMLC model possess if it is to be successful. Here's my list:

- APF requires a new mindset—one that thrives on change.
- APF is not a "one-size-fits-all" approach—it continuously adapts to change.
- APF utilizes a just-in-time planning approach.
- APF adapts tools, templates, and processes from TPM and xPM approaches.
- APF is based on the principle that you learn by discovery.
- APF guarantees "if you build it they will come."
- APF seeks to get it right every time.
- APF is client-focused and client-driven.
- APF is grounded in an immutable set of core values.
- APF delivers maximum business value.
- APF eliminates all non-value-added work.
- APF approaches are less costly and require less time to execute than do TPM approaches.
- APF meaningfully and fully engages the client as primary decision maker.
- APF is based on a shared partnership between client and team.
- APF works—100 percent of the time! No exceptions!

Do I have your attention? Good! Read on and find out how APF approaches can significantly improve your company's project performance and bottom-line impact.

Business Process Life Cycle

APF will have to integrate with other processes. They include software and systems development life cycles, product development life cycles, process improvement life cycles, and problem solving life cycles. There may be others as well. APF should be integrated into these business processes rather than having the business processes integrated into APF.

Project Management Life Cycle

As a project-management approach, APM must adapt to the project. It will not work effectively if it forces the project into its own set of rules and conventions. There will be several APM approaches that might be chosen for these projects. Among the current APM approaches, the industry includes the following software-development models:

- Adaptive Project Framework (APF) (the one discussed in this book)
- Adaptive Software Development (ASD)
- Feature Driven Development (FDD)
- Dynamic Systems Development Method (DSDM)
- Evolutionary Development Waterfall
- Prince2
- Scrum
- Rational Unified Process (RUP)
- Microsoft Solution Framework (MSF)
- Crystal
- xP
- and several others

Except for APF, a detailed discussion of these APM models is beyond the scope of this book. For more detail on TPM, APM, xPM, and MPx, see my book *Effective Project Management: Traditional, Agile, Extreme, Fifth Edition*.[3]

---

[3] Robert D. Wysocki, Ph.D., *Effective Project Management: Traditional, Agile, Extreme, Fifth Edition*, (New York: John Wiley & Sons, 2009).

Profile of the Project Team

Alignment between the project-management approach and the team's skills and competencies is essential for project success. For example, if the project is very complex and will require a lot of creativity and outside-the-box thinking on the part of the team, then choosing a team filled with professionals who like to follow a recipe won't work. If this is your team's profile and you have an APM or xPM project, this may require using an approach that isn't the best fit for the project but does match the team strengths and preferences.

All APM approaches require a project team consisting of senior-level professionals who can work unsupervised. An APM project is no place for a rookie project manager or team member. Many APM project teams must be colocated. While there are some workarounds to avoid having a colocated team, they come with attendant risks. We'll discuss the implications in Chapter 9: APF Frequently Asked Questions.

Profile of the Client Team

Just as the chosen approach must align with the team, it must also align with the client. For example, clients of the take-charge type that are quite comfortable with the lead position might resist an approach where they have little or no say in what happens. If they are capable of taking charge, choose an approach where they can take charge (Scrum, for example). You will always be there as backup if they tend to stray outside of scope.

Supporting Technology

I've always remembered what a friend and colleague used to say: Don't kill mosquitoes with a sledge hammer. She was of course referring to the use of technology. I've run projects where the best-fit technology was a whiteboard with sticky notes and marking pens. Use the appropriate technology. Most APM projects can use a low-tech approach very successfully. Just because the computer is there, it doesn't mean you have to use the latest and greatest toys. Your focus for an APM project should be on creating business value from what you deliver, not on how you deliver it.

Project Management Is Organized Common Sense

I keep things simple and intuitive. One way to simply and intuitively define project management is that it is a set of tools, templates, and processes designed to answer the following six questions:

1. What business situation is being addressed by this project?
2. What do you need to do?
3. What will you do?
4. How will you do it?
5. How will you know you did it?
6. How well did you do?

Let's quickly look at the answers to these questions.

1. What Business Situation Is Being Addressed by This Project?

The situation is either a problem that needs a solution or an untapped business opportunity. If it is a problem, the solution may be clearly defined and the delivery of that solution should be rather straightforward. If the solution is not completely known, then the project-management approach must accommodate the learning and discovery of that solution. Obviously, these will be higher-risk projects than TPM projects, simply because the deliverables are not clearly defined and may not be discovered despite the best efforts being extended.

A project to take advantage of an untapped business opportunity can be done in several ways, discussed in Chapter 1: Overview of the Adaptive Project Framework.

Keep in mind that your project may be competing for resources with other projects that are addressing the same business situation but from a completely different perspective. For example, your project may be attacking one part of the problem while another project is considering a different part of the problem. It would be good if you knew this, because integrating the two projects into a single program may be cost beneficial. At least you would have more points of view to consider. The importance to senior managers of finding that solution or taking advantage of that untapped business opportunity will also compete with the importance of other project proposals.

2. What Do You Need to Do?

The obvious answer is to solve the problem or take advantage of the untapped business opportunity. That's all well and good; but given the business circumstances under which the project will be undertaken, it may not be possible. Even in those rare cases where the solution is clearly known, you might not have the skilled resources to do the project; and if you do have them, they may not be available when you need them. When the solution is not known or only partially known, you might not be successful in finding that heretofore-unknown solution. In any case, you need to document what needs to be done.

3. What Will You Do?

The answer to this question will be framed in your project goal and objectives statements. Maybe you and others will propose partial solutions to the problem or ways to use the untapped business opportunity. In any case, your goal and objective statements will clearly state your intentions.

4. How Will You Do It?

This answer gives your approach to the project and your detailed plan for meeting the goal and objective statements discussed above.

5. How Will You Know You Did It?

Your solution to the problem or approach to the untapped business opportunity will deliver some business value to the organization. That is your success criterion. It will have been used as the basis for approving your doing the project. That success criterion may be expressed in the form of

Increased Revenue or Avoided Costs or Improved Services. IRACIS is the acronym for these three areas of business value. Whatever form that success criterion takes, it will be expressed in quantitative terms so that there is no argument as to whether you achieved the expected business results or not. As part of the post-implementation audit, you will compare the actual business value realized to the estimated business value stated in the project plan that justified doing the project in the first place.

6. How Well Did You Do?

There are really four questions that comprise this question. The first and most important is, how well did your deliverables meet the stated success criteria? The second is, how well did the project team perform? The third is, how well did the project-management approach work for this project? The fourth is, what lessons were learned that can be applied to future projects? The answers are all part of the post-implementation audit.

Project Management Is Organized Common Sense

The answers to the above six questions reduce project management to nothing more than organized common sense. If it weren't organized common sense, then why would you want to do it at all? So a good test of whether or not your project-management approach makes sense lies in your answers to these six questions.

Why I Wrote This Book

Project failure rates upwards of 65 percent (the most recently reported statistic[4]) are just unacceptable. This is not a new problem, but little seems to be happening to improve the likelihood of project success. Project managers continue to force-fit new project situations into old project-management approaches. What a waste of time and resources! A few years ago, I did

---

[4] Standish Group 2007.

some serious retrospective thinking about project failure, and asked myself what could be done. Quite by accident, I had two separate but concurrent client engagements that were good examples of the problem situation where the solutions were only partially defined. I knew a TPM approach would not work. I used those two engagements as the impetus for designing an approach to project management that accommodated the fast-paced, high-change business environment we were living in and would embrace convergence toward the solution using an iterative approach. The result became known as APF. APF is in the APM category of approaches.

How This Book Is Structured

The book consists of this introduction and ten chapters. The first chapter defines APF and puts it in context among project-management approaches. The next five chapters (Chapters 2 through 6) are each devoted to one of the five phases of the APF life cycle. Chapters 2 through 6 are all structured the same way. Each chapter begins with an overview of the phase. Its artifacts, processes, and deliverables are then discussed. The chapter ends with a section on one or more of the four case studies introduced below, as appropriate, a summary of the chapter, and several discussion questions for the academic market. Chapter 7 describes variations in the application of APF. Chapter 8 relates APF to Extreme Project Management approaches. Chapter 9 is a collection of frequently asked questions and answers. Chapter 10 takes a step back and positions APF in the context of the project-management landscape, with more of a future orientation.

Case Studies

As examples of the use of APF outside the software-development arena, I will be referring to the following four case studies. They are all examples of actual client engagements where APF was the approach. I have taken some editorial license to better illustrate APF's characteristics. For the protection of my clients, I have disguised all of the names and the businesses. However, I have tried to preserve the nature of the engagement along with its failures and successes. Any resemblance to actual people or businesses is strictly coincidental.

Snacks Fifth Avenue: Kiosk Design

Snacks Fifth Avenue was looking for a way to create more interest for its shoppers and draw more traffic into its ten New York stores. The company viewed itself as somewhat of a boutique, and attracted high-end customers to its shops. It offered the most complete line of international snack foods and party products of any of its competitors. The kiosk had not yet been widely introduced in retailing, and here was an opportunity to do so profitably. My partner and I developed an approach to support the changing needs of the project and the discovery of the solution through iteration. That approach eventually became the initial version of APF that we successfully used for new-product development, and in this case resulted in a shopping kiosk that located food items, accepted orders, and assisted customers with maps and other directional aids. Interest in the shopping experience began to slowly increase as shoppers accepted and used the new technology. Store managers reported increases in activity as customers began to integrate use of the technology into their shopping experience.

Kamikazi Software Systems: Systems Development Project Management Process Design

Kamikazi Software Systems, a business-to-business and business-to-consumer Web site software development firm, built its reputation on fixed cost/time bids for custom designed internet/intranet sites. The development environment was obviously high risk. Recent trends showed that Kamikazi was not making its margins on smaller projects; in fact, the trend was definitely in the wrong direction. Through project reviews, Kamikazi learned that the number of change requests was growing and the process for managing those changes wasn't holding up. The company approached us to help design, develop, and implement a project-management process that would work in its systems-development environment.

The development teams were seldom able to complete client projects within either budget or timeline parameters. Despite the fact that they had an established project-management process at CMM level 3, senior managers were unable to isolate the problem and correct it. What they did learn is that the internal clients were generally satisfied with the deliverables, but only after one or two unplanned revisions beyond the original specifications. Since these were not budgeted, these outcomes were not met by senior management with any joy or celebration. Because of this, APF's just-in-time planning and iterative cycles were developed as a potential stopgap measure. The following results were achieved:

- Budget and timeline constraints were more consistently met.
- At first, the client's representatives were uncomfortable with a variable scope, but because of their integral involvement in priority decisions and cycle planning, they were satisfied with the final deliverables.
- The general consensus was that projects finished in less time and with higher client acceptance than would have been the case if the old traditional approaches had been used.
- Having the client involved made problem solving and conflict resolution a much more productive exchange between the team and the client.

Pizza Delivered Quickly: Order Entry and Home Delivery Process Design

Pizza Delivered Quickly (PDQ) is a 40-year-old, family-owned, local chain of four eat-in and home-delivery pizza stores. PDQ's stores are located in Woodville, a growing Midwestern city of 200,000. Recently, PDQ has lost 30 percent of its sales revenue, due mostly to a drop in home-delivery business. The company attributes this solely to its major competitor, a national pizza chain with ten stores, which started operation in Woodville 18 months earlier and is promoting a program that guarantees 45-minute delivery service from order entry to home delivery. PDQ advertises one-hour delivery, PDQ currently uses computers for in-store operations and the usual business functions, but otherwise is not heavily dependent upon software systems to help receive, process, and home-deliver customers' orders. Pepe Ronee, PDQ's Supervisor of Computer Services, has been charged with developing a software application to identify optimal "pizza factory" locations and with creating a software system to operate them more efficiently. In commissioning this project, Dee Livery, PDQ's president, said to pull out all the stops.

She further stated that the future of PDQ depends on the success of this project. She wants the team to configure the business to deliver pizza unbaked and "ready for the oven" in 30 minutes or less or deliver it pre-baked in 45 minutes or less. Given their current application of computer technology this was a daunting challenge but essential to the survival of PDQ.

Try & Buy Department Stores: Curriculum Design, Development, and Delivery

Try & Buy Department Stores is among the largest discount department stores in the world. Its Information Systems Department (ISD) comprises over 10,000 professionals, of whom approximately 2,000 were project managers. The systems development staff was organized along customer/product/service lines. There were 184 such groups. Each customer/product/services group operated independently, with its own processes, tools, and templates. There was a very strong sense of team and pride within each group. Despite cross-group project problems, of which there were several, the independent organizational structure did allow ISD to develop expertise in each customer group. Much of the success of Try & Buy was attributable to that unique structure. There were a number of problems, however. Projects were generally late, seldom completed, and poorly tested, and produced high-maintenance results. Adopting a project-management methodology that all 184 teams would be required to use was quickly dismissed as impractical and a waste of time and money. ISD senior managers felt that a training solution was what they needed.

Who Should Read This Book?

In general, this book will be of value to several different professional groups, but they all have a few things in common. You are creative thinkers. Rather than blindly following a task list, you ask, "Why?" If tasks don't make sense, you either delete them or replace them with tasks that do make sense. You are fixed on delivering client-acceptable business value. You strive to do this in concert with your clients, not separate from them. This collaborative effort is the major strength of your approach. You are open to new ideas and concepts of effective project management. You are team players. You realize that only through a collaborative effort with your client will you have any chance of success. If you are struggling to deliver "knock-your-socks-off" service and know that you need some help, you have come to the right place. If this describes you, then you should continue reading. I have some great stuff to add to your toolkit! If this does not describe you, you need to do some serious reflection. The world is about to pass you by.

Project and Program Managers

These professionals are the primary beneficiaries of this book. As they encounter projects that just don't meet the requirements of the traditional approaches, APF may be their best alternative. This book will give them a model that does.

Software Developers

APF is, after all, an agile software-development management process. There is much to learn about requirements gathering and what to do with the results. Meaningful client involvement and collaboration is a must. The change process is not the enemy. It can be a great asset if used correctly. All of these issues are discussed.

Product Developers

There is little mention in the literature about using APM models for product development. APF is designed primarily for that audience. Each of the case studies describes a non-software development application of APF.

Process Designers

One of the original applications of APF was a process-design project. The Kamikazi Software Development Company is the case study that traces the development of APF through the eyes of a systems-development process project. The case study provides an interesting look at a company that had been hell-bent on making its square peg fit a round hole, and it was costing dearly at the bottom line. It even took some time after the process was finished for the company to realize that it was the solution it had been looking for but was too blind to see. In retrospect, APF may have been the primary reason why this company survived the dot-com debacle and flourishes to this day.

Business Analysts

APF is a powerful tool for process-design and process-improvement projects. The investigative nature of the APF cycles is designed to uncover feasible process changes for measurable improvements.

Process Improvement Professionals

APF is a powerful tool for process-improvement projects. The same comments apply as above.

Research & Development Professionals

APF, xPM, and MPx share a lot in common. As the goal becomes fuzzy, the choice of approaches should migrate from APF to either xPM or MPx. The interesting commonality is that the structure of the phases of xPM and MPx is the same. Both xPM and MPx are also designed for discovery of both the goal and the solution to that evolving goal. Even at completion, the remaining question is, "Does the business value generated from the xPM or MPx goal/solution contribute acceptable business value?"

Problem Solvers

There are many problem-solving models; APF is one of them. In the typical APF project, you want to find a complete solution to a complex problem.

Putting It All Together

APF is a bold step forward in project-management approaches. To be successful requires that you reach inside yourself and summon up all the creative juices and outside-the-box thinking that you possibly can. APF requires the same from the client. APF is not for the faint of heart. It requires seeing the project as the unique entity that it is and drawing upon a vetted collection of tools, templates, and processes to craft the best-fit management approach for your project. There is no silver bullet, so don't expect one. There is no recipe, so don't look for one. But take solace in the fact that you are about to become a chef and not just a cook! If you apply what I have to offer, you will be prepared to effectively manage any project, no matter how complex and uncertain it might be. I've been there and done that many times, and I know that what I am advocating here works all the time!

In this book, I prepare you for an exciting, challenging, and rewarding career.

Chapter 1

Overview of the Adaptive Project Framework

It is a mistake to look too far ahead. Only one link of the chain of destiny can be handled at a time.

—*Winston Churchill*

There is no data on the future.

—*Laurel Cutler, Vice Chairman, FCB/Leber Katz Partners*[1]

We have reached a crossroads in our journey to make a better world through our project-management efforts. Before we go any further, I want to ask you to stop and give some thought to how we should proceed on our journey. What I want to share with you is new, and is my conclusion after having been on this journey with you for the past 40 years. I'm not advocating the overthrow of the project management world, but rather asking you to stop and think about what has been happening and how you have reacted to it. It's time to pay attention to the signals coming from the changing business

---

[1] Quotations at the heads of chapters are from Lewis D. Eigen and Jonathan P. Siegel, *The Manager's Book of Quotations* (New York: AMACOM, 1991).

environment and learn how to adapt to the fast-paced, constantly changing, complex, and uncertain demands of today's business world, and how best to manage the projects that support it. It's time for the renaissance project manager. It's time for a new project-management process model. The new model should not be a static one, but rather one that is very dynamic—one that must adapt to the changing project characteristics, environment, and culture within which the project is to be done, to the team and its external support staff, and finally, to the clients (who always seem to be changing their minds). And even these are likely to change from the time the project starts until the time it ends. Therefore, an effective project-management approach must be one that constantly assesses the total project environment and adapts to changing conditions and situations. The renaissance project manager is an outside-the-box thinker—one who instills creativity and courage into the development team and the client team.

Advice

To those businesses that have only recently realized the pain of not having an effective project-management process in place and are struggling to adapt traditional practices to nontraditional projects, I say, "Stop wasting your time!"

The effective project manager I envision is more like a chef than a cook. A cook follows a recipe and is not trained to make exceptions to the recipe. As long as things progress according to the recipe, everything is fine with the cook. The chef, on the other hand, is trained to *create* recipes, and can adapt any recipe in order to meet a changing set of circumstances and a changing set of constraints. I assume you are already a cook. In this book, I will give you the tools you need to be a chef!

The Fundamentals of the Adaptive Project Framework

Let's face it: The world will not stand still just because you are managing a project. So the challenge is to adopt and adapt an approach to managing your project that anticipates constant and unexpected change and can adjust with minimal disruption to the project, the team, the client, the enterprise, and the market.

Client or Customer?

Let's first clear up some vocabulary. To me, a **customer** is someone to whom we are going to sell a product or service. A **client**, on the other hand, is someone with whom we are going to collaborate in order to solve a problem or take advantage of an untapped or new business opportunity. For an APF project, **client** is the correct term, and is the term that I am using throughout this book.

The APF Project Team

The APF project team is composed of a client team and a development team. For some APF projects, the client team may be a single individual with decision-making authority. For larger APF projects, the client team may have several members in order to cover the business processes or functions involved. Client-team membership may change over the life of the project. The client team should have a single member in charge with decision-making authority. This person will serve as co-manager for the entire project, along with the development-team leader. The development team comprises the technical professionals who are responsible for producing the deliverables. Development-team membership will most likely change over the life of the project, although there is usually a core development group that stays with the entire project. The development team will have a single individual in charge with decision-making authority. This person serves as co-manager of the project along with the client-team manager.

The two co-managers share equally in the success or failure of the project, and they both must have decision-making authority with respect to this project. Your APF project would be seriously handicapped if the client co-manager had to get approval from company management all through the project. This project-manager model is unique to APF and is a critical success factor for such projects. The most important characteristic of this management model is that both parties are equally vested and responsible for the project.

The APF project team is a very special team. Its members are mostly senior-level professionals who can work without supervision. The project they are undertaking is complex and filled with a great deal of uncertainty, so they must be creative people as well, if they are to find an acceptable solution. Creative people are generally very independent and may not make good team players. This will present challenges to the co-managers of the project. Along with creativity comes the need to be independent and unfettered by organizational constraints and rigid processes.

I'll refer to the **development team** or **client team** when that specificity is required. When I use the term **project team,** I am referring to the single team formed by the client team and the development team.

First Look at APF

The project strategy you will explore in this groundbreaking book is what you already know I am calling the Adaptive Project Framework (APF). This is definitely not your father's project management. It's new. I don't even use the word "management" to describe it. It is a framework within which effective management takes place. If I had to choose a term, I would prefer "leadership," not "management."

As you will discover, APF represents a shift in thinking about projects and how they should be run. For one thing, it eliminates all of the non-value-added work time that is wasted on planning and re-planning activities and tasks that are never performed. Why plan the future when you don't know what it is? You certainly shouldn't base your project plans on guesses about what that future might be. What a terrible waste of time and money that would be. Furthermore, the impact on project risk could be substantial. In APF, planning is done just-in-time. That sounds like an oxymoron, doesn't it? The plan is based on only what we know or have learned about the solution since the last plan was built. So, APF planning is incremental.

APF demands a creative mind-set—one that thrives on change rather than one that avoids change. A characteristic of every APF project is that the complete solution is not known at the start of the project; it must be discovered and learned during project execution. The process of discovery will require a new set of tools not present in any other agile approach. This means the APF project management process must have within it the provision for learning and discovery. The resulting learning and discovery is turned into added functions and features in the solution. So the solution grows cumulatively until the project ends. This cumulative building of the solution is common to all agile approaches. In APF, the learning and discovery process is structured. In other agile approaches it happens by chance.

In an APF project, you start out with an incomplete definition of the solution. You may know a lot about the solution or very little. The less you know about the solution, the higher the risk of not finding a solution that has acceptable business value. One characteristic common to all APF projects is that the best solution will be found, within the given time and cost constraints, through the creative and collaborative energies and expertise of the client members of the project team and the development members of the project team.

Providing mechanisms for learning and discovery introduces something into your project-management process that does not exist in the traditional approaches—nor, as a matter of fact, in any other agile approach. In collaboration with your client, you have to experiment with possible additions to the solution that has been defined at that point in time. I call these initiatives **probative swim lanes**, and they are discussed in detail in Chapter 3: How to Plan an APF Cycle. The probative swim lanes create the learning and discovery. When a probative swim lane is successful in identifying another part of the solution, that part is integrated into the solution in a later cycle, in what I call an **integrative swim lane**. These two swim lanes define a unique relationship in APF not present in any other agile approach.

APF is obviously not a one-size-fits-all approach. Rather, it continuously adapts to changing business conditions and project status as it learns and discovers more of the solution through each cycle. APF is based on the principle that form follows function. APF adapts tools, templates, and processes from traditional linear and extreme approaches to fit the needs of the project at the precise moment in time when the need arises. APF is a framework based on the principle that you learn by doing, and one that guarantees, "If you build it, it is what they need and they will come."

Unlike an xPM project, which seeks to get it right the last time (and so it should), an APF project seeks to get it right every time. Each cycle produces a working version of the solution as it is known at that moment in time. This is very similar to creating production prototypes. Whenever an APF project is terminated, there is always business value to deliver from the then-current solution.

APF is client focused and client driven, and is grounded in a set of immutable core values discussed later in this chapter. APF ensures maximum business value for the time and dollars expended. APF is efficient: It has squeezed out all of the non-value-added work that it possibly could have. APF is a framework that meaningfully and fully engages the client as the primary decision maker. APF creates a shared partnership with shared responsibility between requestor and provider. APF is a framework that works, 100 percent of the time. No exceptions!

Finally, APF projects are high-risk projects. That isn't the result of the process; it is the nature of the project itself. These are projects whose successful completion is critical to the enterprise but whose solution has so far avoided discovery. Maybe that is because the problem is unsolvable, or maybe it is because no one has been able to successfully find a solution that waits to be discovered. If it can be discovered through effective project management, it will be discovered using APF.

Goal, Solution, Functions, and Features

As already stated, APF is designed for those projects whose goal is clearly stated and documented but whose solution is only partially known. Figure 1.1, a version of which also appeared in the Introduction, shows where APF is positioned in the project landscape. APF can be used on any project in the Agile Project Management (APM) quadrant (clear goal, unclear solution), and is an adaptive PMLC model.

Many situations fit this profile. These range from the simplest, where perhaps only minor parts of the solution are not known, to the most complex, where very little of the solution is known. Perhaps the solution is simply an algorithm for assisting with a decision. At the other extreme would be a solution that is almost entirely unknown because the problem is a first-time problem about which little is known, or is a recurring problem whose solution has so far been elusive. APF addresses the entire range of solution uncertainty. In some cases, APF can also be used when the goal is not clearly specified and an extreme approach is not available.

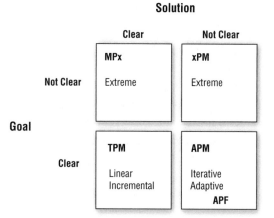

Figure 1.1
The Project-
management
Landscape

The extent to which the solution is known is expressed objectively in terms of the functions and features that define each requirement. These are the building blocks of the Requirements Breakdown Structure (RBS), which is discussed in detail in Chapter 2: How to Scope the APF Project. **Requirements** are the first-level decomposition of the goal in the RBS, **functions** are the second level, and **features** are the lowest level of decomposition, as shown in Figure 1.2.

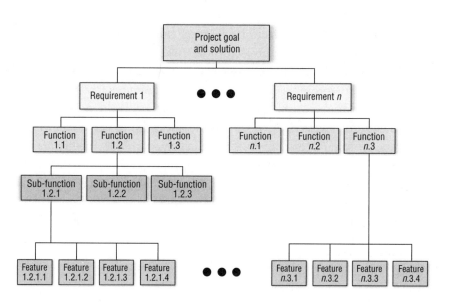

Figure 1.2
The Require-
ments Break-
down Structure

You may have noticed the similarity between the RBS and the deliverables-based Work Breakdown Structure (WBS). Essentially, the RBS answers the question, "What are we going to deliver?" The WBS expands the RBS and answers the question, "How are we going to deliver it?" Therefore, the deliverables-based WBS includes the RBS as a subset. In other words, beginning with the RBS, you can continue its decomposition, and at the lowest level of decomposition create the deliverables-based form of the WBS. There are of course several other architectures that the WBS can follow. Refer to my book *Effective Project Management: Traditional, Agile, Extreme*[2] for details on WBS architectures and how to build a complete WBS.

If the client team and the development team are certain that the solution is completely described by the RBS, then the traditional project management (TPM) category is the correct choice, and some traditional linear or incremental approach would probably be chosen. It is only when the RBS is not complete, or suspected to be incomplete or unstable in the sense that change is likely during the project, that it will be appropriate to use an APM approach such as APF. The missing parts of the RBS could be one or more features (which would result in a straightforward application of APF), or the missing parts could be one or more functions (which would result in a more-challenging application of APF).

Unfortunately, if the RBS is not complete, you and the client may not be aware of that. Most project-management pundits would agree that to generate a complete RBS at project initiation is not possible. If you align with that thinking, it would be wise to adopt some agile approach such as APF for all your projects. In the extreme, a requirement could even be identified during the course of the project. As long as the goal is clearly defined and documented, APF will be the approach of choice. It will no longer be necessary for the project manager to cobble together some hybrid version of a linear or incremental approach in the hopes that it will work. APF can even be used in cases where a TPM approach could have been used. We'll discuss that situation later. What sets APF apart from every other project management approach is that APF is guaranteed to

---

[2] Wysocki, Robert, Ph.D. *Effective Project Management: Traditional, Agile, Extreme, Fifth Edition* (New York: John Wiley & Sons, 2009).

work—100% of the time. The fact that about 65 percent of all projects fail[3] doesn't even affect APF project managers, because they are using a failure-proof project-management approach!

Traditional Project Management (TPM)

As we have already discussed, a TPM approach requires a complete and clearly defined RBS. The reason why TPM variations require complete requirements is so that the complete WBS can be generated and the complete project plan created. A complete WBS will identify all of the work that has to be done to meet specifications and scope.

There are reasons why one would want a complete plan. These include

- To be able to document exactly what will be delivered
- To estimate the human-resource requirements
- To develop the project budget
- To build a complete project work schedule so resources can be committed

It is nice and comforting to have such a list at the beginning of a project. However, that rarely occurs. What happens more often than not is that changes are requested, and if they are approved, then resource requirements may change, and the project plan may need to change as well. Do you begin to see all of the labor and time wasted putting together the original resource requirements and project plan? APF saves all of that wasted time!

Among the TPM approaches, there are two general models. All other TPM approaches are specific examples of one of them. These general models are defined below, with at least one specific example of each type given.

---

[3] Standish Group, *Chaos Report 2007: The Laws of CHAOS* (Boston: Standish Group International, 2007).

Linear Models

These models have a number of phases that operate in sequential order with no feedback loops. The interested reader can consult Chapters 3–9 in my book, *Effective Software Project Management,*[4] for details. Figures 1.3 and 1.4 show two popular TPM models. Note that both models are linear—there are no feedback loops.

Standard Waterfall Model

The Waterfall model has been around for more than 50 years, and is discussed in any good book on systems development life cycles. While it was originally meant for software-development projects, it has applications in non-software development as well.

Figure 1.3
The Standard
Waterfall Model

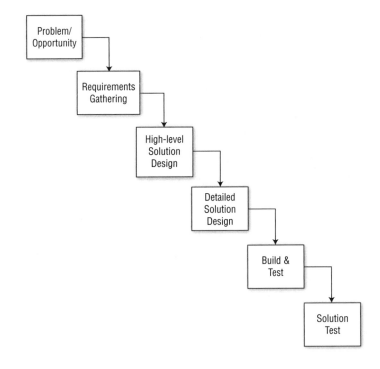

---

[4] Wysocki 2009.

Rapid Development Waterfall Model

The Rapid Development Waterfall model is more recent, and is frequently used to get products to market faster by grouping development into parallel and nearly independent "swim lanes." Do not confuse the Rapid Development Waterfall model with Rapid Application Development (RAD). The two are very different. Grouping for effective and speedy development is challenging. It requires swim lanes that are as independent of one another as possible. The linearity of the process is maintained with these parallel swim lanes. Figure 1.4 depicts the parallel swim lanes. There are several things to consider in creating such a development schedule. The first is risk. Squeezing the work into a shorter timeframe increases the incidence of errors and staff scheduling conflicts. The amount of work has not decreased; it just must be completed in a shorter timeframe. Allocating the work to concurrent swim lanes shortens the project duration, but increases the risk to completing the project. Cramming more work into a shorter time box allows less time to recover from mistakes. Having parallel swim lanes in the project

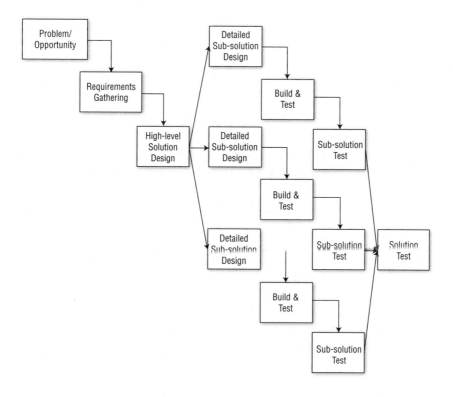

Figure 1.4
The Rapid Development Waterfall Model

schedule raises the possibility of further aggravating any resource scheduling conflicts that were present in the initial schedule. The last parallel swim lane that is completed determines the completion date of the development project. It is clear that the risk in following a Rapid Development Waterfall model is greater than that of the Standard Waterfall model.

Incremental Models

Incremental models are really just a variant of Linear models, but deserve separate discussion. Just as the Linear models require clearly defined and documented goals and solutions, so do Incremental models. Whereas Linear models build and release deliverables all at one time, Incremental models build and release deliverables in stages over time. For marketing and early sales reasons, these models are often chosen. For example, to release a product in stages to test market acceptance and other variables, an Incremental model is often used. The downside of Incremental models is that the client is tempted to introduce scope-change requests between increments. That's okay, but the original project timeframe will have to allow time for such scope-change requests to come forward from the client, be evaluated, and be acted upon. **Management reserve** is a time contingency added as a task to the end of the project schedule to accommodate the time needed to process and incorporate changes. This is an often-overlooked detail in Incremental models. Also, having downtime for the development team between increments creates a temptation for resource managers to temporarily reassign team members elsewhere. There is always the promise that they will return to the team when the next increment is ready to start, but that rarely happens. As a form of insurance to protect against the loss of a team member, hand-off documentation is usually prepared. That adds work not found in the Linear models.

Staged Delivery Waterfall Model

When considering using an Incremental PMLC model, you need to give some thought to the added risk. Figure 1.5 illustrates an example of a Staged Delivery Waterfall model.

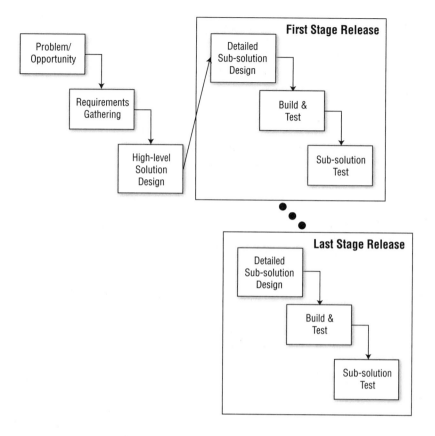

Figure 1.5
Staged Delivery
Waterfall Model

The Staged Delivery Waterfall model suffers the same risks as any other Incremental model. A constraint of the model is the content of each increment. The deliverables from Increment **n** must have all predecessor deliverables built in the previous n-1 increments. This is likely to compromise, or delay, increments having business value sufficient to warrant release to the end user or the market. At best, the process is cumulative; that is, not every increment will contain sufficient business value, but the last several increments since the last release might offer sufficient business value to be released.

For details, see Chapters 10–16 in my book *Effective Software Project Management.*[5] Incremental models encourage scope change but should not be used to further identify missing parts of the solution or improve an existing solution. That is a job for APF.

---

[5] Wysocki 2009.

Feature-Driven Development Model

The Feature-Driven Development (FDD) model (see Figure 1.6) is similar to the Staged Delivery Waterfall model except that "swim lanes" are defined around the technical dependencies among the functions and features assigned to each lane. Because FDD is technology focused, it does not necessarily deliver business value at each iteration. FDD first appeared in *Java™ Modeling in Color with UML®* by Peter Coad, Eric Lefebvre, and Jeff DeLuca.[6] A more-comprehensive treatment of FDD can be found in *A Practical Guide to Feature-Driven Development* by Stephen R. Palmer and John M. Felsing.[7]

Note that the solution must be known in order to use FDD effectively. A model of the solution is developed and used to create the functional WBS. The functional WBS contains a very detailed list of features. The features list is grouped into similar features based on technical dependencies and prioritized for development. FDD iterates through the design and building of the groups of features.

Much like the Rapid Development Waterfall model, FDD prioritizes parts of the solution. But in FDD, the prioritization is based on feature dependencies. With the addition of feature code to the solution, the solution grows in terms of business value. Intermediate production solutions can be released as part of this approach. Just as in the Rapid Development model, there can be multiple design/build swim lanes running concurrently in the Feature Driven Development model.

Figure 1.6
Feature-Driven
Development
Model

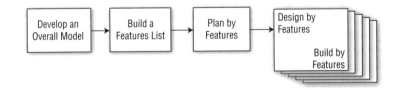

---

[6] Peter Coad, Eric Lefebvre, and Jeff DeLuca, *Java™ Modeling in Color with UML®: Enterprise Components and Process* (Upper Saddle River, NJ: Prentice Hall, 1999).

[7] Stephen R. Palmer and John M. Felsing, *A Practical Guide to Feature-Driven Development* (Upper Saddle River, NJ: Prentice Hall, 2000).

FDD provides for the early release of chunks of features so that the customer can begin to realize business value without having to wait for the single release of the complete solution. There may be several cycles of development before the client is satisfied that the cumulative features list has enough business value to be released as with the Staged Delivery Waterfall model. FDD models may use concurrent swim lanes, sequential phases, or some combination of the two.

Agile Project Management (APM)

For TPM projects, change is the exception. For APM projects, change is the norm. This difference is significant, and results in completely different approaches to managing projects. While the TPM project will follow some form of Linear or Incremental PMLC model as discussed above, the APM project will employ some form of Iterative or Adaptive PMLC model, as discussed below. When the solution is not clearly and completely defined, you will have to approach the project as some type of agile project and use the appropriate Agile PMLC model.

Agile projects come in two flavors.

- **Most of the solution is known.** These are projects whose goals are clearly defined and documented and whose solutions are complete up to the point of specifying the final rendering of one or more features. These projects are what I would call **minimalist agile projects**. These projects should use an Iterative PMLC model, but could also use an Adaptive PMLC model as described and illustrated later in this chapter.

- **Most of the solution is unknown.** These are projects whose goals are clearly defined and documented but whose solution features and functions are not clearly defined and documented. In other words, much of the solution has not been identified. These projects are what I would call **maximalist agile projects**. These projects should use an Adaptive PMLC model as described and illustrated later in this chapter.

Evolutionary Development Waterfall and Rational Unified Process (RUP) are minimalist agile approaches as defined in this book. That is, they are more effective when much of the solution is known. Scrum and APF are maximalist approaches. That is, they are more effective when much of the solution is unknown. In practice, I have seen project managers force-fit maximalist adaptive projects into minimalist approaches. While they may have some success with that approach, it would be better to use a maximalist agile approach which is designed for such projects.

Iterative Models

Iterative models are minimalist agile approaches. The Iterative PMLC models are most effective where we still know all of the functions but some of the features are not known as definitively as the client would like. A good example of such models is the Evolutionary Development Waterfall model shown in Figure 1.7.

Evolutionary Development Waterfall Model

In this approach, the project begins much like a project following the Standard Waterfall model. The known parts of the solution are developed based on current requirements. Through the Evolutionary Development Waterfall model, iterations on the details of the solution will be undertaken. As the features and functions needed to deliver the requirements are developed, the requirements may well change, but few additions or deletions to the original requirements are expected. The WBS for the current version is created along with duration, cost, and resource requirements. This model closely resembles the production-prototype approach that has been quite popular for many years.

Unlike with the traditional models, it should be obvious that the meaningful involvement of the client is critical to the success of agile models. The client members of the project team, not the developers, are the subject-matter experts (SMEs) on the project. The client works with a version of the solution and provides feedback to the project team for further enhancements and changes to features and functions. This process continues as version after version is put into place, until at some point the client is satisfied that all requirements have been met. Also note that this model always presents the client with a production-ready version of the solution.

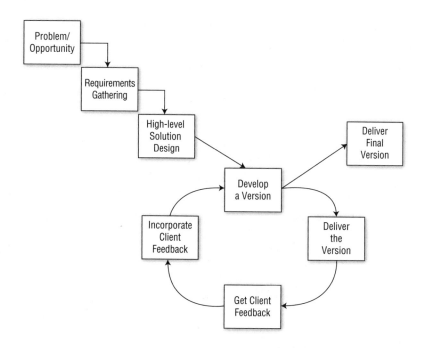

Figure 1.7
Evolutionary
Development
Waterfall Model

In the Evolutionary Development Waterfall model (see Figure 1.7), the learning and discovering experience is obvious. With each iteration, more and more of the depth of the solution is revealed. This follows from the client and developers having an opportunity to play with the then-solution. For simple and obvious enhancements this approach works just fine.

There is one variation worth mentioning here. There may be cases where iteration through solution designs might precede iteration through versions. While these tend to be the early efforts for an adaptive model, they can be used here with good effect. Iteration on design helps the client move up the learning curve of understanding the solution concept. Armed with that understanding, the client is better prepared to participate in iterations through versions. Design iteration is done quickly. If you have the right design tools, in my experience design iteration can be done in a matter of days, not weeks or months.

The discovery of additional features is a process that fully engages the client in meaningful exchanges with the developers. Both client and developers work with the prototypes—sometimes independently and sometimes in collaboration. Collaboration would be done to decide how to go forward with new or redefined features in the next and subsequent iterations. For details, see Chapters 17–23 in my book *Effective Software Project Management.*[8]

The Evolutionary Development Waterfall model works fine for those situations where only a small part of the solution has not been clearly defined. Choosing how to represent a feature in the solution would be an example of where a small part of the solution is not clear. The development team merely presents the client with renditions of the alternatives and asks for a decision as to which alternative is preferred, then implements it in the solution. But when the missing parts of the solution are more significant, as in determining how to make a particular decision, then a more-powerful approach is needed. This more-powerful approach would be some form of Adaptive PMLC model.

Rational Unified Process (RUP)

The Rational Unified Process (RUP) is a completely documented software engineering process for building a solution in an iterative fashion. One might argue that RUP belongs in the maximalist-approach category. I have chosen to put it here. There is an extensive library of books and Internet resources available. A good starting point would be Krutchen's *The Rational Unified Process: An Introduction, Third Edition.*[9]

RUP, illustrated in Figure 1.8, consists of four concepts: Inception, Elaboration, Construction, and Transition. For a visual representation of how these four concepts are related to Figure 1.8, refer to Krutchen, especially his Figure 2.2.

RUP is probably the most well-known of the iterative software development processes. It adapts quite well to process approaches that range from documentation-heavy to documentation-light. The foundation of RUP lies in a library of reusable code, requirements, designs, and so forth. That library will have been built from previous project experiences. This means that RUP can have a long payback period. The library must be sufficiently populated in order to be useful from a return-on-investment perspective. Four to five completed projects may be enough to begin to produce some payback.

---

[8] Wysocki 2009.

[9] Philippe Krutchen, *The Rational Unified Process: An Introduction, Third Edition,* (Boston: Addison-Wesley, 2004).

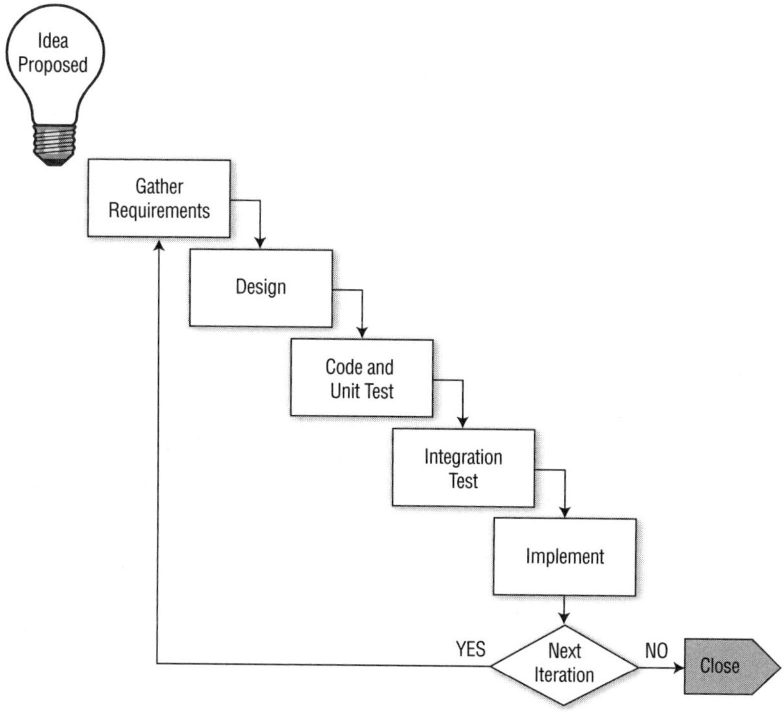

Figure 1.8
Rational Unified
Process Model

RUP ranges widely over the project landscape. When complexity and uncertainty are low but the solution is not fully defined, RUP is a heavy process. It requires considerable documentation, especially for code reuse.

Note that each iteration begins with a requirements-gathering session. The presumption is that the previous iteration will have clarified future directions for the project to take, to be fleshed out in the next requirements-gathering exercise. The direction a RUP project takes tends to be reactive to the requirements-gathering activity. APF, on the other hand, is a proactive model that seeks out missing solution parts through probative swim lanes. APF does not depend totally on discovery of the solution, which is passive, but also depends on proactive initiatives, which are activities designed to learn about the solution. It is this property that sets APF apart from all other Agile PMLC models.

RUP consists of four concepts which run concurrently through all iterations.

Inception

Through a series of requirements-gathering sessions in each iteration, an understanding of the scope of the development effort is agreed to and a cumulative solution as to how the scope will be developed can begin to be developed. Whatever parts of the solution have not been implemented are expected to be uncovered in the requirements-gathering sessions at the start of an iteration.

Elaboration

Whereas the Inception phase focuses on *what* is to be done, the Elaboration step focuses on *how* it will be done. This is a technical design activity, with the appropriate technical specifications and plans as deliverables. RUP is an architecture-centric process, so these technical specifications must integrate with the deliverables from all previous iterations. RUP is not a client-centric process as is APF. In the APF world, these first two RUP concepts are equivalent to the Version Scoping phase and the Cycle Planning phase, respectively.

Construction

This is the build phase of a RUP iteration. It is equivalent to the Cycle Build phase of an APF project.

Transition

The then-solution may be released into production if the client is satisfied that such a release has business value and can be supported by the organization. This is the same as the release decision in an APF project.

Adaptive Models

Whereas Iterative PMLC models work well in situations where only minor parts of the solution (typically features) have not been implemented in the solution, Adaptive PMLC models are most appropriate for situations where sizable parts of the solution have not yet been identified. In the most complex situations, incompleteness could even extend to requirements. APF is one example of an Adaptive PMLC model. There are several others. Some of the more familiar ones that are briefly discussed here are:

- Adaptive Software Development (ASD)
- SCRUM
- Dynamic Systems Development Method (DSDM)

These well-established models work well for what they were designed to do, but their limitation is that they were all designed for software-development projects. The following sections give a brief overview of each of these models. APF can be used for software-development projects as well, but it has a much wider range of applications. Even though it is a member of the APM category, APF was first designed for use on non-software development projects, which is the focus of this book. APF was initially defined for a process design project (see the Kamikazi Software Systems case study) and a product design project (see the Snacks Fifth Avenue case study).

Adaptive Software Development (ASD)

Adaptive Software Development (ASD) is fully described in a book by James A. Highsmith III, *Adaptive Software Development: A Collaborative Approach to Managing Complex Systems*.[10] ASD has three phases: Speculate, Collaborate, and Learn. These three overlapping phases are shown in Figure 1.9.

Speculate

The Speculate phase is nothing more than guessing at what the final goal and solution might look like. Its result may be correct, or it may be far from the mark. It really doesn't make much difference in the final analysis, because the self-correcting nature of ASD will eventually lead the team to the right solution. "Get it right the last time" is all that matters.

---

[10] James A. Highsmith III, *Adaptive Software Development: A Collaborative Approach to Managing Complex Systems* (New York: Dorsett House, 2000).

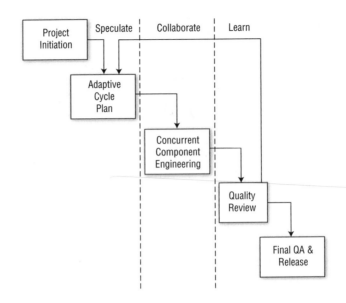

Figure 1.9
Adaptive Software Development Model

Collaborate

The Speculate phase has been completed, and it is time to take stock of where the team and client are with respect to an ultimate solution. The client team and the development team must collaborate on their journey to discover the solution. What great "aha"s did the entire project team discover? What direction should the project take in the next and succeeding iterations?

Learn

What was learned from the just-completed phase, and how might that redirect the team for the next phase?

The ASD Life Cycle Model

Figure 1.9 also shows the detailed phases of ASD.

Project Initiation The objective of the Project Initiation phase is to clearly establish expectations among the sponsor, the client, the core project team, and any other stakeholders. This would be a good place to discuss, agree upon, and approve the Project Overview Statement (POS). For a project of some duration (more than six months), it might be a good idea to hold a kick-off meeting, which might last 2–3 days. During that time, requirements can be gathered and documented and the POS can be written. As part of project initiation, a brief statement of objectives for each iteration is prepared. These are expected to change as the solution detail develops, but at least the sponsor, client, and development team have a sense of direction for their efforts.

Adaptive Cycle Plan   Other deliverables from the kick-off meeting might include the project time-frame, the optimal number of cycles and the time box for each, and objective statements for the coming cycle. Every cycle begins with a plan for what will be done in the coming cycle. These plans are high-level. Functionality is assigned to sub-teams and the details are left to them to establish. This is as opposed to TPM, which requires organized management oversight against a detailed plan. ASD is light when it comes to management processes.

Concurrent Component Engineering   Several concurrent swim lanes are established for each functionality component. Each sub-team is responsible for some part of the functionality planned for the present cycle.

Quality Review   This is the time for the client to review what has been completed to date and revise accordingly. New functionality may emerge; functionality is reprioritized for consideration in later cycles.

Final QA and Release   At some point, the client will declare the requirements met and there will be a final acceptance test procedure and release of the product.

Scrum

Scrum is a term taken from rugby. Scrum involves the team as a unit moving the ball down field in what would appear to be an *ad-hoc* or even chaotic manner. Of all the iterative approaches, Scrum would seem to define a chaotic development environment. The Scrum software development team is self-directed, operates in successive one-month iterations, holds daily team meetings, continually offers the client demos of the current solution, and adapts its development plan at the end of each iteration. For a complete discussion of Scrum and software development, refer to *Agile Software Development with Scrum* by Ken Schwaber and Mike Beedle.[11]

Of all the development models discussed in this book, Scrum is clearly a client-driven approach. It is the client who defines and prioritizes the functions and features which the team prioritizes into phases and builds a phase at a time. The process allows the client to change functions and features as more of the solution depth is uncovered through the previous iterations.

The Scrum process flow is shown in Figure 1.10.

Figure 1.10
The Scrum
Process Flow

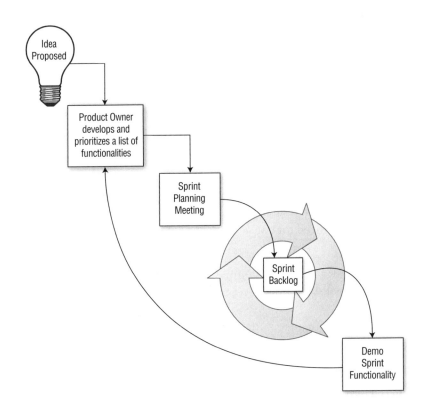

---

[11] Ken Schwaber and Mike Beedle, *Agile Software Development with Scrum* (Upper Saddle River, NJ: Prentice Hall, 2001).

Idea Proposed

The original idea for the system may be vague. It may be expressed in the form of business terms. A function-level description can be developed as part of the scoping phase, but not to the depth of detail that the client requires. It is not likely to be expressed in system terms.

Product Owner Develops and Prioritizes a List of Functionality

The Product Owner is responsible for developing this list, which is called the **product backlog**. It will help team members understand more detail about the idea and help them form some ideas about how to approach the project.

Sprint Planning Meeting

This is an eight-hour meeting with two distinct four-hour parts. In the first part, the Product Owner presents the prioritized product backlog to the development team. This is the opportunity for the team to ask questions to clarify each element of functionality. In this first part of the meeting, the team commits to the Product Owner the functionality it will deliver in the first 30-day **sprint**. The team then spends the remaining four hours developing a high-level plan for how it will accomplish the sprint. The work to be done is captured in the **sprint backlog**. The sprint backlog is the current list of functionalities that are not yet completed for the current sprint.

Sprint Backlog

This is the running list of tasks that must be completed to deliver the product backlog for this iteration.

Demo Sprint Functionality

At the end of the sprint, the team demos the solution to the client. Functionality is added or changed, and the product backlog is updated and reprioritized for the next sprint. This entire process continues until the product backlog is empty or the client is otherwise satisfied that the current sprint version is the ultimate solution, or the budget has been expended.

> **Observation**
>
> Scrum has often been characterized as a methodology that does not require a project manager. In fact, the position of project manager does not exist, but the role does. It is assumed primarily by the team of senior developers, which operates as a self-managed team. The Scrum Master carries responsibility for facilitation of and compliance with the process. Collocation of the Scrum team is critical. Scrum teams of more than ten members tend to be dysfunctional.

One of my clients reported an interesting application of Scrum. You be the judge, but keep an open mind. All of this client's software-maintenance projects are allocated to a **product maintenance backlog** file and prioritized by the Product Maintenance Backlog Manager, who is also responsible for estimating the effort and resource requirements for each maintenance project. This is a project-management consultant assigned to their Project Management Office (PMO). Not all developers are assigned 100 percent to Scrum projects. There will be delays between their Scrum project assignments. During these delays, they are responsible for periodically checking the product-maintenance backlog and working on maintenance projects found there. The objective is to empty the backlog. Periodic reports of the backlog size and dates provide objective measures of attainment.

Dynamic Systems Development Method (DSDM)

Dynamic Systems Development Method (DSDM) is what the Standard Waterfall model would look like in a zero-gravity world. Feedback loops are the defining features that separate DSDM from the Standard Waterfall model. DSDM advocates would claim that a DSDM approach will deliver results more quickly, with higher quality and less cost than any TPM PMLC model. DSDM is an adaptive model. The feedback loops help guide the client and the project team to a complete solution. The business case is included as a feedback loop so that even the fundamental basis and justification for the project can be revisited. DSDM claims to be the only publicly available framework that covers the entire systems life cycle from end to end.

The list below contains the nine key principles of DSDM. Note that these principles are quite similar to those we have previously identified as good practices. Active user involvement is imperative.

1. DSDM teams must be empowered to make decisions.
2. The focus is on frequent delivery of products.
3. Fitness for business purpose is the essential criterion for acceptance of deliverables.
4. Iterative and incremental development is necessary to converge on an accurate business solution.
5. All changes during development are reversible.
6. Requirements are baselined at a high level.
7. Testing is integrated throughout the life cycle.
8. A collaborative and cooperative approach between all stakeholders is essential.

Most Agile PMLC models can subscribe to these principles. With minor variation, these principles are common to the APF PMLC model too, and will be further commented on in the context of APF in the next section.

Figure 1.11 highlights the DSDM method.

The distinguishing feature of the Dynamic Systems Development Model (DSDM) is the incremental release and implementation of a production system at the end of each cycle. Note that iterations around the Design & Build Iteration all follow with an implementation phase. DSDM delivers business value to the client as part of its overall process design. Other approaches may do the same as a variation, but DSDM does it as part of the design of the approach itself.

Pre-project: Idea Generation

This phase includes some type of project overview, charter, or high-level business case designed to support the decision that the project should be undertaken. Once the decision to approve the project is made, the project is funded and the feasibility study can begin.

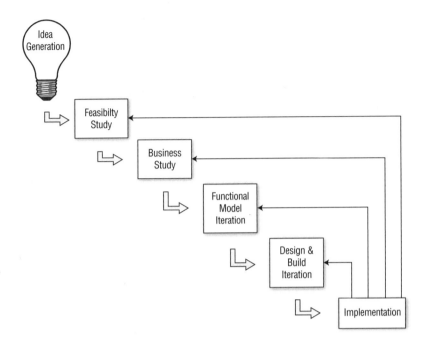

Figure 1.11
Dynamic Systems Development Method

Feasibility Study

A decision must be made as to whether or not to use DSDM on this project. The typical feasibility study is done, but with the addition of the question of the appropriateness of DSDM. As part of answering that question, consideration is given to the support of DSDM that can be expected from the organization and the capabilities of the available project team members. The DSDM feasibility study is not an exhaustive treatise, but is quite high-level. Two weeks at most should be allocated to the Feasibility Study phase. Remember: You want only to decide whether or not to use DSDM.

Business Study

The client team in collaboration with the developer team will do a high-level investigation of the business processes affected by the project and identify information needs. The investigation is best conducted in a workshop environment with the appropriate SMEs involved. High-level process and data-flow diagrams are often produced. Requirements are documented. System architecture is defined, but with the proviso that it will probably change as the project progresses. Finally, a high-level plan is developed. It will identify expected prototyping (if any) during the Functional Model Iteration and Design & Build Iteration phases.

Functional Model Iteration

In this phase, the functional model and information requirements are refined through repeated cycles of the following tasks:

- Identify what you are going to do in this next cycle.
- Decide how you are going to do it.
- Do it.
- Check that you did it right.

Design & Build Iteration

These iterations will select prioritized requirements and design and build them. Production prototypes are commonly developed as well. A partial solution is delivered at each iteration, and the complete solution is a deliverable from this phase.

Implementation

This is the hand-off from development to production. All of the typical implementation activities take place in this phase. Those activities include installation, training, documentation, operations support, and user support.

Post-project

A post-implementation audit will follow after a suitable period of use has passed. Revisions and other system changes are accepted and built into the system through new releases.

DSDM in Non-IT Projects

While DSDM is clearly a systems-development framework, it can be applied to projects that have nothing to do with IT. That is our interest here. The Try & Buy Department Store case study will illustrate the application of DSDM to a training curriculum development project. Because the Information Systems Department was organized along 184 customer groups and each group had developed its own project-management approach along with the tools, templates, and processes to support it, curriculum development would be a challenge. The final curriculum had to support this environment, so a DSDM approach was chosen.

Case Study: Try & Buy Department Stores—DSDM Approach

The Feasibility Study included an assessment of the skills profile of all 2,000 project managers and a gap analysis to identify the skills-development needs. The Systems Architecture Definition provided the overall structure of the curriculum, the courses, and their formats. Existing courses were mapped into this structure. In order to get meaningful involvement in the development effort, the Functional Iteration was conducted entirely within a workshop setting. It required only a few iterations to define specific courses, course content, collateral materials, support services, and the development schedule. Four development teams were put in place for the Design and Build Iterations. Each team focused on a different project manager position class: team leader, project manager, senior project manager, and program manager. Every two weeks, a course prototype was produced by each team. Once the prototypes stabilized, all four teams were brought together to finalize the course prototypes. The build phase followed. The teams decided that a phased roll-out was the best implementation strategy. Later versions of the solution included establishing coaching and mentoring services and course revisions.

From this example, you can see that DSDM is a framework that can be adapted to a given situation.

Adaptive Project Framework

I'm sure I have tested your patience by putting you through the project landscape discussion, including the brief discussion of specific models, but it was necessary. You can now put APF in the context of project-management models and understand how it fills a void left by all other models. APF presents an entirely different way of managing mission-critical projects with poorly defined solutions than do other agile PMLC models. The major distinction is that APF is an active model for searching out solutions, whereas all other Agile PMLC models are basically passive. By that I mean that for them, solution discovery emerges rather than being designed into actual initiatives. To search out the missing parts of the solution, APF uses probative swim lanes that run concurrently with swim lanes that integrate discovered solution components. The probative swim lanes can be of several types. Probative swim lanes are unique to APF. These are discussed later in this section.

APF is still a work-in-progress. It was first introduced in 2001. It is an industrial-strength model designed for a maximalist adaptive project. It is a five-phase approach designed to deliver maximum business value to clients from every cycle within the limits of client-imposed time and cost constraints. In this section, I discuss some of the major differences between APF and other models. I want to plant some early ideas and concepts so that you will understand the relevance of later discussion. As I develop the concepts and practices of APF, I would ask that you keep an open mind. Don't saddle yourself with old practices and worn-out tenets. APF can open a whole new world of possibilities for you.

APF's Roots

APF had its beginnings in two consulting engagements that were running concurrently and by coincidence had much in common. The first engagement was with a retailer who wanted to install kiosks in its stores. The kiosks would offer the latest information on product specials, give store-location information for products, and provide other customer services. Snacks Fifth Avenue is the case study of that company's use of the initial version of APF. The second engagement was with a software-development company that designed and built internet and intranet applications for its clients. Kamikazi Systems Development Company is the case study of that company's use of the initial version of APF. Both of these case studies are included here, but the names and industries have been changed to protect the companies' true identities.

Even though these two projects were quite different, they did have one characteristic in common. Both companies knew the final goal, but neither knew the solution in detail. The question for both projects was, "How do you proceed with managing such projects when neither a complete Requirements Breakdown Structure nor a complete Work Breakdown Structure could be established as the basis for the project plan?" Both organizations followed more-or-less the traditional linear approach to project management. Both could see that that approach wasn't going to do the job. But what *would* do the job? Something different was needed.

That need was the impetus for the development of APF concurrent with the projects themselves. Both projects were completed successfully, and APF became a reality. Since then, APF has been used successfully in a number of different organizations. I am aware of its use in developing new financial products for a large insurance company, designing and building computer-based commercials and short-subject videos, conducting new-product research and development (R&D) for a consumer-products company, engaging in drug research, and other applications.

I still consider APF a work-in-process, and will expand and embellish it through my own consulting engagements as well as experiences shared by others. All of my learning and discovery about APF will eventually find its way into the literature. This book is the initial work. In a sense, the development of APF is an APF project!

APF represents several departures from more-traditional systems.

Scope Is Variable

The first departure of APF from the traditionalist's mindset is that in an APF project scope is variable. This can be disturbing to many more traditionally thinking project managers and clients. APF maximizes business value by adjusting the scope of the solution as part of each completed cycle. It does this by making the client the central figure in deciding what constitutes maximum business value and putting the client in charge of deciding what changes should be made. At the completion of a cycle, the client has an opportunity to change the direction of the project based on the cumulative learning from all previous cycles. This means that an APF project's course is constantly corrected to ensure the delivery of maximum business value. At the completion of the final cycle, when time or money or both have been used up, the deliverable will have the most business value that could have been produced from the collective wisdom and learning of the client team and the development team. A **Scope Bank** will have been established to house all ideas emanating from the previous cycles but not yet acted upon, so that at the completion of the APF project the Scope Bank may still contain additional features and functions that can be integrated into the solution as time, money, and resource availability permit. These unrealized features and functions serve as material for "version 2" of the solution. And so we see that change through learning and discovery is not only embraced, but is a critical success factor for all APF projects.

APF Just-in-time Planning

Because scope is variable, APF project planning takes on a whole new meaning. The basic concept underlying an APF project is not to plan the future. The future is unknown: Leave it that way. Part of the solution lives in the future and is waiting to be discovered. As it is discovered, it will be integrated into the solution. APF planning does not forecast the future and then plan for it. APF is not a passive model. It does try to discover the future through what I will call "probative initiatives" (but more on that later—see Chapter 3: How to Plan an APF Cycle). Trying to forecast the future is a waste of time, and merely increases the non-value-added work already present in the project.

Initial planning in APF is done at a high level and is functionally based. TPM planning is activity- and task-based. In APF, planning at the micro level is done within each cycle. It begins with a mid-level component- or function-based RBS, and ends with a micro-level activity- and task-based WBS. I like to think of it as just-in-time planning. A key phrase to keep in mind when applying APF is, "When in doubt, leave it out!"—meaning that you include within each cycle only the detailed planning of those activities that clearly will be part of the end result. That is, in each cycle, include in your detailed plan only what you know to be factual. Thus, planning is done in segments, where each cycle includes work that will require only a few weeks to complete. A cycle is so short that it typically will not meet the duration requirements to be called a project. Therefore, while a cycle will use many of the tools, templates, and processes of a more-traditional approach, it is a unique artifact of an APF project.

Caution
When in doubt, leave it out!

Change Is Expected

Unlike the Linear and Incremental PMLC models, where we treat scope as fixed and hope to avoid change, the Adaptive and Extreme PMLC models require change in order for the project to be successful. In these two model types, change is what leads to the discovery and learning of missing features and functions needed to fully define the solution (in Adaptive PMLC models), or clearer focus on the goal (in Extreme PMLC models). Two useful metrics to track from cycle to cycle are the number of additions to the Scope Bank at each cycle and the number of additions that result in further defining the solution at each cycle. These metrics are discussed later in this section.

Change in an APF project is encouraged through frequent release of products or processes in order to collect input for further change. Without that input, an APF project will fail. The meaningful involvement and collaboration of the client team is critical to that change process.

The APF Project Contract

This is perhaps the most difficult part of an APF project to justify to managers whose mindset is in the TPM world. Simply put, an APF contract says that with meaningful client involvement the project will deliver the most business value within the limits of client-specified time and cost constraints. Stated another way, clients don't know exactly what will be delivered at the end of the project, only that it will offer the most business value possible and that they will have played a critical role in that determination. For the time and money invested, clients will get as much of a solution as they possibly can with the knowledge they and the development team have of the situation. What this all boils down to is the need for trust and openness between the client team and the development team as well as between the co-managers of the project.

Remember that in an APF project, you can't wait until somebody figures out what the requirements are; that will never happen. You must proceed with the project based on the information you have. Your expectation is that the approach you have chosen will bring the missing functions and features into focus and the project can deliver acceptable business value.

An APF Project Is Mission Critical

It is unlikely that an APF project is anything but critical to the enterprise. The situation is this:

- No complete solution is known
- The risk of not finding a complete solution is high
- The success of the project is critical
- None of the familiar Linear and Incremental PMLC models will work
- APF is the only model that offers any hope of finding an acceptable solution

So while APF may not be the silver bullet you are hoping to find, it is your only alternative. An APF approach will deliver as much business value as possible. Through a collaborative effort between the client team and the development team, the best solution humanly possible will emerge. It may not be a perfect solution, but it will be the best that can be done. The expectation is that with actual experience using the solution, a second and succeeding versions can be justified.

The Roles of the Client and the Project Manager in an APF Project

It would be foolish to use an APF approach in the absence of meaningful client involvement. In fact, without meaningful client involvement, it would be risky to undertake any project, regardless of the model used. Every PMLC requires some level of client involvement. For an APF project, however, there is much more to say about the role of the client co-manager and the role of the development project co-manager. It is best to think of the two as sharing the responsibilities of the project manager—they become co-managers of the project, with distinct responsibilities.

The first difference between traditional project management and APF management is that traditional project managers have to quickly get used to the fact that they are no longer in charge of the project—at least not by themselves. They now share that responsibility with the client. There is no finger-pointing, except at themselves. Different, isn't it? In an APF project, the manager of the development team assumes more of an advisory role. The manager keeps the client team pointed in feasible directions and advises the client on the best choice from among a number of feasible alternatives. The client, however, makes the final decision among the set of alternatives. For some traditional project managers, this role will be difficult to accept. Rather than being in charge, they are going to have to share responsibility for leadership and decision making. For some clients, too, this role will be difficult to accept. Rather than deferring to the project manager, they are going to have to be meaningfully involved and make decisions. Project success or failure is shared between the client-team manager and the development-team manager.

From the client side, the role is different than the project manager would be accustomed to. Client-side accountability is one of the strengths of APF. The client is the business SME. The developer is the technical SME. Both the development-team manager and the client-team manager have vested interests in the success of the project. What otherwise might have been an obstacle to implementation success fades into oblivion.

The second difference is that clients have to be willing to step forward and clearly and openly state their opinions. Their relationship with the project team must be open. They must feel like equals with the team. They can no longer hide behind the excuse that this is a technology project and they don't understand technology. This is a business project, and they have as much say and as much authority as does anyone else on the project team. A great synergy can be created between two parties with totally different perspectives on the same project. Find a way to leverage that power to the advantage of your organization.

APF Is Not a Recipe to Be Blindly Followed

I am not in the recipe business. You won't find endless lists of things to do in an APF project. That would be a waste of time and the APF user doesn't waste time. As you read and study the pages that follow, expect to learn how you, the APF project co-managers, need to start thinking about what you are doing and how you are working together. If something either of you is doing doesn't make sense, it probably should be changed or not done at all. As an APF project co-manager, you will know how to recognize these situations and invoke the proper change. For some traditional project managers, this continues to be a difficult adjustment. They would rather not have to think about what to do, but be able to merely follow a recipe. I want you to start thinking about *creating* a recipe from the ingredients you have at your disposal. That way you will be able to take charge of the project rather than being victimized by it.

If you need a recipe to manage your project, APF is not for you. The effective APF project co-manager is a senior-level manager who not only has command over an extensive collection of tools, templates, and processes, but more importantly, knows when to use them, how to use them, and how to adapt them. This type of co-manager is the chef I wrote about earlier!

Why Do We Need APF?

APF offers a unique approach to types of projects that other approaches and models do not. First of all, APF can be used for software-development projects, but it was designed for non-software development projects, and has been used successfully on process and product design and improvement projects and a variety of R&D projects as well. These are mission-critical projects whose solutions are not completely known ahead of time and can only become known through doing the project. These are projects for which TPM approaches will not work. They are projects that must be done, and some way of doing them effectively must be devised. You have no choice! That need gave rise to APF.

APF is not the only Agile Project Management methodology. I listed several others earlier. But APF is unique in that it was designed for any type of project, not just software development as all of the other agile methodologies were. Project co-managers, the Scope Bank, and probative swim lanes are three of the unique artifacts of an APF effort and set APF apart from all other Agile PMLC models.

Benefits of APF versus TPM Approaches

APF brings a lot of business value to the table as compared to other approaches.

APF Projects Always Finish Sooner than TPM Projects

If it were possible to do the same project twice—once using a TPM Linear model and once using APF—the APF project would finish sooner every time. This is a claim made by all APM approaches. The reason for this is obvious. Because APF squeezes out all non-value-added work, it produces less to do than those projects that follow more-traditional approaches. The time spent planning is a good example. Linear and Incremental models plan the entire project, and then when change comes along and is approved, the plan has to be redone from the point of the change to the end of the project. That situation is repeated several times throughout a project, making much of the original planning into non-value-added work. The more changes that are approved, the more non-value-added work there will be. APF has none of this excess baggage, and is therefore guaranteed to finish sooner than traditional approaches.

APF Projects Are Less Expensive than TPM Projects

Non-value-added work costs money. There is at least a labor cost for the time spent planning activities and tasks that are never done due to frequent scope changes. This wastes money in the end.

APF Projects Have a Better Business Termination Policy than TPM Projects

Most distressed or failing TPM projects are terminated too late, because by the time it is discovered that the project isn't producing the desired results and should be terminated, the available budget and time are nearly expended. That happens because the first deliverables come very late in the project life cycle, after most of the money and time have already been spent. Not so with APF. APF delivers early and often. If anything is going awry, it will be discovered earlier than in a TPM project, giving the project co-managers information on which to decide to terminate the project before any additional time or money is spent needlessly. This doesn't mean the project won't be done. It means that the project won't be done in the way it was originally planned: Some other approach using APF is needed, and the time and money saved by this early termination will be invested in the new direction.

The APF Project Produces Higher-quality Deliverables than the TPM Project

The elevated level of client involvement in an APF project means that the client will have a look at intermediate deliverables early in the project and have an opportunity to adjust them. The quality of the final product will therefore exceed that of a TPM project.

TPM projects all suffer from the effects of scope change. The initial design will be compromised due to the changes. The more frequent the changes, the more the design is compromised. The final TPM solution, if there even is one, will be a patchwork.

The APF Project Delivers Maximum Business Value for the Time and Cost Invested

The continual adjustment and redirection of an APF project means everything that is delivered is needed and is of the quality expected by the client. The client, in collaboration with you, decides what goes into the solution at every iteration. Poorer-than-expected deliverables will not survive the APF project life cycle. If an APF project is terminated, at least you will have a partial solution with some business value.

Core Values of APF

As you can see, APF is more than just a framework. It represents a way of thinking about clients and how best to serve them. The client is the center of attention in an APF project. The client controls the direction of the project and determines where business value can be created or increased. APF projects continue at the clients' discretion and with their approval.

This way of thinking is embodied in the following six core values. These core values are immutable. They must be practiced in every APF project—no exceptions. In time, APF teams will be recognized for the visible practice of their core values. I have had occasion to work with teams that periodically reward team members for practicing the APF core values above and beyond the call of duty. The core values are that important.

1. Client-focused

While I was looking for the appropriate name for this core value, the phrase "walk in the shoes of the client" was always on my mind. It still is an operative part of truly being client-focused. This value is the most important of the core values. The needs of the client must always come first, as long as they are within the bounds of ethical business practices. This value can never be compromised, and APF teams must go beyond simply keeping it in mind: It must be obvious throughout your interactions with your fellow development-team members and all of the members of the client team.

A client-focused attitude will be a radical behavioral change to those few project managers who are clinging to old practices. I have some clients who provide templates for their clients to use to submit a description of what they want and of what business value it will offer. I've seen questions such as: "What other systems will the requested system impact?" How they expect the client to answer that question is beyond me. Others will make the process a little less painful by assisting the client with filling out the document. That approach is better, but not the best. It still assumes that clients can in fact state what they want (or to be more precise, what they need). Few clients will be able to do that because of the complexity and uncertainty that pervades today's projects. The simple projects have all been done many times. Best would be to engage the client in discussions about their needs, and from that start, forge a strategy for going forward. That is the APF strategy we explore in this section and in the remaining chapters.

Don't think that I am advocating passive acceptance of whatever the client might request. Such acceptance would border on dereliction of duty. "Client-focused" means going way beyond doing what clients ask of you. It also means protecting their best interests. In a spirit of openness, you are obligated to challenge ideas, wishes, and wants whenever you believe such challenges are called for. Your goal is to maximize business value to your clients, even if you have to push back on their requests. You have to own the solution just as much as the client has to own the solution. To do otherwise is not part of being client-focused. You want to do the right things for the right reasons, and to always act with honesty and integrity.

2. Client-driven

One of the guiding principles of my business has always been to engage my clients in every way that I can. I want them not only to be meaningfully involved, but also to have the sense that they are determining the direction the project is taking. At the extreme, this value would mean having the client take on the role and responsibilities of the project manager. I've been in such situations a few times in the last 20 years of practicing project management. Such an extreme will not happen very often, but there are occasions when it will occur. An effective arrangement I insist on with my clients is to have project co-managers—one from the client side and one from my organization. I have insisted on this for my entire career in project management. In this arrangement, both individuals share equally in the success or failure of the project. There is a clear and established co-ownership. My own practice with my clients tells me that this is a key to successful implementation. The client will have a vested interest in the success of the project and will do whatever is necessary to assure success. The client's reputation and credibility are on the line, just as mine are on the line. This is critical for a successful APF project.

For many clients, early in the history of APF adoption by their organizations there is a learning curve that you will have to pay attention to. The first APF project you undertake with a client should be prefaced by a workshop to help the client not only understand what APF is and why APF is being used, but more importantly, how to be a good client in an APF project. For the second and later projects, you can expect more from this client. Eventually, you may even move the client to the position of project manager, with you acting as advisor, coach, and mentor. Being the product owner in a Scrum project would be the final step in the growth and development of the client as a contributing member of an agile project team.

3. Incremental Results Early and Often

In the spirit of prototyping, in an APF project you want to deliver a working solution to the client as early and often as possible. Early delivery is especially valuable when there is any question that the real needs of the client have not yet surfaced despite your best efforts. The functionality of the first cycles of the project may be very limited, but useful in any case. In some cases, the first iteration might be a proof of concept. (See Chapter 7: Adapting APF for more on this point.) It should deliver business value even though it is of very limited functionality. It gives the client an early feel for the final deliverables. Giving clients opportunities to work with something concrete is always better than asking them to react to some vague concept or sketch on the back of a napkin or buried in a lengthy functional specification.

Early-and-often delivery helps get clients meaningfully engaged, and keeps them engaged throughout the project. It creates an ownership on the part of the client. This is critical to the success of the project. Without the client's meaningful participation, an APF project is doomed to failure. Clients must understand this, and you must facilitate it. If you can't get that involvement, use some other approach; APF is not the way to go. See Chapter 9: APF Frequently Asked Questions for advice and guidance on getting and sustaining meaningful client involvement from the very beginning of a project.

4. Continuous Questioning and Introspection

This core value speaks to an openness and honesty that must exist between the client team and the development team. Both parties must be committed to making the best business decisions possible. That can happen only with honest and open dialog. Personalities have to be put aside if this environment is to be realized.

Building a solution iteratively affords the opportunity to be creative. It creates the opportunity to adjust as better and more valuable features or functions are discovered. As the cycle build proceeds, both the client team and the development team should be looking continually for improvements in the solution or the functionality and features being offered. Look back at previous cycles and ask whether what was done was the best that could have been done. All of this learning and discovery will be captured in the Scope Bank (see Chapter 4: How to Build the APF Cycle for a detailed discussion of the Scope Bank) and will come together in the Client Checkpoint phase. Here is where the client and your project team propose, discuss, and approve further solution-development efforts.

A true spirit of openness must exist. Neither party should be afraid to offer or challenge an idea or the real value of some present or future deliverable. I've frequently told teams that if any one of their members had an idea and didn't share it with the rest of the team, I would consider that dereliction of duty. Some think that coveting knowledge is a source of power. In the APF project, that is the kiss of death! The same is true for the client. The successful practice of this core value is heavily dependent on the existence of a true team environment.

5. Change Is Progress to a Better Solution

Dave Crane, one of my colleagues, is often heard saying, "You're always smarter tomorrow than you are today." He is referring to improving task duration estimates over time, but his comment applies to APF as well. The Version Scope phase begins with the requestor and provider coming to a definition of what is needed and what will be delivered through the Conditions of Satisfaction (COS) experience. (See Chapter 2: How to Scope the

APF Project for a detailed discussion of COS.) Despite their best efforts, all the two parties have done to this point is make the best guess they can as to what will be done. That guess may turn out to be a very good guess or only partially on target, but that is not important. What is important is that by working with the deliverables from the earlier cycles, both parties will get a better picture of what can still be delivered. They will be smarter as a result of their experiences with the deliverables from the earlier cycles. The result is to improve the solution going forward into future cycles.

While change is needed to reach the best solution, too much change sends a very different message. One of the metrics I advise my clients to use is the frequency of change requests over time. The expectation is that the interim solutions are converging on the ultimate solution. This is evidenced first by an increasing number of change requests from cycle to cycle, and then a decreasing number of change requests later in the project. If this is not happening, there is a likelihood that the project is not converging on an acceptable solution, but rather is diverging. See Chapter 5: How to Manage the Client Checkpoint for more on the topic of monitoring project progress.

6. Don't Speculate on the Future

There will always be the temptation to envision some ideal state and convince oneself that achieving it is realistic. An APF team must resist that temptation. APF strips out all non-value-added work. Guessing only adds non-value-added work back in. When in doubt, leave it out. APF is designed to spend the client's time and money on client-defined business value, not on non-value-added work.

> **Caution**
> When in doubt, leave it out.

If you find yourself building the RBS or the WBS and you are, or the client is, guessing at what should be included, you are probably using the wrong approach. The RBS is your best checkpoint against the choice of approach. If there is any guessing at all, you might want to think about APF as the better-fit approach.

Overview of the APF Life Cycle

The stage is now set for our first detailed look at APF. Figure 1.12 is a graphic portrayal of the five phases of APF. First, note that APF is an iterative process. You iterate within a cycle and between cycles. Every cycle presents the team and the client with a learning and discovery opportunity. APF is crafted to take advantage of these opportunities. As you continue to study each phase, you will come to realize that defining the cycle content for learning and discovery is its real strength. It sets APF apart from all the other APM models.

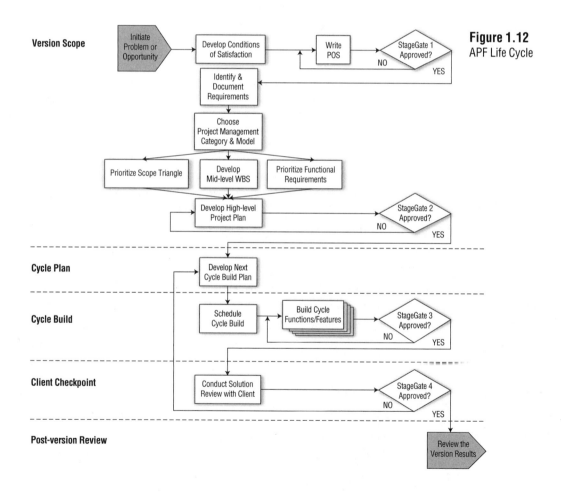

Figure 1.12
APF Life Cycle

Version Scope

As shown in the Version Scope portion of Figure 1.12, the Version Defining phase and the Version Planning phase both contain approval points, which I call StageGates. There are four StageGates in every APF Project:

- StageGate 1: Approval of the POS so that requirements can be gathered (part of the version-defining process)
- StageGate 2: Approval of the high-level project plan so that the project may begin (end of the version-planning process)
- StageGate 3: Cycle approved as having met the cycle-completion criteria (required at completion of every cycle)
- StageGate 4: Version approved as having met the version-completion criteria (end of the version)

Version Scope defines the boundaries of the project. I have chosen to use the term **version** to indicate that a subsequent project might take the solution to the next level of development. An APF project begins with a stated business problem or opportunity. This beginning is the same as for a TPM project. A request has been made to develop a solution to the stated problem or a way to take advantage of a stated business opportunity. At this point, you are not at all sure what kind of project this might be, or how you might approach it from a methodology perspective. A Conditions of Satisfaction conversation takes place between the requestor and the provider to define more clearly exactly what is needed and what will be done to meet that need. A requirements-gathering session may be held in which an RBS may be constructed. The RBS is input into the decision process regarding which project-management category the project belongs in: TPM, APM, xPM, or MPx. Once the category is chosen, the project characteristics are used to decide which model is a best fit. For the sake of this section, assume you have discovered or suspect that the RBS is not complete. There is no formula or survey to determine the degree of completeness. It is a feeling, a very subjective call on your part and that of the client. In any case, because of the suspected missing functions and features, an APM approach is chosen and you have decided upon APF, so a project-scoping document—specifically, a Project Overview Statement—is written. A POS basically summarizes the COS and RBS, if either is available. The POS is a brief document (usually one page, with perhaps an attachment) that contains the following five sections:

- A statement of the problem or opportunity (reason for doing the project)
- A goal statement (what will generally be done)
- A statement of the objectives (general statements of how it might be done)
- The quantifiable business outcomes (what business value will be obtained)
- General comments on risks, assumptions, and obstacles to success

For a more-detailed discussion of Project Overview Statements, see my book *Effective Project Management: Traditional, Agile, Extreme*.[12]

The second deliverable from this phase is a prioritized list of the functionalities that have been requested and agreed to in the COS. The RBS contains this information. Both parties recognize that this list may change and is probably incomplete, but at this point in the project, the list reflects the best information available. There may be additions, deletions, and changes as the project commences.

The third deliverable from this phase is the mid-level Work Breakdown Structure. Since the RBS is incomplete, the WBS will also be incomplete. If an RBS exists, it may be used as the starting point for defining the WBS. The RBS will specify what is to be done, and the WBS will further decompose the RBS to define how it will be done. For present purposes, a mid-level WBS is one that shows the goal at level 0, major functions at level 1, and sub-functions at level 2. Generally, such a WBS would have a two- or three-level decomposition. The number of levels is not important. What is important is to have at least one level of decomposition to the work level for as many functions and features as have been identified. Any more WBS detail at this point is not considered useful. The reason for this will become clear in the Cycle Plan phase.

The traditionalist would have a problem with this approach, because the entire foundation of traditional project planning and scheduling is based on having a complete WBS. I contend that the time spent trying to create a complete WBS at this stage is largely wasted. Again, I remind you of the question, "Why plan for the future when you don't know what it is?" In this

---

[12] Wysocki 2009.

case, the piece that is missing is that you are not exactly sure how you are going to deliver the functionality. You do know what functionality has to be delivered, and you are using that information to generate a mid-level WBS, but not a complete WBS. The complete WBS will eventually be generated when we know enough to generate it. That will happen with repeated iterations through the Cycle Plan, Cycle Build, and Client Checkpoint phases. You will generate the complete WBS when you need it and not before; and when you do generate it, you will know that it is correct and not a guess. Again, since the RBS focuses on what needs to be done while the WBS focuses on how it will be done, if the RBS is incomplete, the WBS must also be incomplete.

The fourth deliverable from this phase is a prioritization of the variables that define the Scope Triangle (**time**, **cost**, and **resource availability** determining the scale of the **scope** and **quality**). This prioritization will be used later as an aid to decision making and problem solving during the Cycle Build phase.

Cycle Plan

Once the POS has been written and is presented along with a prioritized list of known functionalities that the client and the project manager believe are needed to take advantage of the business opportunity or solve the business problem, some high-level planning is done very quickly to prioritize the functionality into a number of time-boxed cycles for development. Typical cycle length is two to six weeks. The cycle length is documented and agreed to by both parties—along with the expectation that it will change as project work commences.

The Cycle Plan phase will be repeated a number of times before the project is complete. The first Cycle Plan phase has as input the POS, the prioritized Scope Triangle, the functionality that will be built in this cycle, and the mid-level WBS. Each subsequent Cycle Plan phase will also have a Scope Bank as input.

So far, we have been discussing specific cycle contents that relate to adding detail to the evolving solution. There is another aspect of the cycle contents that is equally important. Think of a cycle as containing two major swim lanes. (In this book, a **swim lane** defines a stream of work whose activities are related to the development or exploration of a single function or feature. These are streams of build activities that occur in parallel.) One type of swim lane is devoted to adding more detail to the evolving solution. These are called integrative swim lanes. The other type of swim lane is devoted to discovering aspects of the solution heretofore unknown. These are what I call probative swim lanes. There may be several occurrences of each type of swim lane in a single Cycle Build phase. They might comprise the search for answers to questions like: "I wonder if this is the way to solve that part of the problem?" or, "I wonder whether this would work?"

In the probative swim lanes we call on the problem-solving and creative skills of the client team and development team. In the integrative swim lanes we call on the implementation and process skills of the client team and the development team. Different skill sets are needed for the two types of swim lane. The challenge is to build a team that has both sets of skills.

I don't dismiss this as an easy exercise. It definitely isn't. Most of the difficulty stems from either the client team or the development team not approaching reprioritization with an open mind. People tend to become wedded to their earlier ideas, and are hard-pressed to give them up in favor of others. To be successful with APF, both the development team and the client team must have open minds, and not display pride of authorship on any functionality that was discussed previously.

One of the greatest benefits deriving from this approach is the meaningful and continuous involvement of clients. They are the decision makers in all activities going forward. They participate with full knowledge of what has taken place to date and with the collaborative support of the development team. They understand how business value can be achieved via changes in functionality, and they are in a position to take action. Their presence will be a constant reminder to the development team of the business aspects and value of what they are doing, and what changes should be made to protect that business value. Client involvement is a very important point to remember. It ensures that what is eventually built will meet client needs.

Cycle Build

Contrary to what you might think, the creation of the Cycle Build plan is a low-tech operation. While you certainly could use project-management software tools, I have found that a whiteboard, sticky notes, and marking pens are just as effective. This approach does keep the maintenance effort for a project file down considerably, allowing the team to focus on value-added work. This advice may sound heretical to those of you who are project-management software aficionados, so let me explain. Cycle length generally falls within a two- to six-week frame. There will likely be several small teams (a typical small team being one or two developers), working in parallel but independently, each on a separate piece of functionality. Each of these small teams will plan the cycle build in this phase and then conduct the cycle build in the next phase. Based on this description, a minimal planning effort is all that makes sense.

The cycle-planning effort might go something like this:

1. Under the guidance and advice of the client team, identify those activities that define the features and functionality that will be built in this cycle.
2. Decompose the activities, extracted down to the task level.
3. Establish the dependencies among these tasks.
4. Partition the tasks into meaningful groups and assign a team to each group.
5. Each team develops a micro-level schedule with resource allocations for the completion of its tasks within the cycle time and budget constraints.

This planning focuses on parts of the solution that will be implemented (i.e., it comprises integrative swim lanes). For the probative swim lanes (See Chapter 2: How to Scope the APF Project), repeat the steps, focusing on establishing whether certain proposed features and functionality would enhance the current solution. If they would, then these will become part of a future cycle plan.

There is no critical path to calculate and manage. The longest-duration swim lane is the critical path. Pay attention to it! The cycle is so short that too much planning and analysis leads to paralysis and, worst of all, non-value-added work. Take the low-tech approach; it will work just fine here. You don't need to clutter the cycle with non-value-added work. The entire effort can be whiteboard, sticky-note, and marker-pen based. A dedicated war room would be helpful (about 300 square feet of floor space should be adequate). Here the team can post plans, work schedules, Scope Bank, issues log, and so on, and have daily 15-minute updates, weekly status meetings with the client, and problem-solving sessions.

Detailed planning for producing the functionality assigned to this cycle is conducted. The cycle work begins and is monitored throughout the cycle, and adjustments are made as necessary. The cycle ends when its time has expired. Any functionality not completed during this cycle is reconsidered and reprioritized for later consideration. The cycle build time box is never changed once the Cycle Build phase begins.

The first activity in the Cycle Build phase is to finish the cycle build schedule and resource allocation. With everything in place and understood by the team, work begins. Every team member has a daily task list, and posts task status updates at the completion of each day. Any variances are caught early, and corrective-action plans are put in place. Nothing escapes the attention of the project co-managers for more than one working day. A Scope Bank is created to record all change requests and ideas for functional improvements. An **issues log** records all problems and tracks the status of their resolution.

Client Checkpoint

Without a doubt, this is the most important phase of APF, for in this phase the client team and the development team come together and assess what has been accomplished, what has been discovered and learned from the just-completed cycle, and what should be done in the cycle to come. The client team and the development team jointly perform a quality review of the features and functionality produced in the just-completed cycle. These are compared against the requirements and their part in the solution and the overall goal of maximizing business value. Adjustments are made to the high-level plan and next cycle work as appropriate. The sequence Cycle Plan→Cycle Build→Client Checkpoint is repeated until the time and cost budgets for this version have been expended, or the project is terminated because it is not converging on an acceptable solution, or an acceptable solution has been reached for this version and no further work is needed.

The Client Checkpoint phase is a critical review that takes place after every Cycle Build phase is completed. During the Cycle Build phase, both the client team and the development team will benefit from several discovery and learning episodes. Variations to the version functionality will surface; alternative approaches to delivering certain functionality will be suggested, and each team will learn through continuous involvement with the other team. A definite synergy will develop between the two teams. All of this must be considered, along with the functionality that had originally been assigned to the next cycle. The result is a revised prioritization of functionalities for the next cycle. The most important thing to remember is not to speculate on the future. For the next cycle, prioritize only functionality that you are certain will be in the end result. The newly prioritized list will be input into deciding on the integrative swim lanes for the coming cycle. The learning and discovery from the just-completed Cycle Build phase will be input into deciding on the probative swim lanes for the coming cycle, while the available resources and the resource requirements of the prioritized integrative and probative swim lanes will dictate the contents of the coming cycle.

Post-version Review

During the Version Scope phase, you developed measurable business outcomes in discussion with the client. These became the rationale for why the project was undertaken in the first place. Think of these outcomes as success criteria: That is, the undertaking can be considered a success if, and only if, these outcomes are achieved. In many cases, these outcomes cannot be measured until some time after the project has been completed. Take the case of a project impacting market share. It won't happen next Tuesday. It may happen several quarters later, and this timeframe must be part of the success-criteria statement.

When the budget and time allotted to this version have been spent, that marks the end of the project. Some functionality that was planned to be completed may not have been. It will be archived in the Scope Bank for consideration in the next version. The main purposes of the Post-version Review are to check how you did with respect to the success criteria, to document what you learned that will be useful in the next version, and to begin thinking about functionality for the next version.

What the client team and the development team believe to be the best mix of functionality has been built into the solution. The project is done. The deliverables are installed, and the solution is in production. At this stage, three questions need to be answered:

1. Was the expected business outcome realized?
2. What was learned that can be used to improve the solution?
3. What was learned that can be used to improve the effectiveness of APF?

The business outcome was the factor used to validate the reason for doing the project in the first place. If it was achieved, chalk that one up on the success side of the board. If it wasn't, determine why not. Can something further be done to achieve the outcome? If so, that will be input into the functional specifications for the next version. If not, kill the project right now. No need to send good money after bad.

There is also a lesson here for everyone. If projects are limited in scope and they fail with no way to rescue them, you have limited the dollars lost to those failed projects. The downside of undertaking larger projects is that you risk losing more money. If there is a way of finding out early that a project isn't going to deliver as promised, cut your losses. The same logic works from cycle to cycle. If you can learn early that an approach will not work, kill the project and save the time and cost of the later cycles. TPM would find out a project wasn't working only after all the money was spent, and then a great deal of trouble might be involved in killing the project. The traditional thought goes, "After all, there is so much money tied up in this project, we can't just kill it. Let's try to save it." How costly, and unnecessary!

The APF Scope Triangle

The APF Scope Triangle is defined by five variables (**time**, **cost**, and **resource availability** forming the borders of the triangle, and **scope** and **quality** comprising its area). You may be familiar with the "Iron Triangle." It is defined by scope, time, and cost, and is a more-primitive form of the APF Scope Triangle. Both models are valid. The five variables that define the APF Scope Triangle form an interdependent set and define the project as a system in balance at the beginning of the project. If one of these variables should change for any reason, at least one of the others must change in order to restore balance to the system. For example, if the client changes the project-completion deadline by reducing the time allowed, then at least one of the following must be done in order to restore balance to the system (the project):

- Increase the budget
- Increase the development-team size
- Reduce quality
- Reduce scope

Five Project Variables

The five variables that define the project (system) form an interdependent set that works together to keep the project moving forward in an orderly fashion. Figure 1.13 represents the APF Scope Triangle.

Scope

Scope defines the depth and breadth of the deliverables the project is intended to produce. The functions and features that define these deliverables are not all known at the beginning of the project—the reason why you are using APF. Scope will therefore change as the project work commences, and this is not unexpected. The changes bring the project closer to an acceptable solution and therefore are for the good of the project.

Figure 1.13
The APF Scope
Triangle

Scope changes in an APF project would throw the project out of balance. A larger scope results in a larger area occupied by scope and quality. Since time and cost are fixed, those cannot be adjusted to restore balance. The project manager does not have control over resource availability; that is the responsibility of the resource managers. That leaves scope and quality as the factors that have to change to restore balance to the project. So an increase in scope due to the addition of new features or functions will result in deprioritizing less-important features or functions in the Scope Bank—at least for the time being. Remember that maximum business value is the goal of an APF project.

Quality

Scope and Quality are linked. Changes in quality are considered changes in scope.

Cost

Cost is a constraint established by the client. The investment clients make is a statement of what they are willing to pay for a solution to their problem. The development team treats cost as fixed for the duration of the project. For business reasons, the client may change it. For example, if the project is complete but more business value could still be added to the solution, the client may increase the monies available and extend the project. On the other hand, if the project is not converging on an acceptable solution, the client may reduce the dollars available, even to the point that the project must be terminated.

Time

Time is a parameter established by the client. The amount of time clients are willing to give the development team is a statement of how long they are willing to wait for the solution to their problem. The development team treats time as fixed for the duration of the project. For business reasons, the client may change it. For example, if the project continues to add business value but the timeframe for the project has run out, the client may extend the project for one or more cycles. On the other hand, if the project is not converging on an acceptable solution, the project may be terminated.

Resource Availability

Those of you who are Project Management Body of Knowledge (PMBOK) aficionados will recognize the above three variables as defining the so-called **PMBOK Iron Triangle**. PMBOK does not separate quality from scope, so the Iron Triangle is defined by cost, time, and scope. PMBOK would say: "Fix any two and the third is determined." APF would say: "Fix time and cost and the size of scope is fixed, but not its content." For years I have contended that there are really five variables, the fifth being resource availability. Time, cost, scope, and quality can all be in balance, just as they should be, but the project may still be unable to proceed. If resources are not available during the window of time in which the project work is to be done, the project goes nowhere. If resource availability changes for the worse due to competing priorities, the project is slowed or stopped unless at least one of the remaining four variables is adjusted so as to restore balance to the project (the system).

Using the APF Scope Triangle

Figure 1.13 depicts the project as a system in balance before any work begins. The three sides of the triangle are exactly long enough to form a triangle that exactly encloses the area taken by scope and quality. (Don't try to draw this triangle. It is a conceptual model only.)

You would use this model as follows. Suppose competing priorities result in reduced resource availability. The resource availability side of the triangle is shortened; the three sides no longer enclose scope and quality. To restore the balance to the system, at least one of the remaining sides must be lengthened, or the area inside the triangle must be reduced in size.

Several other permutations are possible. Some examples:

- Due to market forces, the client is forced to change the deadline for project completion to an earlier date.
- The schedule slips.
- There is a budget cut.
- Team members are lost to the project.
- Due to market forces, the scope of the project is increased

In all of these cases, one or more factors must be changed to restore balance. In all of my training classes, I advise the attendees to burn this graphic into their brains. The APF Scope Triangle is an excellent model for understanding scope-change requests and problem-resolution strategies. It has guided my problem-resolution strategies for many years.

Prioritize Project Variables

Despite all efforts, the project work can still be compromised. The need to make adjusting decisions can arise rather unexpectedly. These decisions may impact the work of the project going forward. Rather than wait for the unexpected, I strongly suggest being proactive. In the case of APF, that means prioritizing among the five project variables. Think in terms of prioritizing the five variables, beginning the list with the variable you and the client are willing to concede first if the situation warrants.

An example will help.

Case Study: PDQ Prioritized Scope Triangle

Starting with a table that contains no X's, the project team decides the priority order of the five elements. Table 1.1 reflects these decisions.

Table 1.1   PDQ Prioritized Elements of the Scope Triangle

	Firm (1)	(2)	(3)	(4)	Flexible (5)
Scope			X		
Quality		X			
Cost					X
Time	X				
Resource Availability				X	

So the prioritized list reads Cost, Resource Availability, Scope, Quality, and finally Time. No ties are allowed! That can be tough, because everything is important. If the client had to choose which variable to compromise, what would be the pecking order? The table entries reflect that thinking. In other words, the client would be willing to add more dollars to the project as the first choice for change. An extension of time would be the last resort.

How should we interpret this information with respect to project deliverables? Because of the deterioration in home-delivery sales, the solution must be put in place as soon as possible. For all intents and purposes, that makes the planned project completion date sacred. Sooner would be even better! All other variables would be relaxed before the Time variable would change. Next in priority order is Quality. Maintaining quality of product and service are critical success factors for this type of business. Next in priority order is Scope. What can be postponed until version 2? Next in priority order is Resource Availability. Most of the development team will be contractors, and their numbers can be increased or decreased as the situation dictates. Last is Cost. Dee is willing to invest more if the added business value justifies it.

Applications of APF

There are five distinct application areas for APF. The case studies provide examples of these. The five application areas are described in the following subsections.

Software Development

There is a lot of similarity between APF and the five Adaptive PMLC models discussed earlier in this chapter. All of the latter were designed for software-development projects. APF works well for software-development projects, with the added benefit that it was designed for projects that are not software-development projects. The APF probative swim lanes, which do not have an analog in any of the other five models, allow for the planned exploration and discovery of software solutions.

New Product Development

APF was originally developed for new product/process development projects. For these types of projects, early APF cycles are used for business validation, proof of concept, product design, model building, prototyping, and focus groups. Later cycles actually build and test market the product/process.

Case Study: Snacks Fifth Avenue Kiosk Design
It wasn't at all obvious how the kiosk should be designed. Several questions needed answering.   • Should the input be keyboard or touch screen?   • Will customized recipes be available with printed output an option?   • Should the kiosk be linked to the physical product location in the store?   • Can orders be placed through the kiosk?   • Is there an application for real time audio feedback through a device mounted on the shopping cart?   • Should the checkout service be linked to the shopping cart device?   There will certainly be other questions that arise during the course of the project.

Process Design, Development, and Deployment

There is little difference between the variant of APF that is used for new-product development and that used for new-process design. In this example, process design was treated as an APF project. The development phase used an Evolutionary Waterfall model, and deployment uses a traditional linear model.

Process Improvement

Perhaps the most powerful use of APF is for process improvement. Process improvement draws heavily upon learning and discovery through experimentation within each cycle. Ideas for improvement are suggested, prioritized, tried in priority order, further developed, and eventually implemented if they result in measurable process improvement.

Case Study: Kamikazi SDPM Improvement

The initial release of the new systems development project management (SDPM) model was the best that could be done given the precarious situation Kamikazi found itself in. The company had to act quickly because it was losing money on just about every project. On go-live day, Kamikazi was already planning the process-improvement project. The only approach to process improvement that made sense was to closely monitor actual process performance in the field and use that to identify process-improvement changes. The primary metric tracked would be profit margin. Additional metrics would be defined to measure phase performance.

This is clearly an APF project. Field experience would suggest areas for improvement to be carefully explored, with probative swim lanes initiated, process changes implemented, and their performance impact tracked. Management knew that this would be a never-ending APF project.

Problem Solving

Problem-solving and process-improvement processes have a lot in common in the early stages. Both identify, evaluate, and prioritize alternatives. Problem solving generally picks one alternative. Process improvement, as in the Kamikazi case study, consecutively picks alternatives and lets their results affect process performance cumulatively until some target process performance level is reached or no further improvement ideas have surfaced.

Extreme Project Management

The Extreme Project Management (xPM) model is best described as the R&D model. Neither the goal nor the solution is clearly defined and documented. The project heads out in a direction where the goal and some solution are thought to be found. They might or might not have successfully been identified. If they have not been, then further investigation is warranted. If they have been found, then a new direction is chosen. At some point in time, a goal and its solution are both defined. Obviously, extreme projects are very high risk.

For example, the rough stated goal of a project might originally have been to cure cancer. Through iteration, the scope of the final goal may have evolved to curing breast cancer in Asia using a ginseng-root compress. Figure 1.14 illustrates the INSPIRE process: **IN**itiate, **SP**eculate, **I**nnovate, and **RE**view. I developed INSPIRE as the APF version for xPM projects. There is a lot of commonality between xPM and APF. One of my clients is in the drug research and development business, and has successfully applied APF to xPM projects.

For details on INSPIRE, see Chapters 31–37 in my book, *Effective Software Project Management.*[13]

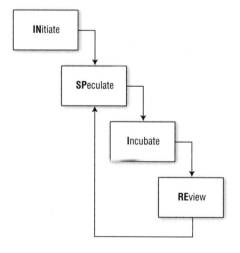

Figure 1.14
INSPIRE

---

[13] Wysocki 2009.

Emertxe Project Management

Emertxe projects are Extreme projects, only backwards: The solution is known but the goal is not! While this might look nonsensical at first blush, it really isn't if interpreted properly. You need to think of time being reversed. Does the solution have any business value? In other words, does the solution support a goal that has business value?

My favorite example is from a project conducted by Wal-Mart to determine whether Radio Frequency Identification (RFID) technology (the solution) could deliver business value when applied to warehousing operations (the goal). Initially it was determined that the reliability and accuracy of the technology was below the minimum needed to meet Wal-Mart's standards. Because Wal-Mart was and still is the 800-pound gorilla in the room, RFID got better, and is now used routinely in warehouse stocking and pulling operations.

The simplest example I can think of would be a project to evaluate a commercial software package for use in your company. Suppose a major vendor of human resource management systems (HRMS) announces a new version of its product that it claims can be used for career and professional development and project staffing (the solution). The APF project is to evaluate the software package for application in your soon-to-be-released resource constrained project portfolio management system (the goal).

The most complex example I can think of would be to research a juice extracted from a tree that grows only in Borneo and is suspected to have some medicinal value to the natives for whom it is a daily part of their diet. Unlike with the previous example, you aren't sure how to start such a research project.

In between these three examples is a whole family of projects that are equivalent to a solution (or some variant of it) looking for an application (the goal)—hoping that the solution has business value. One of my clients uses APF for xPM projects and has also used APF for MPx projects. Both xPM and MPx projects consist of an initial goal and an initial solution converging on a final goal and ultimate solution. If the final goal has business value, the project is considered successful. Obviously these are very high-risk projects—not because of any shortcomings on the part of the project team but because the solution, if there is one, is elusive.

Putting It All Together

In this first chapter, I have set the stage for the rest of the book. The rationale behind APF has been briefly explored, and I have given you a high-level overview of what APF involves. This introduction could well meet the needs of the senior manager who simply wants to understand APF at a high level and has no need for the details. For those at the program- or project-manager level, you are off to a good start. With this understanding in place, I can now proceed to peel back the layers of the onion—the layers of APF. In Chapters 2 through 6, you will discover and come to understand the most granular of details for each of the five phases of APF. My intent is that you have a working knowledge of APF when you are finished. I also expect you to be able to create a recipe for success using APF, rather than just following a pre-defined TPM recipe and hoping for success.

Discussion Questions

The following questions are posed for your use. Use them to test your understanding and potential application of the materials presented in this chapter. If you are using this book for a course you are teaching, the questions will provoke good class discussion.

1. Under your leadership, your organization has spent considerable effort to adopt a traditional approach to project management. It has reached maturity level three—that is, there are fully documented project management processes and templates, and everyone is following them. PMBOK is the recognized standard. You have earned a good reputation among your management colleagues. You have noticed a number of projects where the client has requested and gotten approval for several changes throughout the project. These have cost significant money and time, the loss of market share, and the subsequent loss of revenues. As Director of the Project Support Office, you have come to realize that APF is the approach that should have been taken on this project. You are convinced that by using APF these types of projects could have been completed earlier, at less

cost, and with much better end results. What strategy would you suggest to introduce and institutionalize APF in your company? What obstacles do you foresee?

2. You are a senior project manager in your company. You have 15 years' experience with the company and a solid reputation for delivering successful projects. What might you, acting on your own, do to get your organization to appreciate the value of APF? What plan might you follow to bring APF into the company? What obstacles might prevent you from going forward with your plan? How do you feel about stepping outside the box?

Chapter 2

How to Scope the APF Project

Invention breeds invention.

> —*Ralph Waldo Emerson, American essayist and poet*

Define the problem before you pursue a solution.

> —*John Williams, CEO, Spence Corporation*

Version Scope is a phase that is done once for every APF project. It is a challenge, because the project is already known to be very complex and its successful completion is critical to the business. There is a great deal of uncertainty associated with every APF project, because you are heading into the unknown and must discover the missing parts of the solution through the tasks and activities that you build into the project plan. This distinguishes an APF project from any project you may have worked on in the past. The Version Scope phase brings together, maybe for the first time, a representative group from the client organization and a representative group from the development organization. Together these two groups form the project team that will be charged with solving a currently unsolved problem or taking advantage of a heretofore untapped business opportunity. The project is critical to the business, and since it remains unsolved, it must be complex or it would have been solved through an earlier effort. If it is an untapped business opportunity, the project is complex or it would have been completed through an earlier effort. In either case, the APF project will be a complex project. The information about the solution available to the team initially will be quite incomplete. Part of the team's challenge will be to complete the solution while working together within given time, cost, and resource constraints.

Overview of the APF Version Scope Phase

The APF Version Scope phase initiates the APF project on a challenging course that will often tax even the most creative and skilled project teams. An APF project is an adventure into the unknown. Figure 2.1 is the same as Figure 1.12 from Chapter 1, except that the Version Scope phase is highlighted for easy reference.

For several years, I have been concerned about how informal and disconnected we often are in the initial task of defining and planning a project with our clients. We frequently treat this process too casually, and do not question the client as we should. Lots of untested assumptions and suppositions are made by both parties in an effort to get going on the work of the project. Filling in all the required fields on a form seems to be the common practice and driving interest. Once that is done and the form is submitted for approval, the defining activities are considered done. Whether or not the result makes business sense doesn't seem very important. How unfortunate!

Later in the project, when things start to go wrong, participants might question what happened. We know that the history of project management is characterized by failure rates that are unacceptably high. What doesn't make any sense to me is that we don't seem to learn from our mistakes. We just keep on doing the same things project after project. Someone[1] once defined insanity as doing the same thing over and over again and somehow expecting a different result. So let's agree right now that we will take version scope very seriously.

---

[1] Usually attributed to Albert Einstein.

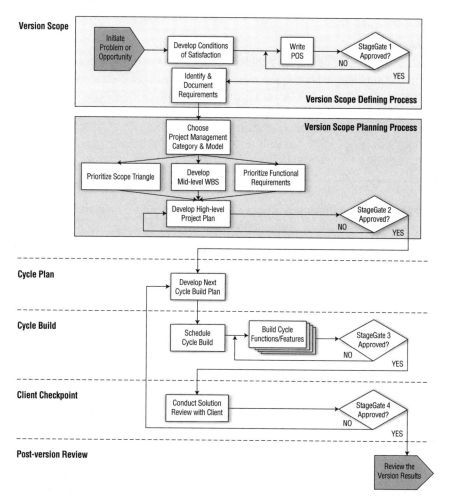

Figure 2.1
The APF Life
Cycle with the
APF Version
Scope Phase
Highlighted

An APF Version Scope phase follows a formal discipline of working collaboratively with clients to define the project. What I am going to share with you I developed long before APF came along. There is a certain amount of structure needed during initiation activities, and my approach will give that to you. It preserves the flexibility needed in APF projects. From personal experience, I know it works, and I use it to initiate every project I undertake. I have made version defining an integral part of the APF Version Scope phase.

The most significant feature of the Version Scope phase is that, from the very start, it meaningfully involves the client in all of the tasks that make up the version scope defining and planning activities. All too often we experience difficulty in meaningfully engaging the client. It's not a perfect project world out there. If you remember one thing from this chapter, remember this: Don't start the Version Scope phase unless and until you get a commitment from your clients to be appropriately involved. The extent to which they will be involved depends on the type of project. As project manager, it is your responsibility to get that commitment. This is so important that, whenever it makes sense, I recruit a client representative to co-manage the project with me. We share the rewards of success and we share the pain of failure, and we do it as equals. If you are able to do this, you will have created a real partner with a vested interest in the success of the project. Meaningful client involvement is almost a sure bet. In those few cases where I was not able to get that commitment from the client, I postponed the project until the clients decided the project was important enough for them to get involved. That's playing hardball, and not to be taken or treated lightly, but it's that important.

---

[2] Standish Group, *Chaos Report 2007: The Laws of CHAOS* (Boston: Standish Group International, 2007).

Two major processes make up the APF Version Scope phase: the Defining Process and the Planning Process.

APF Version Scope Defining Process

The APF Version Scope Defining process produces two documents: the Project Overview Statement (POS) and the Requirements Breakdown Structure (RBS). Both of these documents are described later in this section. Together these two documents describe as much as is known about what needs to be done and why. The activities leading up to StageGate 1[3] approval are usually done by single representatives from the two major groups that make up the project team: the client group and the development group. For small or simple projects, these groups may each have one member; with larger or more-complex projects, I have experienced client groups as large as 10–15 members. Regardless of their size, they must be representative of their constituencies and must speak for them in all project decisions. The critical factor is that they not only represent their constituencies but can make decisions for their constituencies. Once StageGate 1 approval is granted, the last activity in the APF Version Scope Defining process is to identify and document the known requirements, in the form of the RBS. StageGate 1 approval should be obtained before requirements gathering is initiated. Requirements gathering can be very labor intensive; holding off on it makes sense until you have some indication that the project makes business sense. That is the determination you get from StageGate 1 approval.

Requirements gathering is an activity done by all the known team members from both the client side and the developer side. Others, such as resource managers and other functional managers, may be added as needed or requested.

APF Version Scope Planning Process

Once the known requirements have been documented, the project moves immediately into the APF Version Scope Planning phase. The beginning

---

[3] Refer to Figure 2.1.

activity in this part is to decide upon the project-management category and model that will be used to manage the project. The project will be classified as TPM, APM, xPM or MPx, and a specific Linear, Incremental, Iterative, Adaptive or Extreme PMLC model will be chosen. The RBS is the major input into this decision. This is the first time APF will have been mentioned, and marks the actual beginning of an APF project. All activities that have led up to StageGate 1 approval and the creation of the RBS will apply to all projects. The PMLC model you will use to manage the project cannot be determined until the RBS has been defined and documented.

The inputs into the APF Version Scope Planning process are the outputs from the APF Version Scope Defining process—that is, the COS, POS, and RBS. While the APF Version Scope Defining process documents as much as is known about what needs to be done, the APF Version Scope Planning process documents as much as is known about how it will be done. How it will be done is embodied in the major deliverable from this process: the high-level project plan.

A formal planning meeting is required to generate the high-level project plan. The APF Version Scope Planning meeting should be attended by the sponsor, the client team, the development team, and the appropriate resource managers. In most cases, the development team will not be completely identified until the project plan is completed and the project budget approved. In such cases, the initial development team will be a core team of client and development professionals who will remain with the project until it is completed.

APF Version Scope Phase: The Defining Process

The APF Version Scope Phase Defining process can be applied to any project. The RBS is the major deliverable from APF Version Scope Phase Defining process. It is input into the APF Version Scope Planning phase. The steps in the Defining process are discussed in the sections that follow.

Initiate Addressing a Problem or Opportunity

A sponsor (usually an executive from the client organization) makes a request of senior management to undertake a project to solve a mission-critical problem or take advantage of a significant-yet-untapped business opportunity. Whether addressing a problem or an opportunity, the organization is presented with a major challenge. The challenge arises from the fact that the problem may not have a defined solution, or it may be unclear how to take advantage of the untapped business opportunity. A representative from the development organization is assigned to work with the client sponsor. Usually this individual will become a project co-manager, and someone from the sponsor's business unit will become the other project co-manager. This could be the sponsor, but usually is a line manager from the client business unit. Whoever is chosen must represent, and have decision-making authority for, the business unit.

Develop Conditions of Satisfaction

At the first meeting between the client representative and the development representative, a seemingly unstructured conversation takes place wherein both parties come to an understanding of the situation and how it will be approached. I call this conversation the Conditions of Satisfaction (COS) discussion. I am told that the COS originated with IBM Canada. Others have told me that it originated with the Fox Consulting Group, a New England-based practice. I've never been able to verify where it originated. All I know is that it works, and it should be in the toolkit of every project manager. I've been using COS for more than 20 years, and wouldn't consider starting a project without going through a COS session with my client.

The COS (see Figure 2.2) is a purposed conversation between the project manager (or a representative group from the development side) and the client sponsor (or a representative group from the client side). At one extreme, the COS may be a brief one-on-one conversation between two people (the project manager and the client sponsor). In some cases it might be a multiple-day planned meeting with several participants. At the other extreme, it might involve prototyping and even functional specification.

Figure 2.2
Conditions of
Satisfaction
Discussion

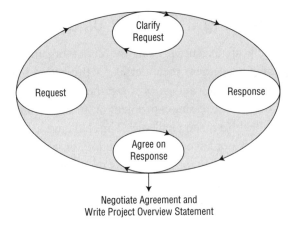

Negotiate Agreement and
Write Project Overview Statement

The COS process should be thought of as an approach to be adapted to the situation.

Whatever approach you decide to use, it must be conversationally based. I maintain that the conversations cannot be replaced with a stream of e-mails, so don't even think about accepting a stream of e-mails as a substitute for a face-to-face conversation. There is something foreboding about the written word (regardless of its intended message) in that it becomes set in stone once delivered. There is always a risk that what you wrote (or what was believed that you said) will be misinterpreted. That may trigger another e-mail, and an endless stream of e-mails follows. Avoid that trap by having face-to-face conversations, where misunderstandings are far less likely to occur, and if they do are easily cleared up.

COS Benefits

Two important benefits accrue to the project from the COS. The first benefit is that you and the client will have established a vocabulary—a common language that you will use for clear communications throughout this project, and all future projects with this client. It amazes me, when I test the accuracy of communication between parties, how often the message sent is not the message received. We carelessly assume that the receiver of our communication has the same understanding of the terminology we use as we do. People are often embarrassed to admit that they do not understand something you have said or written. Some cultures are particularly adverse to admitting they don't know or understand. That doesn't excuse you from making sure that the message you send is the message received.

Let me give you an example from one of my training classes that will drive home the importance of a common language. I asked the attendees (they were all software developers in this example) to write down their definitions of the word "implementation." They could do so by simply listing what is included, or what is not included. Then they compared definitions. Would you be surprised to find out that there were about as many definitions of the word "implementation" as there were participants in the exercise? This is amazing to me because those of us in the information-technology field can hardly speak a sentence without using the word "implementation," yet we really don't know what others are saying when they use the term, nor what they are hearing when we use the term.

With reference to your own projects, can you say that you and your client really understand one another? Maybe you both do—but probably not. The COS is a tool you can use to assure a good channel of communication between the development team and the client team. It is a great insurance policy against a failure to communicate clearly and completely. With COS, you can have a conversation about the project and know that each party understands the other. While this may sound trivial, it definitely is anything but trivial.

The second benefit is that after the COS process, you have a negotiated, though tentative, agreement with your client, and you can both approach the project based on that agreement. The negotiated agreement becomes the foundation on which the project proceeds. You use it for problem solving, conflict resolution, and decision making. It is used to bring others on board as the project proceeds. Most important of all, it is the basis on which APF planning is built and prioritization decisions are to be made. If you do this right, you are well on your way to a successful project. If you do this wrong, there is a very high probability of significant problems, or even project failure. You make the choice.

How you will come to that agreement is illustrated by way of the following simple example. One thing I want you to note in the example conversation that follows is the preciseness employed. It is critical that both parties to the COS assure that preciseness.

An Example of a COS Conversation[4]

Suppose the client (the requestor) wants a certain model of widgets in forest green to ship to its warehouse by December 1, 2009. The client decides to visit the manufacturer (the provider) to make this request. The conversation would go something like this:

Requestor: I would like you to build five prototypes of the new forest green widgets and ship them to my warehouse no later than December 1, 2009.

Provider: You are asking if we can get five green widget prototypes into your warehouse by December 1, 2009?

Requestor: Actually, if you can get them shipped by December 1, 2009, that will be acceptable. But remember they have to be forest green.

Provider: So if on December 1, 2009, I can ship five forest green widgets to your warehouse, you will be satisfied.

Requestor: Yes, but they must be the new model, not the old model.

Provider: The new model?

Requestor: The new model.

Provider: I believe I understand what you have asked for.

Requestor: Yes, I believe you do.

Provider: Because of my current production schedule and the fact that I have to change paint colors for your order, I can ship two forest green widgets on November 25, 2009, and the remaining three on December 8, 2009.

Requestor: If I understand you correctly, I will get five prototypes of the new forest green widgets in two shipments—two prototypes on November 25 and three on December 8. Is that correct?

Provider: Not exactly. You won't receive them on those dates. I will ship them to your warehouse on those dates.

Requestor: So, let me summarize to make sure I understand what you are able to do for me. You will build a total of five forest green prototypes

---

[4] This example is taken from Chapter 3 of Robert Wysocki, Ph.D. *Effective Project Management: Traditional, Agile, Extreme, Fifth Edition,* (New York: John Wiley & Sons, 2009).

of the new widgets for me and ship two of them on November 25 and the remaining three on December 8? You will of course use our agreed shipment schedule so that the items will arrive two days later.

Provider: That is correct.

What has been accomplished by both parties at this point is an understanding of what has been requested and what can be provided. There may not be agreement, but at least there is an understanding, and the differences can be negotiated until there is an acceptable agreement.

Expectation Setting

Because of the uncertainty and complexity that surrounds an APF project, it is critical that you clearly set expectations with your client. A strong and forceful sponsor or client can often put you in the position of adding new deliverables within time and budget constraints that are not feasible. Meeting your client's needs is uppermost in your mind, but don't compromise beyond what is realistic. In every agile project, solution scope is variable and not clearly definable at the beginning of the project. Scope is learned and discovered as part of the project work. The client must understand and accept the implications of this uncertainty and complexity, including the attendant risks. A client might be locked in the TPM world, which is focused on defining deliverables up-front. That is not the APM world, and you should consider educating them to the differences. Those differences are profound!

I have negotiated a number of contracts for APF projects, and my biggest stumbling block has always been defining deliverables. The contract language says something roughly like:

Message to your client: "In an agile project, scope is variable."
Neither you nor I can define exactly what will be delivered at the end of the project, but we know that it will offer the maximum business value you and I can deliver given the time and budget constraints you have established. Your only choice is to use an agile approach to create that business value.

In other words, this partnership will work to deliver the best solution possible. Having that partnership is a critical success factor for every APF project.

Requestor-driven Conversation

In the preceding example, the requestor (the client) states and describes the request using her or his own language. The provider makes sure he or she understands the request by asking questions, and eventually feeding back the request in his or her own language. At some point in this conversation, you want the requestor to be able to say to the provider, "You clearly understand what I am asking you to do." The conversation now shifts to the provider-driven side of the conversation.

Provider-driven Conversation

The provider responds by stating and describing what can be done to meet the requestor's request. The requestor asks questions to frame the answer, and eventually describes the response in his or her own language. At some point in this conversation, the provider is able to say to the requestor, "You clearly understand what I can provide."

Results of the Two-way Discussion

We should now have the makings of an agreement, with a clear understanding of what is being asked and what can be done. There will usually be some negotiating to reach closure on the agreement, and you shouldn't assume that everything is in sync until finishing the process. Note that the requestor and provider, through their earlier conversations, have established a common language. Each understands the other, which will smooth the negotiating that will later take place. This understanding is one of the major benefits of COS; a clear communication link is now established between the two parties. This communication link is very important, especially when the project does not have a clear solution. It will take the best efforts of both the development team and the client team to fashion a solution that meets the expectations of the organization.

The COS Is a Dynamic Process

The COS process is not a one-time event. It occurs repeatedly throughout the project. At each client checkpoint or other project milestone, the COS is revisited with the participation of the client team and the development team. Because of the learning and discovery that has taken place, something surely will have changed that renders the previous agreement out-of-date and in need of revision. Revisiting the COS provides your guarantee of always staying in alignment with what the client needs. It is also the pathway for moving clients from what they want to what they need. Remember, APF embraces change, and here is the place where change enjoys the light of day.

Wants versus Needs: A Warning and Suggestion

What the client wants may not be what the client needs! I would be willing to bet that despite the Chaos 2007 report[5] of the top ten reasons why projects fail, the root cause of many project failures is the project manager assuming that what the clients say they want is what the clients actually need. Nowhere on the Chaos 2007 list is that reason given or even alluded to. After more than 40 years of project-management experience, I have come to the conclusion that many of the clients' wants are not much more than their attempts at solving problems they have, but whose definition neither of you is privy to. The clients' solution landscape is limited to their areas of expertise, which may not include the solution to the problem. Unless I have evidence to the contrary, my going-in assumption is that wants do not reflect actual needs. So my advice to you is to make sure that the client's wants and actual needs are the same.

I have done that quite successfully by applying a form of Root Cause Analysis during the required COS session. (Any good text on business analysis will provide a detailed treatment of Root Cause Analysis.) For every want expressed by the client, I ask, "Why do you want that?" By repeatedly asking "why" questions, I eventually get to the real reason for the want, and no further "why" questions are asked about that particular want. I have found a need. There may be several wants for you and the client to explore. Eventually you and the client together will have identified all of the needs. Through the collection of needs, you and the client will be able to define the problem, and through the project eventually find a solution. Figure 2.3 captures my point.

---

[5] Standish Group 2007.

Figure 2.3
The Wants
versus Needs
Dilemma

What the client wants is probably not what the client needs.
The project manager's job is to discover what the clients need
and convince them that they want it.

A further suggestion is to be careful in your questioning that the client does not feel like they are on the defensive. Why questions can be softened by saying instead "What do you expect that to do for you?" That might lead you to questions like "Can we try to find something that works better?" If you are going to build a meaningful relationship with your client, they need to feel like you are both on the same team and are working toward the same goal.

Write a Project Overview Statement

The deliverable from the COS is a negotiated agreement. The Project Overview Statement (POS) is the documented and approved statement of that agreement. The POS is brief—one page is always sufficient. It has five parts. A POS template with an example is shown in Figure 2.4.

After more than 40 years of managing projects, I can honestly say that I have always been able to write a one-page POS regardless of the scope of the project. Being able to write a one-page POS means that you really understand the project and can communicate it intelligently to senior management. If you think of it as a two-minute "elevator speech," you won't go far astray. I've seen project-initiation documents as large as 70 pages. I'm not sure who reads these, if anyone. If they do, do they really understand the project at the level of detail needed for granting approval to create the project plan? I doubt it! A document of that length may be of value to the project team,

PROJECT OVERVIEW STATEMENT	Project Name Common Cold Prevention Project	Project No. 02-01	Project Manager Carries deCure

Problem/Opportunity
There does not exist a preventative for the common cold.

Goal
Find a way to prevent the occurrence of the common cold.

Objectives
1. Find a food additive that will prevent the occurrence of the common cold.
2. Alter the immune system to prevent the occurrence of the common cold.
3. Devine a program of diet and exercise that will prevent the occurrence of the common cold.

Success Criteria
The solution must be effective for at least 90% of persons of any age.
The solution must not introduce any harmful side effects.
The solution must cost the consumer less than $20.00 per dose.
The solution must be accepted by the FDA.
The solution must be obtained over the counter at any pharmacy.
The solution must return at least 20% gross profit.

Assumptions, Risks, Obstacles
Assumption: The common cold can be prevented.
Risk: The solution will have harmful side effects.
Obstacle: Drug manufacturers will hinder the search for a cure.

Prepared By Earnest Effort	Date 11-14-2009	Approved By Hy Podermick	Date 11-16-2009

Figure 2.4
A Typical POS Template with Example Data

but not to the sponsor, and certainly not to the executive who will be approving it.

The POS has five parts, which are discussed next.

Identifying the Business Problem or Opportunity

A well-defined need and a clear solution pathway to meet that need define a project that the traditionalist expects. A rather vague idea of a want coupled with a vague idea of how it will be satisfied define a project that the **agilist** (one who aligns the project-management approach with APM or xPM) expects. Every project in-between these two extremes belongs to the province of the APF project manager. The problem or opportunity that our project is going to respond to must already be recognized by the organization as a legitimate problem or opportunity that must be attended to. If anyone in the organization were asked about it, he or she would surely answer, "You bet it is, and we need to do something about it." In other words, it is not something that needs a defense; it stands on its own merits. Furthermore, the problem or opportunity statement must be couched in terms that anyone in the organization who would have a reason to read the statement could understand without the need for further explanation.

Defining the Goal of This Version

The goal of this version will be a simple yet definitive statement about what this project intends to do to address the problem or opportunity. It might be a total solution, but more realistically, it is most likely to be a solution that addresses a major segment of the problem or opportunity. I say this because all too often we define projects that are far too large in scope. Sure, you would like to cure cancer, but be realistic: Maybe curing one form of cancer would be a lofty-enough goal. Having too ambitious a goal will open the project to scope reduction as the project is framed in a more attainable way. Furthermore, there can be changes in the environment that render ambitious goals ineffective or unattainable. By defining the goal of this version to be a reachable target rather than a lofty or unattainable ambition, we protect the client and the team from scope reduction and significantly increase their chances of delivering business value. I'm sure that overly ambitious scoping has a lot to do with the high incidence of project failure. It may sound too pedestrian to some readers, but I believe that you will be far more successful in the long run by biting off less than you think you can chew. Management didn't appoint you project manager expecting heroic efforts—just successful ones.

Writing the Objectives of This Version

As an analogy, think of the goal statement as a pie and the objective statements as slices of the pie. If you would rather have a mathematical interpretation, think of the objectives as necessary and sufficient conditions for the attainment of the goal. In either analogy, the objective statements give a little more detail on how the goal will be achieved. They are the boundary conditions, if you will. I would expect to see you write six to eight objective statements to clarify your goal statement. Together, the project statement and the objectives statements define the goal of the project. They will be either a clear or an unclear statement of the goal of the project.

Defining the Success Criteria

The success criteria (or explicit business outcomes) are quantitative statements of the results that will be realized from having successfully completed this project. They are formulated in such a way that they can be clearly determined to have either happened or not happened. There will be no debate over attainment of success criteria. Statements like "Pre-tax profit margins will increase from their current average of 23 percent per month to an average of at least 34 percent per month by the end of the second quarter of operations using the new system" are acceptable. Statements like "Increase customer satisfaction" are not. We would expect to see two or perhaps three success criteria for your project. Success criteria generally fall into three categories:

- Metrics related to increased revenues (IR)
- Metrics related to avoidance of cost (AC)
- Metrics related to increased service levels (IS)

This list is identified with the acronym IRACIS.

Listing the Major Assumptions/Risks/Obstacles

Put yourself in the shoes of the financial analyst who might ask, "I am being asked to invest $10 million in a new process that is supposed to cut operating expenses by 5 percent per month. What risks are we exposed to that might prevent us from achieving that ROI?" What would you tell the analyst? That is what you would list as major risks or obstacles. As another example, you might make senior managers aware that certain staff skill shortages are going to be a problem, or that the ongoing reorganization of Sales and Marketing will have to be complete or there will be serious consequences during system implementation.

Seek StageGate 1 Approval

StageGate 1 is the approval by senior management for the project team to proceed with the last activity in the Version Scope Defining process, the identification and documentation of requirements, and then continue into the Version Scope Planning process. Since requirements gathering is a labor-intensive version-defining activity, it is not done until StageGate 1 approval is granted. There is still a lot about this project that has to be defined before any version planning work can be done, and one more approval step (StageGate 2) must be passed before the actual work of the project is authorized and budgeted by senior management.

There will be occasions when the POS is not approved. This usually means that the sponsor has not made a compelling argument for the business viability of the intended approach to the problem or opportunity. Although the business need may be critical, the risk of failure is weighed against the expected business value of the solution. Expected business value may not justify the cost of the project. That doesn't mean the project isn't important to the executives—just that the approach chosen doesn't make good business sense. Some other approach is needed. The sponsoring business unit is invited to revise and resubmit the POS. Alternatively, the POS may be rejected without further consideration.

Case Studies

Let's look at each of the four case studies. We'll follow one to the point of having a POS.

Case Study: Snacks Fifth Avenue—Kiosk Design

Snacks Fifth Avenue was a tired business. It had remained largely unchanged since its founding in 1960. The customer base was steady with lots of repeat business, but the growth wasn't there. The fiftieth anniversary was coming soon, and something needed to be done to breathe life back into the business. Patty Fours, the founder and current owner, had seen a kiosk in the local shopping mall that allowed the customer to get information about local movies and restaurants. Maybe, just maybe, she could use that technology to bring Snacks Fifth Avenue back to life. She met with T. N. Kauphy, her computer person, and discussed her needs. The POS shown in Figure 2.5 was the result of their conversation.

A couple of things are clear from the POS. First, Patty and T. N. don't know what the kiosk will look like. More importantly, they don't know what services it will deliver. The objective statements are guesses at what their customers might like. Those guesses will have to be tested, and may change before the kiosk is put into production. Even after going into production status, the service offerings will have to prove themselves business worthy. Up to that point, everything will be speculation. Even at this early stage, this

PROJECT OVERVIEW STATEMENT	Project Name Kiosk Design		Project No. 08-01	Project Manager T. N. Kauphy
Problem/Opportunity Snacks Fifth Avenue store traffic was dropping off and sales were down 10% this quarter compared to last quarter. Something had to be done to reverse the trend.				
Goal Increase store sales to their previous level by creating a more interesting in-store experience for shoppers and drawing more traffic into the store.				
Objectives 1. Design a multi-purpose in-store kiosk offering several shopping aids to customers. 2. Provide a store map to direct customers to specific products. 3. Provide custom-designed and off-the-shelf party packs. 4. Provide catalog ordering. 5. Provide party menus for specific types of parties. 6. Provide party planning services.				
Success Criteria 1. Restores lost sales to their previous quarter high within two quarters of launching the kiosk. 2. Offer a minimum of 4 services on the kiosk with each one generating a minimum of 5% of sales. 3. Survey customers to establish a 50% approval rating of the kiosk service. 4. Survey customers to identify a minimum of 3 new service ideas, which results in at least one new service that generates 5% of sales by the end of the second quarter of implementation.				
Assumptions, Risks, Obstacles 1. Shoppers are not comfortable using the kiosk.				
Prepared By T. N. Kauphy	**Date** 01-01-08	**Approved By** Patty Fours		**Date** 01-03-08

Figure 2.5
Snacks Fifth Avenue POS

is already beginning to show signs of being an APM project. We'll know more once we have built the RBS.

Case Study: Kamikazi Software Systems— Systems Development Project Management Process Design

Kamikazi Software Systems was one of the few survivors of the dot-com catastrophe of the 1990s. Company officials felt they owed their success to the fact that Kamikazi was a fixed-bid vendor. They were willing to assume the risk of not bidding an engagement correctly. They were very successful until client-requested changes seemed to take over the Web applications development business. Clients looking to build B2B and B2C Web sites weren't really sure what they needed, but were not bashful in stating what they wanted. The lack of clear specification of needs led to uncontrolled change requests. Many of the changes were approved at the cost of reduced profit margin. It was a client market, and if Kamikazi wasn't willing to deliver, someone else would. Kamikazi was trapped in its own bidding model. Business took a radical downturn. The company went through three rounds of layoffs in less than a year. Something radical was needed to save the business, and it had to happen quickly.

Harry Kerry, the CEO of Kamikazi, met with Crash dePlane, his Director of Client Services, to look for a solution. The result of that conversation is summarized in Figure 2.6.

The goal statement is clear, but ambitious. It must be met to save the business. That means any reasonable idea should get executive support. Whether or not it was attainable is another question. The solution could be very elusive. This is clearly an APF project.

Case Study: Pizza Delivered Quickly—Order Entry and Home Delivery Process Design

Dee Livery, the president, met with Pepe Ronee, the Director of IS, to identify how computer technology could be used to make PDQ more competitive.

Figure 2.6
Kamikazi
Software
Systems POS

PROJECT OVERVIEW STATEMENT	Project Name Systems Development Project Management Process Design	Project No. 08-02	Project Manager Crash dePlane

Problem/Opportunity

Kamikazi Software Systems uses a fixed price bidding system for all of its client development work. Recently the number of client change requests have eroded the profit margin to the point where many projects are money losers. This problem must be fixed without changing the fixed bid model.

Goal

Modify the software development project management process to accommodate change without sacrificing profit margin.

Objectives

1. Modify the software development project management process to accommodate change without sacrificing profit margin.
2. Implement the revised system within 12 months of starting the project.
3. Meaningfully involve clients in the project.

Success Criteria

1. Get development team approval of the revised systems development project management process design.
2. Get serious management approval of the revised systems development project management process.
3. By the third completed project using the revised systems development project management process there will be no loss of profit margin due to client changes.

Assumptions, Risks, Obstacles

1. Clients will not accept the revised systems development project management process.

Prepared By Crash dePlane	Date 02-01-08	Approved By Harry Kerry	Date 02-04-08

They talked about a lot of ideas and came to the conclusion that there would have to be four subsystems to get PDQ competitive and restore lost sales. Figure 2.7 summarizes their agreement.

The pizza factories would not have any retail space. The only function would be to receive home-delivery orders, then prepare and deliver the pizzas. The factory location nearest the customer's location would receive the order from a central ordering facility, then process and deliver the order within 30 or 45 minutes of order entry, depending on whether the customer had ordered the pizza ready for the oven or already baked.

There are six software applications that Pepe and Dee identified for the solution. These are obviously very different software-development projects requiring very different approaches.

Figure 2.7
Pizza Delivered
Quickly POS

PROJECT OVERVIEW STATEMENT	Project Name Order Entry - Home Delivery Process	Project No. 08-03	Project Manager Pepe Ronee

Problem/Opportunity
PDQ has lost 30% of sales due primarily to a drop in home delivery business. This is due mostly to a national chain that opened 5 stores in Woodville and guaranteed 45-minute delivery.

Goal
Design and implement a new order entry and delivery process that guarantees 30 minute delivery.

Objectives
1. Restore lost sales within six months of launching the new order entry-delivery process.
2. Achieve 30-minute delivery in at least 90% of the orders.
3. Develop a pizza factory locator subsystem.
4. Acquire an order entry subsystem & GPS Routing Package.
5. Design and develop a logistics subsystem.
6. Design and develop an order submit subsystem.
7. Acquire an inventory management subsystem.

Success Criteria
1. Launch the revised order entry-delivery process within six months of starting the project.
2. Restore lost sales within six months of launching the new order entry-delivery process.
3. Achieve 30-minute delivery in at least 90% of the orders within one month of launching the revised process.

Assumptions, Risks, Obstacles
1. The revised process will cost too much to design and implement.
2. 30-minute delivery is not attainable.

Prepared By Pepe Ronee	Date 03-01-08	Approved By Dee Livery	Date 03-01-08

Pizza Factory Locator Subsystem

The first is a software system to find pizza-factory locations. It is not known how many such factories will be needed, nor where they should be located. The software system will have to determine that. Clearly this system is a very complex application. The goal can be clearly defined, but the solution will not be at all obvious. The system will have to use very sophisticated modeling tools. The requirements, functionality, and features are not at all obvious. Some of the solution can probably be envisioned, but clearly the whole solution is elusive at this early stage. Exactly how it will do modeling is not known at the outset. It will have to be discovered as the development project is underway. This is APF territory.

Order-entry Subsystem

The second application is an order-entry system to support store and factory operations. Telephone orders will come to a single location, be taken there, and then be routed to the appropriate store or factory electronically. This system focuses on routine business functions and should be easily defined. Off-the-shelf commercial software may be a big part of the ultimate solution. This system can utilize COTS (Commercial Off-the-shelf) order-entry software which will have to be enhanced at the front end to direct the order to the closest factory, and provide driving directions for delivery and other fulfillment tasks on the back end. The requirements, functionality, and features of this system can be determined. A TPM approach should work fine.

Logistics Subsystem

The third subsystem is the traffic cop for the entire solution. The logistics subsystem will provide a real-time snapshot of the status and queue length of every workstation in the order entry to order fulfillment process. It will have the capability of looking ahead to any point in time and projecting process status as well as pizza-van and delivery-truck locations, as an aid to decision making. The logistics subsystem will decide where the order will be prepared and which van will deliver it. This is a complex application, whose solution is defined only at a high level. Pepe can envision all kinds of business rules for the decisions that need to be made. He will use APF to investigate when and how these rules should be applied. Some simulation models will be needed to conduct those investigations.

Order-submit Subsystem

The fourth software application places the order into the system and updates the status of all workstations. It is straightforward. A TPM approach is appropriate.

Inventory-management Subsystem

The fifth application will be an inventory-control system to manage inventories at all stores, factories, and pizza vans, and automatically reorder from the single vendor PDQ has been using since it first started in the business. PDQ has been informed by the vendor that it can earn discounts by using the automatic-reordering feature. This application should also be a commercial off-the-shelf application. PDQ wishes to have inventory delivered to the point of use. This will create some complications with restocking pizza vans. An Iterative PMLC model built around a commercial inventory management application may be the best approach.

Routing Subsystem

The sixth application is straightforward, and will probably involve having GPS systems installed in all the delivery trucks and pizza vans with commercial software integrated. A TPM approach should work just fine.

Case Study: Try & Buy Department Stores—Curriculum Design, Development, and Delivery

The high failure rate of Try & Buy projects could not be tolerated any longer. Theopholus Punofall, Vice President of Project Management for the corporation, was convinced that a training solution was the only approach that made any sense. Some of his directors suggested that maybe an enterprise-wide project management process was the solution, but Theopholus dismissed that as too radical. The project-management processes that each client group developed were developed around the specific needs of their client groups, and changes would not be accepted. The best approach was to offer best-practices training and work with each group (through training) to offer changes that would positively impact project success for its customer group. The result of that conversation is shown in Figure 2.8.

Try & Buy engaged EII to design, develop, and deliver a comprehensive project, program, and portfolio instructor-led curriculum to take project management to the next level company-wide. All 2,000 project/program managers would be able to participate in the training. It was essential that the curriculum deliver best-practice tools, templates, and processes that could be fully implemented without further training.

Delivering an effective curriculum in the face of such a unique client organization was a challenge. A needs analysis would be done, but EII

PROJECT OVERVIEW STATEMENT	Project Name Curriculum design, development, and delivery		Project No. 08-04	Project Manager Hal C. N. Daize

Problem/Opportunity

Projects were often late, over budget, and did not meet client expectations. Much of this was attributable to the client service group structure of the IS Department. Every client group followed its own processes, tools, and templates. There was little collaboration and poor learning opportunities. Cross group projects rarely succeeded.

Goal

Design, develop, and implement a training solution for all 2,000 project managers.

Objectives

1. Conduct a needs analysis across all 184 client groups.
2. Design a 6 course instructor-led curriculum that integrates the client groups.
3. Develop the curriculum with client collaboration.
4. Pilot test the curriculum beginning 3 months after project start and revise as needed.

Success Criteria

1. The current 60% project failure rate will be reduced to 30% within six months of curriculum delivery.
2. At least 90% of the project managers will have completed the curriculum on schedule.
3. A pre-post test survey will measure learning and behavioral changes that resulted from the training.

Assumptions, Risks, Obstacles

1. IS client development teams have a stronger allegiance to their client groups than to the IS Department.
2. IS client development groups are resistant to changing processes, templates, and tools.

Prepared By Hal C. N. Daize	Date 04-01-08	Approved By Theopholus Punofall	Date 04-01-08

Figure 2.8
Try & Buy Department Stores POS

expected that the curriculum would have to be field tested under live conditions and revised several times. APF was the clear choice for the project-management model for the curriculum-development project. The 2,000 participants would be divided into 80 cohorts of 25 participants each. A cohort would have representation from several customer groups. The delivery of the training program presented a rare opportunity for cross-group fertilization and process sharing. Every two weeks another cohort would begin studying the curriculum, and follow the complete curriculum as a group.

In effect, the curriculum would be developed in parallel with its offering. As each course in the curriculum was completed by a cohort, it would be analyzed and revised as necessary in time for offering to the next cohort.

Three to four revisions per course were anticipated before the curriculum would be considered complete. ISD management limited the curriculum to six courses totaling 15 instructor-led days. Three courses would be of two days' duration, and three courses would be of three days' duration. Each cohort would follow a schedule that allowed it to complete the six courses in 12 weeks. The content and format would be determined by EII.

Approaches to Requirements Elicitation

Requirements have to be discovered through a carefully planned engagement with the client. Of all the requirements-elicitation approaches, I recommend eight that work particularly well with my concept of the RBS. These eight are widely used methods for generating requirements. It is usually the case that more than one method is chosen to generate the requirements on a project. Selection of the best methods to generate potential requirements for the project is the responsibility of the project manager, who must evaluate each method for costs, ease of implementation, reliability, and client comfort level with the chosen process and risks. Further, selection of a particular method should be based on specific product and project needs, as well as proven effectiveness. Certain methods have been proven effective for specific industries and products. An example is physical, three-dimensional modeling in product development and construction.

Table 2.1 lists the more-popular methods and provides some detail on their properties.

Choosing a Requirements-elicitation Approach

There are several points to take into consideration in deciding which approach to take:

- The experience of the client team
- The experience of the development team
- The complexity and nature of the project
- The experience of the session facilitator

Table 2.1 Requirements Elicitation Approaches

Method	Strengths	Risks
Facilitated Group Sessions	Excellent for cross-functional processes Detailed requirements can be documented and verified immediately Resolves issues with an impartial facilitator	Use of untrained or biased facilitators can lead to a negative response from users Time and cost of planning/executing session can be high
Interviews	Gets client participation early High-level description of processes, functions, and features provided	Descriptions may differ from actual detailed activities Without structure, stakeholders may not know what information to provide Real needs ignored if analyst is prejudiced
Observation	Specific/complete descriptions of actions provided Effective when routine activities are difficult to describe	Documenting and videotaping may be time consuming and expensive, and may have legal overtones Confusing/conflicting information must be clarified Misinterpretation of what is observed
Requirements Reuse	Requirements quickly generated/refined Redundant efforts reduced Client satisfaction enhanced by previous proof Quality increase Reinventing the wheel minimized	Significant investment to develop archives, maintenance, and library functions May violate intellectual rights of previous owner Similarity may be misunderstood

Continues

Table 2.1   Requirements Elicitation Approaches (Continued)

Method	Strengths	Risks
Business Process Analysis	Excellent for cross-functional processes Visual communication Verification of "what is/what is not"	Implementation of improvement is dependent on an organization open to changes Good facilitation, data gathering, and interpretation required Time consuming
Prototyping	Innovative ideas can be generated Users clarify what they want Users identify requirements that may be missed Client-focused Early proof of concept Stimulates thought process	Client may want to implement the prototype Difficult to know when to stop Specialized skills required Absence of documentation
User Stories	Written from the perspective of the user of the product/service Keeps the client involved Emphasize verbal rather than written communications Understandable by the client and developers Good fit for iterative development	Newness has resulted in some inconsistencies Information may be missing from scenario description Long interaction required Training is expensive
Use Case Scenarios	State of system described before entering the system Completed scenarios used to describe state of system Normal flow of event/ exceptions revealed Improved client satisfaction and design	Newness has resulted in some inconsistencies Information may still be missing from scenario description Long interaction required Training expensive

The Experience of the Client Team

If the client team has memorable and effective experiences with any of the requirements-gathering approaches, try to select from among them. To the extent possible, you should put the clients in their comfort zone, so they can focus on the work of defining requirements.

The Experience of the Development Team

If the development team has memorable and effective experiences with any of the requirements-gathering approaches, try to select from among them. Given the choice of two or more approaches, choose the one that favors the client.

The Complexity and Nature of the Project

The more complex the project, the more you will want to use approaches that give detailed information and are less likely to overlook anything. A formal process should be preferred to a more-informal process. An ordering of the approaches from most informal to most formal might look like this:

- Observation
- Interviews
- Facilitated Group Sessions
- Requirements Reuse
- Prototyping
- User Stories
- Business Process Analysis
- Use Cases

The Experience of the Session Facilitator

First of all, this person should not be a member of either the client team or the development team. This may come as a surprise to some, but there are good reasons to back it up. The facilitator's job is so critical that you need someone with facilitation experience and with no biases regarding the project. The facilitator's job is to facilitate, not engage in politics. The client team leader and the development team leader need to focus their attention on the deliverables from the requirements-gathering exercise, not on the process of getting them, so they are not good choices. If there is no one internal to the organization that meets the criteria, hire an outside consultant. This is no place to cut expenses. The more critical and complex the project, the more you should favor the use of an outside facilitator.

Representing Requirements: The Requirements Breakdown Structure

So far, we have defined requirements from the perspective of what those requirements have to do. Functions and features offer us the details of that definition. Given that understanding, our requirements fit into a structure much like that shown in Figure 2.9. Those familiar with WBS will see that this is quite similar to a functional-based WBS. And it is, so nothing is new there. The RBS is a noun-based hierarchy. It identifies *what* must be done. The WBS is verb-based. It defines *how* it will be done. What is new in APF is what we do with the RBS. It becomes the basis on which you decide how to structure the project-management approach you will use for a project with this type of RBS (the reference here is to complexity, completeness, and uncertainty of the RBS for the project at hand).

Figure 2.9
The Requirements Breakdown Structure (RBS)

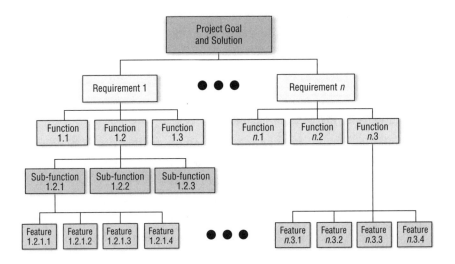

The RBS will be useful as an aid in deciding which strategy is best for the project-management process we will follow. In other words, the nature of the project as viewed through its RBS is the best guide you will have to the best strategy for managing the project.

If you get the RBS right, you are halfway home. This means you should pay particular attention to what you put in the RBS, and make sure you are not yourselves victims of scope creep. We will have enough outside influences attempting to enlarge scope. We do not need to be party to that now.

Beginning with the list of requirements generated from any one of the eight methods identified in Table 2.1, you have to create a deliverables-based WBS. The first-level decomposition will be by functions that define requirements, the second-level decomposition by sub-function, and the third-level decomposition by features that describe sub-functions. In the context of this approach to the RBS, think of features as little sub-functions. I call this the RBS, and it is shown in Figure 2.9.

I advise creating an RBS for every project for the following reasons:

- The RBS is most meaningful to the customer.
- The RBS is a deliverables-based approach.
- The RBS can be used to measure progress toward solution definition.
- The RBS can be used to measure project status.
- The RBS is consistent with the Project Management Institute's Project Management Body of Knowledge (PMI PMBOK).
- The RBS remains customer-facing as long as possible into the planning exercise.

The situation depicted in Figure 2.9 is all well and good if you happen to know the complete RBS. If you don't, you have a situation like the one depicted in Figure 2.10. The circumstance shown in Figure 2.10 is the rule rather than the exception. Some functions and features may not be known, and their absence may not be known at this early stage either. Being able to say that the RBS is complete is based more on a feeling than on hard fact. At the risk of pushing the metaphor too far, APF is designed to move the cloud and expose the complete solution.

The cloud hides some of the functionality, and features that further define the functionality.

Figure 2.10
What Is
Currently
Known about
the Solution

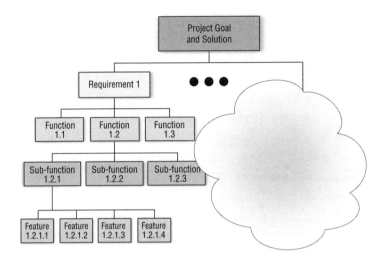

Let's look at the PDQ RBS for the Order-entry Subsystem and the RBS for Try & Buy Department Stores.

Case Study: Pizza Delivered Quickly—Order Entry and Home Delivery Process Design

Pepe realized that PDQ was a mom-and-pop business that had retained its neighborhood flavor for its entire history. It had not taken advantage of technology to improve the efficiency and effectiveness of its operations. In order to achieve 30-minute delivery, it would require a massive revision of its business processes through technology. Its founder wanted to maintain a homey environment, and felt that technology destroyed that ambiance. Since this was the first project of its kind to be undertaken by PDQ, Pepe decided to use Facilitated Group Sessions to create the RBS. The vendor PDQ had been using for years for all of its supplies and food orders recommended a consultant who had considerable experience in running Facilitated Group Sessions. That proved to be a good referral. The PDQ staff responded very well. The facilitator was very familiar with the types of people at PDQ and easily allayed their fears and anxieties about getting involved in a technology project. The RBS they defined for the Order Entry Subsystem is shown in Table 2.2.

Table 2.2 PDQ Order Entry Subsystem RBS

Requirement	Function	Sub-function	Feature
Identify customer	Identify customer	New or returning	
		Purchase history	Frequency
			Products ordered
			Special requests
		Name, address, etc.	
Get order	Get order	Product requested	Thin crust
			Chicago style
			Toppings
			Size
			Baked or unbaked
		Quantity ordered	
		Special order	
	Get delivery info	Delivery address	
		Delivery options	
		Delivery time	
	Pricing	Promotions	
		Calculate cost	
		Maintain pricing table	
	Confirm order	Order status	Accept
			Cancel
			Modify
		Payment type	Credit card
			Check
			Cash
			Coupon
		Display order	
	Submit order		
	Confirm order accept		

Since this was PDQ's first attempt at creating an RBS, Pepe was not at all confident that a complete RBS for the Order-entry Subsystem had been created. He proceeded on the assumption that it had not. This is a lower-risk approach than assuming the RBS is complete. Under the assumption of an incomplete RBS, you would choose an iterative APM approach to the project, while under the assumption of a complete RBS you would choose a TPM approach. I think you can see the potential for problems under the TPM approach. The APM approach is the safer ground. My advice is this: If you are not absolutely certain that the RBS is complete, then act as though it is not complete. You will win in the long run.

Case Study: Try & Buy Department Stores— Curriculum Design, Development, and Delivery

Because of the challenge of developing a curriculum for a decentralized structure such as the Try & Buy IS Department, a comprehensive needs analysis was essential. The curriculum had to address the variety of project situations that arose in any of the customer groups. Interviewing was chosen to define the RBS. After 106 interviews were conducted, no additional requirements, functions, or features surfaced. Table 2.3 contains the resulting RBS.

Table 2.3   Try & Buy Department Stores RBS

Requirement	Function	Sub-function	Feature
Curriculum	Content presentation		
	Discussion-based	T&B topic	
		Case study	
		Team-based	
	Use of case studies	In class	
		Homework	
	Problem exercises		
	Team-based exercises		
	Application to T&B		

Table 2.3 Try & Buy Department Stores RBS (Continued)

Requirement	Function	Sub-function	Feature
	Instructor-led	One instructor	
		Team taught	
		Alternate instructors	
	Course Topics	Project Management Processes	
		Risk	
		Planning & Control	
		Communications	
		Governance	
		Scheduling	
		Team Building	
		Organization	
		Quality	
		Customer Relations	
		Requirements Management	
		Vendor Relations	
		Supply Chain Management	
		Change Management	
		Agile Project Management	
		Software Development Project Management	
	Course Design	Learning Objectives	
		Format	
		Topics	
		Duration	
		Exercises	

Continues

Table 2.3 Try & Buy Department Stores RBS (Continued)

Requirement	Function	Sub-function	Feature
Materials	Student workbooks		
	Case studies		
	Exercises		
	Slide presentations		
	Instructor workbook		
	References		
	Evaluations	Course materials	
		Instructor	
		Participants (pre & post)	

Because of the independent organizational structure of the IS Department development function, this RBS is far from complete. There will be considerable detail specific to each customer group that can only be discovered as part of the process of designing, building, and offering the curriculum. The complete lack of features is a strong indicator that detail is yet to be defined.

APF Version Scope: Planning Process

In general, APF Version Scope will include specifying which PMLC model to use (linear, incremental, iterative, adaptive, or extreme) and which specific model will be used. I am assuming in this discussion that the decision was that this project requires using an Adaptive PMLC model, and that APF is the specific model selected to manage the project.

The APF Version Scope Planning process consists of six activities: choosing the project management quadrant and model, prioritizing the Scope Triangle, prioritizing the functional requirements, developing the mid-level WBS, developing the high-level project plan, and submitting the project plan for StageGate 2 approval. Descriptions of each follow.

Choosing the Project Management Quadrant and Model

The decisions as to which quadrant the project belongs in and which specific PMLC model is the best fit are based on weighing several variables and how they would impact the choice. The ultimate decision is more subjective than objective; generally, you would choose the alternative that is least risky.

Choosing the quadrant and the model within that quadrant does offer some flexibility. Table 2.4 summarizes the conditions under which specific decisions might be made. (I make no suggestion that the list in Table 2.4 is exhaustive of all possible models. I've included most of the commonly known models.) For example, if the goal is clear but the solution is not clear, the correct quadrant would be the APM quadrant and would require either an Iterative PMLC model or an Adaptive PMLC model. Further, if the organizational environment is in flux and the project profile is dynamic, then the appropriate quadrant would be an Adaptive PMLC model. Further, if the development team or the client team (or both) are experienced but not senior, then from Table 2.4 the best-fit model would be either APF or ASD. If the project is software development, then either APF or ASD would be the best-fit model. If the project is not software development, then APF would be the best-fit model. There are of course other considerations, such as prior experience with the client, that may change your choice of PMLC model. For example, suppose all of the conditions point to APF as the best-fit model, but the client team will be composed of less-experienced members. You might consider still using APF but holding concurrent training sessions to make up for the lack of experience.

Keep in mind that the selection is not fixed for the duration of the project. Conditions change, and the choice of quadrant and specific PMLC model might change as well. For example, say you initially chose APF. Several functions were not well-defined, and their features were not even identified. As the project commenced, the missing functions were identified, and you felt that all of them had been identified. Soon after, you felt most features had been identified and the minute details of others were close to being done. The new goal and solution clarity suggests that you might switch to the Evolutionary Development Waterfall model. You would want to weigh the cost of changing the model against the business value that would result. Another variable you might consider would be the impact on

Table 2.4 Choosing a Project Management Quadrant and Model

Quadrant	Model	Goal	Solution	Development Team Profile	Client Team Profile	Organization Profile	Project Profile
TPM—Linear	Standard Waterfall Model	Clear	Clear	Distributed	Distributed	Stable	Static
				Less experienced members	Less experienced members		Not changing
	Rapid Development Waterfall Model	Clear	Clear	Distributed	Distributed	Stable	Static
				Less experienced members	Less experienced members		Not changing
				Needs team leaders			
TPM—Incremental	Staged Delivery Waterfall Model	Clear	Clear	Distributed	Distributed	Stable	Static
				Less experienced members	Less experienced members		Not changing
	Feature-driven Development Model	Clear	Clear	Distributed	Distributed	Stable	Static
				Needs technical team leaders	Less experienced members		Not changing
APM—Iterative	Prototyping	Clear	Not clear	Colocated	Colocated	Stable	Static
				Needs experienced members	Needs experienced members		Feature changes
	Evolutionary Development Waterfall Model	Clear	Not clear	Colocated	Colocated	Stable	Static
				Needs experienced members	Needs experienced members		Feature changes
APM—Adaptive	Adaptive Project Framework (APF)	Clear	Not clear	Colocated	Colocated	Changing	Dynamic feature/function changes
				Needs experienced members	Needs experienced members		
	Adaptive Software Development	Clear	Not clear	Colocated	Colocated	Changing	Dynamic feature/function changes
				Needs experienced members	Needs experienced members		
	Dynamic Systems Development Method	Clear	Not clear	Colocated	Colocated	Changing	Dynamic feature/function changes
				Needs senior members	Needs senior members		

Table 2.4   Choosing a Project Management Quadrant and Model (Continued)

Quadrant	Model	Goal	Solution	Development Team Profile	Client Team Profile	Organization Profile	Project Profile
	Rational Unified Process (RUP)	Clear	Not clear	Colocated Needs senior members	Colocated Needs senior members	Changing	Dynamic feature/function changes
	Scrum	Clear	Not clear	Colocated Needs senior members	Colocated Needs senior members	Changing	Dynamic feature/function changes
xPM— Extreme	INSPIRE	Not clear	Not clear	Colocated Needs senior members	Colocated Needs senior members	Changing	Very dynamic feature/function changes

the team members. If they were really into APF, would it still make sense to change the model? Clients' involvement would change too. They would no longer be participating in the project to the extent that they had been with APF. If getting that participation was a hard-won battle, changing might not make sense.

Prioritize the Scope Triangle

A tradeoff matrix like that shown in Table 2.5 is a simple but elegant tool for facilitating the prioritization discussion, and as a reference later in the project when such information is useful during the Client Checkpoint phase.

Three parameters define boundaries of the Scope Triangle, with two more defining its area. They are prioritized into a list with no ties. That is, each parameter has a unique position in the prioritized list, so the strategy for changing a parameter is clear. The list is used primarily as decision support for processing changes during the Client Checkpoint phase. It is important to have these priority discussions as part of the version-planning part. Postponing such decisions until the Client Checkpoint phase is not good project management. Making the decisions in the heat of battle never gives a fair result.

Table 2.5   Scope Triangle Tradeoff Matrix

		Priority				
		Critical (1)	(2)	(3)	(4)	Flexible (5)
Variable	Scope				X	
	Quality			X		
	Time	X				
	Cost					X
	Resource Availability		X			

Table 2.5 shows the Tradeoff Matrix for Kamikazi Software Systems. The company is bleeding at the bottom line; finding a solution as quickly as possible is a must. Time is therefore the most critical and least negotiable of the five variables. Scope, on the other hand, can be negotiated. Kamikazi would be willing to put a less-than-complete solution into production rather than wait.

Develop Mid-level Work Breakdown Structure

The input into planning the version is the mid-level WBS. The mid-level WBS identifies the functionality that will be built in this version. It is a noun-type decomposition of the goal statement.

The mid-level WBS does not show the tasks that have to be done to build that functionality. To complete the WBS down to that level at this point would define work that might never be done. At this stage in the APF process, we don't know enough about the future to spend the time creating the full WBS to that level of detail. Over the course of all of the cycles, we may end up generating the complete WBS, but we don't know that for sure. In APF, we will build the WBS detail when we know it for certain and when we need it. For our purposes here, we simply decompose the WBS to a level that allows us to reasonably estimate the time and resources needed for each piece of functionality. These are not top-down estimates, nor are they bottom-up. We simply need a reasonable "guesstimate."

Typically, the mid-level WBS is detailed down to Level 2, but this is not mandatory. Level 2 would consist of sub-functions, but these are still noun-type statements. If you find yourself decomposing using verb-type statements, you have gone too far. In the APF mid-level WBS, the lowest level of detail is still a definition of what needs to be built (functionality—a noun-type statement) rather than how it is built (a verb-type statement). This is an important distinction. To define how to build something that may not even be built is a waste of time. Again, why plan the future when you don't know what it is?

Estimating Team Resources

Your resource requirements are determined at either the skill level or the position title as part of the Version Project Plan. The core team will have been assigned after StageGate 1 approval has been granted in order to participate in the requirements-gathering session at the end of the defining part of the Version Scoping phase.

The core team is only part of the project team. The remaining members will be identified by skill or position title in the Version Project Plan. You have only a high-level WBS at this time, so your identification of the resources you will need is quite subjective. You and the client will have to take some risks. You do know the budget and timeline, so that information can be used as a guide to the number of full-time equivalent (FTE) positions you can cover in the budget. Most companies will have a standard cost figure for each staff position, which will help you in estimating your client- and development-team FTE costs.

If the Version Project Plan is approved, the specific team members will then be recruited. An APF team member is assigned 100 percent to the project from beginning to end. That is radically different than in TPM projects, where team members are rarely assigned 100 percent. The APF team is a tight-knit team, and must function together in a very effective and efficient manner if it is to be successful in finding the solution. Team members come to know one another and bond together for the duration of the project. They have a strong commitment to the project and the client. A TPM project team does not typically share that unity of purpose; individual members may focus on the project only during the window of time when they are actively involved in doing work on the project. When not assigned to the TPM project, they are focused on other projects or responsibilities assigned by their home department managers.

Prioritize Functional Requirements

Using the mid-level WBS as a starting point, the core team must determine the priority rankings of the functions and sub-functions identified in the mid-level WBS. Before you can determine the relative priorities of the various functionalities, you need a criterion on which to make those prioritization decisions. Some possibilities are risk, complexity, duration, business value, and dependencies. Let's take a look at each, and discuss some of the reasons why you might want to use it.

Risk

This criterion suggests that high-risk functionality has the highest priority and low-risk functionality has the lowest priority. Why? The strategy goes something like this. If we get started on the tough stuff early and we have problems, we'll have time to make any mid-project corrections. If we leave the higher-risk items until later, we may not have time to solve problems that arise from them before the version timeframe expires.

Complexity

This criterion says that highly complex functionality has the highest priority and low-complexity functionality has the lowest priority. Why? The rationale here is the same as for the risk criterion.

Duration

This criterion says that short-duration functionality has the highest priority and long-duration functionality has the lowest priority. Again, why? If the driving strategy is to get something to the client as soon as possible, this criterion does the job. This criterion also keeps clients' interest at a high level.

You don't want them to wait three months before you produce some working piece of the solution. This strategy allows you to get back to them quickly. They have something to inspect, and you get some input for the next cycle. As you move further into the cycles, cycle length can increase, because by that time you will have the committed interest of the clients, and longer cycles will not be a problem for them.

Business Value

This criterion states that high business value has the highest priority and low business value has the lowest priority. From a business perspective, this criterion makes perfect sense. Get the most business value into the solution as soon as possible, and start to reap the benefits.

Dependencies

There will be cases where functions, and even sub-functions for two or more functions are dependent upon one another. For example, sub-function A1 in function A must be in place in order for sub-function B2 in function B to work. Dependencies like these may suggest that sub-functions A1 and B2 be addressed in the same cycle build, or that A1 be in an earlier cycle than B2.

So which criterion do you use? If you guessed that the answer is "it depends," you are partially right. Actually, the best strategy is to defer to the client for the answer. Of course, you as project manager had better provide a detailed analysis of the pluses and minuses of each choice. Still, this decision is really a business decision, and the client is in the best position to give the answer. In any case, the functionalities get ranked in order of priority.

Prioritization Approaches

Before we leave this topic, we need to spend a few lines on what that prioritization process looks like. The choice of how you establish the priority order of the sub-functions is entirely up to the client team and the development team. If you need some suggestions of rules to use for prioritizing, here are three. I've used these almost exclusively in all my client engagements. They are briefly described in the sections that follow by way of examples.

Forced Ranking

The first approach to prioritizing is called forced ranking. Suppose 10 pieces of functionality have been requested. Number them 1–10 so we can refer to them later on. Let's also suppose that the client team has six members (A–F), and each is asked to rank the functionalities from most important (1) to least important (10). They can use any criteria they wish, and they do not have to describe the criteria they used. The results of their rankings are shown in Table 2.6.

The individual rankings from each of the six members for specific functions (or sub-functions) are added to produce the rank sum for each function (or sub-function). Low-value rank sums are indicative of functions (or sub-functions) that have been given high priority by the members. So, for example, if Function 7 has the lowest rank sum, it is the highest-priority function.

Ties are possible. In fact, the preceding example has two ties (1 and 4, 6 and 9). Ties can be broken in a number of ways. We prefer to use the existing rankings to break ties. Taking the tied function with the lowest rank score and moving it to the next lowest forced rank breaks a tie. In this example, the lowest rank for Function 1 is 6, and the lowest rank for Function 4 is 8. Therefore, the tie is broken by giving Function 1 a rank of 2 and Function 4 a rank of 3.

Table 2.6   Force Ranking of 10 Pieces of Functionality

Functionality #	A	B	C	D	E	F	Rank Sum	Forced Rank
1	2	5	3	2	1	6	19	2
2	4	3	2	7	9	10	35	6
3	7	4	9	8	6	3	37	7
4	1	8	5	1	2	2	19	3
5	3	6	8	4	7	5	33	5
6	8	9	10	9	10	8	54	9
7	5	1	1	3	3	4	17	1
8	6	2	4	5	4	1	22	4
9	10	10	7	10	8	9	54	10
10	9	7	6	6	5	7	40	8

   CHAPTER 2: HOW TO SCOPE THE APF PROJECT

Must-haves, Should-haves, Could-haves, Won't-have-nows (MoSCoW)

The second prioritization approach is a bit less demanding. Here you simply create four buckets: the must-haves, the should-haves, the could-haves, and the won't-have-nows. This approach is called **MoSCoW**, an acronym for the four buckets. Every piece of functionality is assigned to one and only one bucket. Be careful with this one, because there is a temptation to make everything a must-have. To prevent that from happening, you might put a rule in place that every bucket must have at least 20 percent of the functionality in it. Adjust the percentage to suit your taste.

Q-Sort

The third approach to prioritizing is called the Q-Sort. This approach, discussed in *Project Selection and Economic Appraisal,*[6] starts out much like MoSCoW. Functions (or sub-functions) are divided into two groups: high priority and low priority. The high-priority group is then divided into two groups: high priority and medium priority. The low-priority group is also divided into two groups: low priority and medium priority. The next step is to divide the high-priority group into two groups: very high priority and high priority. The same is done for the low-priority group. The decomposition continues until each group has eight or fewer members (see Figure 2.11). As a last step, you could distribute the medium-priority projects to the other final groups.

Develop High-level Project Plan

This planning function will look quite similar to what the traditionalist would do. In APF, however, we stop the process earlier than the traditionalist would. The APF version plan extends only to the mid-level. Any task-level decomposition, even if it is known during the Version Scoping phase, is left for the appropriate Cycle Plan phase. The reason for this is that we don't yet know which cycle this work will be assigned to. Planning to that level of detail during the Version Scoping phase could be a waste of time. In APF,

---

[6] William E. Souder, *Project Selection and Economic Appraisal* (New York: Van Nostrand Reinhold, 1984).

Figure 2.11
An Example of
the Q-Sort

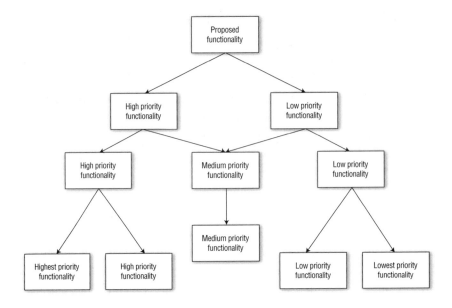

we plan only to the level that we know will happen. Anything below that level is playing with the future, and the APF project manager doesn't play with the future. APF planning is just-in-time planning.

So let's get into the details of the planning part of the Version Scope phase.

Assigning Functionality to Cycles

This is not a required activity in an APF project. Its value lies mostly in the eyes of the client, who thinks of it as a roadmap for the project. Make sure clients understand that this is quite tentative and could change radically from cycle to cycle. For APF projects, where very little is known about the solution, consider assigning functionality to cycles as an optional activity. Using the established priorities, simply map the functionality into the cycles, respecting any between-function dependencies, and then step back and ask the following questions about what you have just done.

- Based on the dependencies between functionalities and the resources available, does this assignment make sense?
- When you finish the first few cycles, will you have a working version of part of the ultimate solution?

- Can you improve on this assignment if you vary cycle length for the early cycles?
- Does this assignment fully utilize your resources in the early cycles?
- Are you practicing the core value to "deliver incremental results early and often"?

There is no substitute for common sense, and we always want to do what is right. Don't make the mistake that a traditionalist might make in making the assignments: Don't plan the details out to the last cycle. You really have no idea what will take place in the late cycles. Focus on the first few cycles and do what makes sense for them. We'll worry about the later cycles in due time.

Holding a Fixed Version Budget and Time Box

In APF, the budget and time box are fixed. The **time box** refers to the window of time within which the project must be completed. The time box includes all cycles, which have their own time boxes too. I try to limit a version time box to less than nine months. Six months is even better. Any longer and you invite many of the problems that plague the traditionalist. There are no rolling schedules. There is no going back to the well for another budget increase. One of the objectives in an APF project is to maximize business value under fixed time and cost constraints. Period. This is a very different approach to the project than the traditionalist would take. As long as the client is satisfied that the maximum business value has been attained for the time and dollars expended, the project has been successfully completed. If the client team and the development team pay attention, this result can be achieved every time. No exceptions!

Unfortunately, the maximum business value attained may not meet the success criteria, but that is an issue for the client to deal with, and should not determine the success or failure of the APF approach. Whatever didn't get done in this version will have to be left for the next version, or not done at all. Hence, we have another reason for keeping scope to a feasible minimum and the time box to less than six months: These restrictions reduce the occasions when schedules are extended or more dollars are needed. These restrictions then also reduce any financial loss to the organization, as compared to the traditional approach. With APF, you can kill a bad project much earlier than you can with the traditional approach, and that accounts for the dollar savings.

Define Cycle Duration and Number

Cycle duration should vary from two to six weeks. Earlier cycles should be shorter. The reason is that you want to solidify client ownership and meaningful involvement. You do that at the beginning of the project, so the first few cycles are critical. Try for two-week cycle duration for at least the first three to five cycles. Keeping the project constantly on the minds of the clients and giving them things to do will go a long way toward creating ownership on their part. For a simple example, suppose the version time box is 12 months. At four weeks' average cycle duration, you would plan for 13 cycles. So let's set 13 cycles as our plan. There are a variety of ways to plan 13 cycles to add up to 52 weeks. Ideally, the agilist would prefer equal-length cycles. In this example, that would mean 13 cycles of four weeks each. One modification that I have often used is to have early cycle durations that are shorter in order to get the client on board and involved. Later cycles can be lengthened in order to accommodate a more extensive deliverable schedule.

Writing Objective Statements for Each Cycle

The objective statements are primarily for the benefit of the clients and their management whose expectations live in the TPM world. You need to be able to tell them what they can expect at each cycle. They must understand that the list is very tentative. The less that is known about the solution, the more tentative is the list. The list will obviously change as learning and discovery take place. The objectives have to make business sense, and that means you may need some further modification of the assignments to each cycle as a result of the clients having reviewed and commented on your plan so far. You also want to make sure that the clients can do something productive with the deliverables from each cycle. They should review these lists with respect to the business value that will result if the objectives are met. Those deliverables are your key to further modifications of the solution scope, which will be discussed at the Client Checkpoint phase following the completion of a Cycle Build phase.

Version Scope Phase Kick-off Meeting

The Version Scope phase is often conducted with a kick-off meeting that has three separate parts, which produce the deliverables needed for StageGate 1 and StageGate 2 approvals. The first part of the kick-off meeting produces an initial version of the Project Overview Statement (POS) and is attended by the client sponsor and the project manager of the development team. The second part of the kick-off meeting reviews and modifies the POS in preparation for StageGate 1 approval and is attended by senior management from the client side, the client team, and the core development team. The third part of the kick-off meeting is a working meeting attended by the core team (the then-known client and development members of the project team). The first major deliverable is the RBS. The second major deliverable is a high-level project plan. Both of these are part of the package that is submitted for StageGate 2 approval.

The core team comprises client and development team members who will be with the project from beginning to end. Even though the project plan is not in place yet, there will be certain professionals who will be members of the project team. These professionals constitute the core team. For an APF project, these members should be colocated and assigned 100 percent if possible.

I have facilitated kick-off meetings where the third part was more like mini-conferences—often lasting several days. These are well-planned with a specific agenda and conducted by an experienced facilitator. Although these sessions may seem to be overkill, they are invaluable, especially for APF projects. This is an excellent opportunity to initiate and build a strong core team focus and to establish ownership on the part of the client members of the core team as they gain some degree of comfort working with the development members of the core team. Don't pass up the opportunity if it presents itself. There is no better way to initiate complex or critical mission projects. For very small projects, it would not be unusual for the kick-off meeting to be replaced by a one-on-one session between the project manager and the client sponsor. These sessions usually last for just a few hours. The best strategy for initiating your APF project will usually lie somewhere between these two extremes. Let the characteristics of the project drive your decision as to how to proceed.

Team Formation

When a group of people come together for the first time, they remind me of a herd of cats. Have you ever tried to herd cats? It can't be done. Fortunately, our situation isn't that hopeless. The client group and the development group have one thing in common: a complex project whose successful completion is critical to the enterprise. Furthermore, exactly how that successful completion is to be realized has so far eluded the best minds in the organization.

Team formation is absolutely essential. In this book, I don't give you even a quick course on team building. For that you can refer to my book *Building Effective Project Teams,*[7] or any of the many books on team building. For the moment, I merely want to raise your awareness of the importance of building an open and honest team. APF asks some different things of the client team and the development team—things that will take them out of their comfort zones. It is critical to have a strong sense of team as a foundation going forward.

Stop and think for a moment about what might be going through the minds of the team members at their first full team meeting. Many of them might be strangers to the other attendees and might not recognize others at the meeting. You, as the project manager (as well as a team member), might wonder what your role will be and whether you are prepared for it. One thing is certain. As the project manager, it is your job to create the team atmosphere that will be needed to succeed. You must create an open and honest environment. Team members must be willing to admit when they are having problems and not keep them secret. Team members must be willing and courageous enough to challenge others when they do not agree. The absence of such challenges can easily lead to "groupthink"—and that is death to an APF project.

---

[7] Robert Wysocki, Ph.D., *Building Effective Project Teams* (New York: John Wiley & Sons, 2002).

Putting It All Together

We hope you are beginning to get a feel for what APF has to offer and how it differs from the traditionalist approach. So far, we've completed our discussion of only the first phase of APF. Some of it is similar to the traditionalist approach, but most of it is quite different. For example, APF uses the WBS, but not to the extent that the traditionalists approach does. Traditionalists develop complete WBS's because they have to show all of the work needed to complete the project. After all, that's what the definition of the WBS says you have to do. The project manager using APF would say that's great as long as you *know* all of the work that has to be done. In APF, we don't know all the work that has to be done, so we take some liberties with the WBS. We define only the early work that has to be done (as discussed in the next chapter). Some of that later work, even though we think we know what it is, may not be done. Why worry about it now? We'll take care of that part of our planning when we need to, and right now we don't need to.

At this point, we have done all of the planning we are going to do for the version. In the next chapter, we complete the planning for the first cycle, and later for all following cycles.

Discussion Questions

The following questions are posed for your use. Use them to test your understanding and potential application of the materials presented in the chapter. If you are using this book for a course you are teaching, the questions will provoke good class discussion.

1. From what you know so far about APF, do you see a conflict between staff, process, and technology? Explain.

2. Clients are always reluctant to get too involved in planning. What might you do to sell them on the idea that their full involvement in APF is needed for the effort to succeed?

Chapter 3

How to Plan an APF Cycle

You've got to think about "big things" while you're doing small things, so that all the small things go in the right direction.

—Alvin Toffler

Let all things be done correctly and in order.

—1 Corinthians 14:40

In a Traditional Project Management project, all planning is done before any work begins. In an APF project, high-level planning is done once, and then detailed planning is done incrementally at the beginning of each cycle. In other words—just-in-time planning. In an APF project we plan only what we know to be part of the ultimate end result. Any other planning would potentially be a waste of time, money, and human resources, and is out of scope for an APF project. An APF project team does not waste time.

Definition: APFist

An APFist is any project manager who chooses to use APF for the current project. It does not imply the person is always an APFist, since there are many agile approaches other than APF.

Although TPM and APF projects use the same basic toolkit, there are two major differences between their planning processes. The first difference is that the traditionalist will do planning for the entire project using an assumed complete version of the Work Breakdown Structure (WBS). TPM makes no room for projects where the requirements are not fully documented and so the WBS is not complete. As noted in the previous chapter, the project manager using APF (the APFist) plans using only those parts of the WBS that contain the prioritized work to be done in the cycle coming up. Anything beyond that would be conjecture on the part of the APFist. The APFist can adapt everything learned about project-management planning from the perspective of the traditionalist to the APF project.

The second difference is that the traditionalist will almost always use project-management software, while the APFist will almost never use project-management software. That may sound as if APF is taking a giant technology step backwards, but it isn't. APF uses the appropriate tools, and that doesn't mean using high-tech tools just because they are there. The APFist will almost always use a whiteboard, sticky notes, and marking pens. Not much more is ever needed. The APFist could use project-management software, but it is not necessary. In fact, using project-management software to do APF cycle planning is like killing mosquitoes with sledgehammers. Remember that cycle length is typically around two to six weeks, and that is the window of time over which the APFist is doing planning. The cycle length is typically less than the minimum length needed for the work to even meet most organizations' definition of a project. I have successfully managed APF projects as extensive as three years with a $5 million budget, and not used any automated project-management tools!

An Overview of the APF Cycle Planning Phase

The Cycle Planning phase is the beginning of an APF cycle (see Figure 3.1) that consists of three of the five APF phases.

- A Cycle Planning phase that is not for building and integrating of one or more functions, sub-functions, and known features into the current solution, but rather for the preliminary investigation of potential functions, sub-functions, and features that might be integrated into the ultimate solution in a later cycle;

- A Cycle Build phase that executes the Cycle Plan; and
- A Client Checkpoint phase that includes a review of the current solution, any learning and discovery from the just-completed cycle, and the prioritization of work for the next cycle, if there is to be a next cycle.

The APF cycle is short (two-to-six weeks). Its time box is initially set as part of the Version Scope phase, and is adjusted during each Cycle Planning phase but then does not change during that cycle. Shorter cycles are

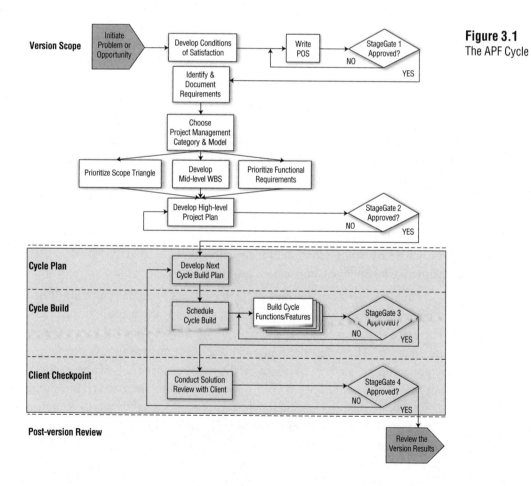

Figure 3.1
The APF Cycle

generally used early in the project to gain the meaningful involvement of the client team and create client ownership of the evolving solution. The less that is known about the solution, the shorter the cycle duration. This allows for prototyping and other quickly executed initiatives that provide a sense of the direction to pursue in the search for the solution. Longer cycle time boxes are used later in the project to allow for the integration or investigation of more-significant parts of the solution.

Clearly, APF planning is just-in-time planning. That term may sound like an oxymoron, but it really isn't. APF planning in each cycle encompasses the integration of only those functions, sub-functions, and features that you are certain will be part of the ultimate solution in some form. This integration takes place in **integrative swim lanes**, discussed later in this chapter.

There is no speculation in APF. To speculate on what will be in the final result and to spend time planning for it is to open the project to the possibility of including non-value-added work. That has the potential for wasting time and money, and the APFist doesn't waste time or money. Not wasting time or money is one of the real strengths of APF, and what results in an APF project finishing earlier and at lower cost than if a TPM model had been used instead.

Since the solution is incomplete and must be discovered and learned during project execution, each cycle will consist of investigative tasks in search of missing components. These searches can consist of any number of activities. I have personally used in-depth discussions of alternatives in an effort to choose (or at least prioritize) likely approaches for later investigation. Prototyping an idea can provide more information on its feasibility before pursuing an in-depth investigation. These activities are called **probative swim lanes**, and are discussed later in this chapter.

Planning of a short duration cycle has to be approached carefully. When it comes to spending time on planning, there are three types of planners. There are those for whom planning is a task looked forward to with eager anticipation. These are the anal-retentive folks among us who easily get wrapped up in "analysis paralysis" and not on results. They can be a serious impediment to an APF team. They waste time. Then there are those among us for whom planning is something to be done once lightly so the team can get going on the real work of the project. They can also be an impediment to an APF team. They haven't sufficiently described their tasks, and may set the team off in a direction that will be a waste of time too. I am reminded of a cartoon from many years ago whose source has since been lost. It shows the project manager going past the programmers' cubicles as she says: "You people get started on the coding. I'm going down the hall to find out what the spec is."

APF planning involves neither of these extremes. It is just-in-time planning, with all of the non-value-added work stripped out. APF planning is a learned skill. It must be adapted to the situation, and is not simply a recipe to be followed blindly. Remember, project management is nothing more than organized common sense!

As highlighted in Figure 3.2, the APF Cycle Planning phase is the phase that begins each APF cycle. There are two types of Cycle Planning phases to

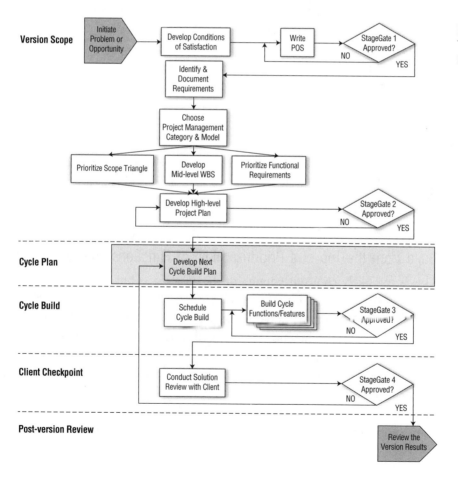

Figure 3.2
The APF Cycle Planning Phase

discuss: the first Cycle Planning phase, and all subsequent ones. They are different, so they are discussed separately.

The First Cycle Planning Phase

The first time we enter the APF Cycle Planning phase, we'll have as input the deliverables from the Version Scoping phase: the POS, the RBS, the PMLC model that will be used, the prioritized Scope Triangle, the mid-level WBS, the prioritized list of known requirements, functions, and features, and the high-level project plan.

For most APF projects, the first cycle should be short. I like to keep it to about two weeks, so don't plan on putting too much into it. At this early stage of the project it is most important to get the client to have a vested interest in the project and to get the development team aligned to the project. To gain and sustain the client's interest and involvement, you need to show something quickly. Since the APF team may be coming together for the first time as a team, you need to spend some time on team development. Who the team members are, why they have been assigned to this project, and what their understanding of the project is should be put on your agenda.

Depending on the depth to which the solution is known, there are four directions that the first Cycle Planning phase might take. They are described below.

Build from the Top of a Prioritized List of Functions and Features

This is the likely choice if enough of the solution is known to produce a meaningful part of the ultimate result for the client to begin envisioning what that end result might look like and to begin working toward it. From the prioritized list of functionality created in the Version Scoping phase, enough functionality for a short cycle of, say, two weeks would be included, starting from the top of the list. Even if a reasonably complete solution is known, stick with two-week cycles for the first few cycles. Your goal in the first few cycles is to meaningfully engage the client, create a sense of ownership, and to begin the task of forming an effective team. Short cycles will make it possible for you to do those. At the same time, you will begin to deliver business value. Also, from the early short cycles you might be surprised to discover that the solution isn't what you thought it would be. Two-week cycles will keep the project heading in the right direction and prevent you from wasting your time and your client's money jousting with windmills.

If your concern is about creating business value as soon as possible, you may have to lengthen the cycle duration in order to build enough functionality to attain even minimal business value. But be careful here, because the longer the cycle, the more likely you will err on the side of including something in the solution that turns out not to be part of the ultimate result.

Including probative swim lanes in the early cycles is low priority when most of the solution is known.

Build a Prototype of the Solution

If very little of the functionality is known, you may not be able to generate an initial solution that is useful to the client. A better choice for the first few cycles might be to build a prototype. The purpose of the prototype is to get a conversation going with the client to begin identifying meaningful solution components. This prototype will be very high-level, and is not expected to contain much detail because that detail is not yet known. It can be created quickly, and it can be very informative. This is the approach I used for the first APF new-product design project, briefly described below. Once a sufficiently detailed prototype is in place, the priority can shift to including probative swim lanes.

Definition: Prototype

A prototype is a throw-away representation of what the known or speculated solution might contain. It is quickly built and used primarily to gain a deeper understanding of what the actual solution might look like. Several versions of the prototype will usually be built until a vision of the complete solution is attained.

Build the Complete Solution as It Is Known at This Time

While this certainly is an approach for the first cycle, it is not high on my list of recommended first-cycle activities for the following reasons.

- It makes the first cycle too long and hampers establishing meaningful client involvement. Establishing meaningful client involvement from the very beginning of the project is the number-one critical success factor for project success, as we learned from the Standish Group's *Chaos Report 2007*[1] on the top ten reasons why projects fail. Even when you know a lot about the solution you have to be patient. Establishing a solid client relationship early will pay dividends later.

- You might have guessed incorrectly as to what is in the ultimate solution, and therefore wasted time. As learning and discovery take place in each cycle, your view of the ultimate solution will change. Certainly more of the solution will be known, but so will earlier understandings change. What was once thought to be part of the solution may no longer be part of the solution. So you will have wasted time integrating that part into the solution and then backing it out of the solution. Wasted time is the bane of all APF projects and to be avoided if at all possible. The timeframe for the project is fixed, so the APFist would rather spend the time on delivering the best solution possible.

Instead of building the solution as known at this time, I prefer to take a more-pedestrian approach and work from the prioritized list. If your initial guess proves to be correct, then those functions and features will eventually find their place in the end result, and nothing will have been lost. If not, my pedestrian approach reduces the risk of having made a bad decision as to the contents of the final result at the beginning of the project and potentially wasted a lot of time.

Create a Business Case

If little of the solution can be envisioned and senior management is a bit hesitant to go forward with the project, a business case might be a good choice

---

[1] Standish Group, *Chaos Report 2007: The Laws of CHAOS* (Boston: Standish Group International, 2007).

for the first cycle. The purposes of the business case are to get senior management on board and to identify what the solution has to do if it is to deliver enough business value to satisfy senior management and the client. The success of the project is critical to the organization, and some project to address the problem or opportunity must be undertaken. Senior management just needs some reassurance that your approach is the best approach. The Objective Statement in the POS might contain some of the information that is already known about the solution, and that will help. The business case can expand on the Objective Statement. What you are looking for are validation of the business idea and guidance on the contents of early cycles. I have had occasion to use prototyping to support the business case.

The Second and All Subsequent Cycle Planning Phases

At the start of the second and all subsequent Cycle Planning phases, we'll have the current solution, an updated RBS, all the deliverables from the previously completed cycles, all learning and discovery that took place in those earlier cycles, and the Scope Bank, which contains all the ideas for change accumulated over all previous cycles but not yet acted upon. As you can see, each Cycle Planning phase is a moment of opportunity when the client team and the development team come together to openly discuss, prioritize, and plan the work to be done in the upcoming cycle. These planning exercises should be lively sessions where ideas are shared in a brainstorming fashion, discussed, challenged, and then brought to closure for exclusion or tabled for consideration in a later cycle. Whatever the disposition, all of the learning and discovery should remain in the Scope Bank for future reference. You can't possibly know what future courses the solution might take, and keeping the project team's cumulative knowledge at hand may prove valuable later on. It doesn't cost anything to keep it, but it may cost to not have it if it is needed later.

Swim Lanes

The basic component of the Cycle Planning phase is what I call a "swim lane." You may be familiar with the term, but I may be using it somewhat differently than you are expecting. In APF, swim lanes are parallel streams of concurrent project work. A number of swim lanes will be used to construct the cycle work plan. Each swim lane must have a total duration less than or equal to the cycle duration. The longest-duration swim lane should command the management attention of the client team leader and the development team leader. This is the critical path for the cycle.

The parallel swim lanes serve the same purpose as the tracks of concurrent work that make up the Rapid Development Waterfall model in a TPM project. They are designed to increase the amount of work that can be done in a fixed timeframe. In a TPM project, the swim-lane approach is used to get deliverables into production faster. In an APF project, the parallel swim lanes are used to get to the end result faster, and to allow the project team to examine more alternatives for inclusion in the solution.

When you are planning to use multiple swim lanes in a cycle, it is good risk-management strategy to construct them so that there is minimal or no task or resource dependency across the swim lanes. This allows for independent task scheduling and usually minimizes the risk of resource-scheduling conflicts. Figure 3.3 illustrates the situation.

Cycle A is clearly easier to manage than Cycle B. There will be fewer problems with Cycle A than Cycle B. Each swim lane in Cycle A can be managed and scheduled independently of the others. The only scheduling requirement is that A7, A8, and A9 are all finished before the Late Start date for A10. (The Late Start date is the latest date when a task could begin without delaying the completion date of the cycle.) Cycle B, on the other hand, poses a number of schedule risks. If B2 is delayed beyond its Late Finish date, then B5 and B6 will be delayed. (The Late Finish date is the latest date when a task could be finished without delaying the completion of the cycle.) If B7 is delayed beyond its Late Finish date, then B9 will be delayed. The final scheduling risk is that B8 or B9, or both, are delayed beyond their Late Finish dates: B10 will therefore not be complete by the end of the cycle time box.

There are two types of dependencies across swim lanes that can affect the scheduling risk of a cycle. They are described next.

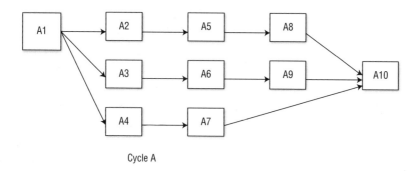

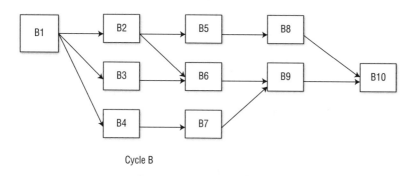

Figure 3.3
Examples of Cycle Swim Lanes

Schedule Dependencies across Swim Lanes

The work within a cycle is tightly scheduled. Having schedule dependencies across two or more swim lanes introduces the possibility that schedule delays in one swim lane will cause schedule delays in a dependent swim lane. Partition the tasks into swim lanes to minimize the possibility that that will happen. If you can actually make the swim lanes independent of one another, consider yourself fortunate. Don't expect the swim lanes to be totally independent of one another. Consider that to be the ideal.

Resource Dependencies across Swim Lanes

This one can pack a double whammy. If the resource becomes unavailable for some reason, then two or more swim lanes are affected. Maintenance of the cycle schedule becomes more problematic.

The other case arises when the resource falls behind schedule with a task in one swim lane and may therefore be delayed in working on a scheduled task in another swim lane. The usual fixes when this occurs are the same as in a TPM project. Those fixes include reassigning resources and requisitioning added resources. In an APF project, you also have the possibility of reducing cycle scope without compromising the overall project schedule. Some of the lower-priority work planned for this cycle can be put back in the Scope Bank for reprioritization and inclusion in a later cycle. That should give you a clue for organizing the work of the current cycle: Try to complete the highest-priority tasks, and leave the lower priority tasks for later cycles if necessary. If they are still important, they will be added to later cycles. This option is not readily available in the TPM project.

Types of Swim Lanes

In an APF project there are two very distinct types of swim lanes. I've labeled them **probative** and **integrative**. They are described below.

Probative Swim Lanes

This is the label I use for those swim lanes whose purpose is to investigate new ideas, or whether a particular variation of a function or feature could be part of the ultimate solution and what it might look like. New ideas are tested for feasibility in a probative swim lane. Probative swim lanes are speculative, in other words. Only as much planning and detailing as necessary for a decision are done in a probative swim lane. Conserving project team resources is important: We want to save resources for integrative swim lanes. Planning for probative swim lanes is minimal. If the decision is such that the potential function or feature can be part of the final result, then either further probative swim lanes will be planned to further define the function or feature, or an integrative swim lane for that functionality will be prioritized for a coming cycle.

The decision as to which approach makes the most sense is subjective. Factors affecting that decision include

- The number of probative swim lane ideas in the Scope Bank
- The number of integrative swim lane ideas in the Scope Bank
- The degree to which the solution is defined

Later probative swim lanes would verify the inclusion of an idea, and at that point an integrative swim lane would be planned.

There could be several probative swim lanes in one cycle, each investigating some new function or feature. You could even have several variations of the same function or feature running in concurrent probative swim lanes. Your objective would be to either eliminate one or more of them from further consideration or have one or more of them emerge to be integrated into the current solution. Ideally, a new function or feature would be identified and would then become part of an integrative swim lane in some later cycle. The deliverable from a probative swim lane will be one or more alternatives from which the client will choose for development in an integrative swim lane in a future cycle.

In my APF experiences, I have used three different kinds of probative swim lanes.

Iconic Prototyping Probative Swim Lanes   I've used these to clarify with the client how a function or feature idea might be rendered in the solution. If the idea looks promising, then the prototype will have established a foundation on which more details can be explored in this or a later cycle. There have been situations when the idea doesn't look promising, but a variant of it might. The variant can be explored in a later cycle.

In-depth Discussion Probative Swim Lanes   A brainstorming session might identify several options for consideration. A probative swim lane can be used to discuss the details and establish specific directions for further investigation.

Information-gathering Probative Swim Lanes   In most cases, the organization provides the information. Its collection comes in response to questions that have arisen in a previous probative swim lane.

Integrative Swim Lanes

This is the label I use for those swim lanes that will be integrating into the current solution new functions and features that are clearly defined from the beginning of the project or from a previous cycle and are now known to be part of the end result. These functions and features may have been known to be part of the solution from the start of the project but never given high-enough priority to be integrated into the solution in some earlier cycle. The necessary testing and documentation are done as part of the tasks in an integrative swim lane. At the end of every cycle, the deliverables will include a working solution with functions and features added since the previous solution. This new solution goes to the Client Checkpoint for evaluation.

Balance between Integrative and Probative Swim Lanes

Successful management of the Scope Bank is essential to the success of an APF project. The cumulative history of the number of integrative and probative swim lanes in the Scope Bank is an aid to management of the project. There should be a healthy balance between the two types of swim lanes.

Suppose most of the solution is known. In this case, early in the project the focus should be on integrative swim lanes. Having as complete a solution as possible integrated early will inform the project team about missing and needed functions and features. As most of these parts are integrated, the focus will shift to probative swim lanes to identify the missing parts of the solution. You should try to keep a good supply of probative swim lanes in each cycle so that there will be a steady supply of function and feature additions being discovered and available for integration into the solution. You are trying to protect yourself from the risk of having an incomplete solution without new ideas for functions and features to be added. As you get close to convergence on the final complete solution or expending all of the time and money allocated to the project, the number of probative swim lanes relative to integrative swim lanes should diminish. Late in the project, you will want to get as much of the solution defined and operational as possible. The client is the final arbiter of what will be integrated, so any thoughts of "gold plating" the solution rather than finishing early should not arise.

An example should help. Figure 3.4 charts an APF project where most of the solution is known at the start of the project.

Suppose very little of the solution is known. There are two strategies I have used successfully. The obvious strategy is to have the first cycle focus on building a prototype, followed by several cycles heavily loaded with probative swim lanes. If you have established good client relationships from previous APF projects, this can work quite effectively. If you don't have that type of relationship with your client, this strategy isn't a good choice for the

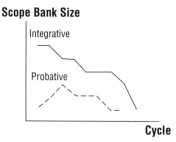

Scope Bank Size

Integrative

Probative

Cycle

Figure 3.4
Size of the
Scope Bank
Over Time
When the Initial
Solution Is
Mostly Known

reason that it doesn't contribute to the early establishment of meaningful client involvement. In my practice, the less I know about the solution, the more I would lean toward prototyping for the first few cycles. Before you can effectively define probative initiatives, you and the client need a sense of direction as to where that elusive solution might be found. Early prototyping cycles will do the job, and will also contribute to building that much-needed client relationship.

For this example, the early cycles consist mostly of integrative swim lanes. As integrative ideas are moved out of the Scope Bank and integrated into the solution, their numbers in the Scope Bank will decrease. As learning and discovery take place, the number of potential probative swim lane ideas waiting in the Scope Bank to be acted upon will increase. That increase is due mostly to learning and discovery about the solution from actually building partial solutions through the integrative swim lanes. By spreading the integrative swim lanes across the early cycles, you might also discover that the lower-priority functions and features that were once thought to be part of the solution may no longer be relevant. You wouldn't know that if you simply used the first cycle to build the entire then-known solution. Give considerable thought to what I just wrote. It may save you from wasting the precious time of the developers.

The project co-managers will want to keep a healthy balance between the two types of swim lanes so that there will always be functions and features to be added or discovered. Probative swim lanes grow the solution by feeding ideas with business value to the list of functions and features waiting for a prioritizing in the integrative swim lanes.

As the project commences, keep the relative number of ideas for each type of swim lane in balance. What is considered balanced is a subjective decision—something the co-managers get a feeling for as the project progresses. At some point in time, the numbers of each type in the Scope Bank will decrease. This means that the solution is stabilizing, and no new ideas are coming forth.

By this point, it is hoped that the solution is stabilizing to one that has acceptable business value. That will always be the final question in an APF project. As the project-completion deadline approaches or as the budget is nearly exhausted, the effort should shift entirely toward planning integrative swim lanes and away from probative swim lanes. Your goal is to get as much of the defined solution implemented as possible. Leave untested ideas for the next version.

Figure 3.5 represents a different type of project. In this example, very little is known about the solution, so the early cycles will be focused on discovering functions and features of the solution. Early brainstorming sessions should be conducted in the Version Scoping phase and the first few Cycle Planning phases. You need to stoke the fires and get as many ideas as possible into the probative swim lanes. Prototyping can be effective in the early cycles.

As probative swim lanes identify parts of the solution, they should be followed by integrative swim lanes as soon as possible. It is important to get even a partial solution in front of the client. The most useful information about the missing parts of the solution will come from the learning and discovery by the client-team members as they work with the then-solution.

Remember that the successful identification of solution components through the use of probative swim lanes feeds the integrative swim lane contents and hence the convergence of solutions into the complete solution. It is the responsibility of the project co-managers to maintain a healthy balance between Probative and integrative swim lanes so that convergence to the ultimate solution is assured. That balance will change as the project progresses through the cycles.

Figure 3.5
Size of the Scope Bank Over Time When the Solution Is Mostly Unknown

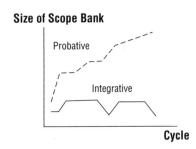

Size of Scope Bank

Probative

Integrative

Cycle

APF Cycle Plan Deliverables

There are two major types of deliverables from an APF Cycle plan. The first is a decision as to which functions and features will be integrated into the current solution in the coming cycle to help converge toward the final result. The current solution is always a working version of the then-known solution. In the early cycles, not much integration may be happening, simply because so little is known of the ultimate solution. In later cycles, this pattern will reverse as several functions, sub-functions, and especially features will be integrated in each cycle. A steady trend of integration should be the pattern. If it is not, there is serious doubt about the convergence toward a final acceptable solution. I'll introduce some metrics in the Cycle Build discussion that will help you assess the extent to which convergence upon or divergence from the solution is happening. I have even seen examples where the metrics indicated that the process was diverging and would ultimately lead to project failure if a termination decision was not made. Often the decision is to terminate the project and start over in a different direction. Serving as an early-warning system has proven to be a real strength of APF.

The second type of deliverable is the selection of new ideas, in the form of functions and features, to be investigated for possible addition into the solution in a later cycle. These deliverables can start out as high-level descriptions of potential solution parts, and can be further investigated for as long as they seem feasible. At the completion of a cycle, these discoveries will be either abandoned and returned to the Scope Bank or added to the priority list for integration into the solution during some future cycle.

Just as I did with the Version Scoping phase, the best way to introduce you to the Cycle Planning phase is from the perspective of its deliverables.

The Cycle Planning phase has seven steps.

1. Update the prioritized functionality list.
2. Establish the contents of the next Cycle Build integrative swim lanes.
3. Establish the contents of the next Cycle Build probative swim lanes.
4. Create the low-level WBS for this cycle's swim lanes.
5. Identify resource requirements.

6. Estimate swim-lane duration.

7. Establish dependencies and finalize cycle schedule.

Let's briefly discuss each one.

Update the Prioritized Functionality List

The input into this list includes the prioritized list from the just-completed cycle, any work planned but not completed from the previous cycle, any ideas or changes in the Scope Bank that have not yet been acted upon, and any new ideas or changes suggested by the client or the development team based on additional learning and discovery from the just-completed cycle.

All of this information is best kept in the Scope Bank. The Scope Bank is the repository of all known functions, sub-functions, features, and ideas or suggested changes not yet acted upon. At the beginning of each cycle, all of the items in the updated Scope Bank are ranked by priority. From this prioritized list, the contents of the next cycle build will be identified.

Establish the Contents of the Next Cycle Build Integrative Swim Lanes

The contents of the next cycle build will take the form of some number of probative and integrative swim lanes. You also have a preliminary estimate of the time box for the coming cycle, so you can determine the cycle contents based on what can reasonably be accomplished within that time constraint. I have the opinion that keeping the cycle time box a fixed duration from cycle to cycle is best. The team develops a certain cadence, and that should be protected. If necessary, you might adjust the time box to accommodate the next item or items on the prioritized list. Apart from any dependencies between the functions, sub-functions, and features, the client team and the development team will jointly decide how much of the prioritized list the development team can address in the coming cycle. The duration of the cycle and the estimated duration of the functions and features to be worked on in this cycle are what you will use to determine what can be worked on in this cycle.

There is a caution here that I want you to be aware of. Technical professionals tend to be optimistic about what they can accomplish in a given time box. There is something about the challenge that gets their juices flowing. That has no place here. APF projects are risky enough; they don't need heroes on white horses arriving in the nick of time to save the project. In the first cycle, don't be too ambitious, especially if your project team members have not had the opportunity to work together on an APF project before. How they have come together as a team may also influence planning for the coming cycle. If they are together for the first time, you should not expect them to be a lean, mean fighting machine. They will stumble at first, so don't burden them too heavily while they are learning to work together efficiently. You are constrained to a fixed time box for this cycle and the available resources of the project team. What can realistically be built within this time box using the available team resources? As the project team gains experience through successfully completed cycles, you can get a bit more aggressive on what can be accomplished in each coming cycle. At that time, you will have direct and relevant experience working with the team on this project and will have a better grasp on what it can be expected to accomplish.

Inside the cycle, think about using tools, templates, and processes from your TPM experiences. For example, you might use the Standard Waterfall model, the Staged Delivery Waterfall model, or the Rapid Development Waterfall model to maximize the deliverables that can be produced in a swim lane in this cycle. You should be on familiar ground here and know what makes sense. When you have identified what will be built in this cycle, you can complete that part of the WBS down to the lowest level at which activities that define how you will build the functionality and features are defined. Remember that even this part of the WBS may not be complete. For a given function, not all features will be known until some later cycle. You surely don't know them all at this point in time.

The first step in establishing cycle contents is to work down the prioritized list of functions, sub-functions, and features, estimating the time to build each. How far down the list to go is a judgment call. (As a guide, you might use the total number of hours of labor available from the project team in the coming cycle. Since the team members are assigned 100 percent to the APF project duration, and labor should be nearly the same. If you feel uncomfortable with this, you might reduce labor hours by some percentage, say 10 percent, and use that as your guide to cumulative hours available in the coming cycle.) The cumulative duration of the work you have estimated can be larger than the cycle duration if the team size is large enough so that parallel work can take place. We'll look at an example later in this chapter. Don't spend time working far down the list past anything that might reasonably be included in the coming cycle. That could prove to be a waste of time. Where to stop is a judgment call; just remember that the APFist doesn't waste time.

Establish the Contents of the Next Cycle Build Probative Swim Lanes

The less is known about the solution, the more important it is to aggressively identify potential solution details. That is the purpose of probative swim lanes. I have often found it helpful to use a prototyping approach in these probative swim lanes to investigate possible additions to the solution. Several iterations of the prototype can be completed within the cycle time box.

Create the Low-level WBS for this Cycle's Contents

You have identified the preliminary contents of the cycle from the perspective of priority and duration. It is now time to build out the WBS for the functions, sub-functions, and features chosen as the cycle contents and to finalize what actually will be included. The list could be compromised by any resource or schedule dependencies between swim lanes. If there are probative swim lanes to be added, they will require resources, and hence will further limit the integrative swim lanes that can be included in the cycle plan.

So far, the known part of the WBS is a mid-level WBS. It is deliverables-oriented, as shown in Figure 3.6. These sub-functions are the most granular decomposition in the WBS that define what will be done. The next and all lower-level decompositions of the sub-functions identify how

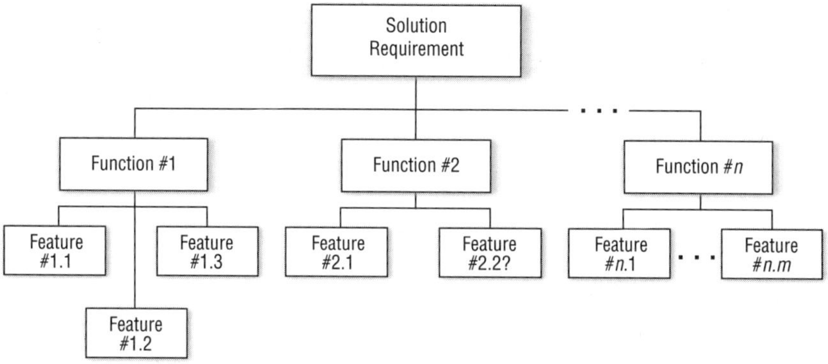

Figure 3.6
Mid-level WBS

the sub-functions will be built. We will create the low-level WBS for each of the functions or sub-functions assigned to this cycle. That means decomposing to the feature level wherever that is appropriate and known. To complete this part of the WBS, we have to decompose features into activities, and finally into tasks that must be performed to produce the feature.

The top-down approach is my clear choice for how to do this. Start with any feature, sub-function, or function if that is the lowest level of decomposition in this part of the WBS and ask yourself, "What major activities (chunks of work) must be done in order to deliver this feature, sub-function, or function?" Think in the broadest sense, and come up with three to five chunks of work. At this level we are defining work, and that means making verb statements. Make sure these chunks of work are defined at a high-enough level so that you can easily tell when they are all completed and hence the activity is completed.

We will continue this decomposition until the completion criteria listed in the following sub-sections have been met. Once an activity meets the completion criteria, we rename it a task; no further decomposition of the task is needed or advised. No other type of activity will have this property, so task is a precise term in our project-management vocabulary. The completion criteria reproduced here were originally defined in the first edition of my book *Effective Project Management: Traditional, Agile, Extreme.*[2]

---

[2] Robert K. Wysocki, Ph.D., *Effective Project Management: Traditional, Agile, Extreme* (New York: John Wiley & Sons, 1995).

Status and Completion Are Measurable

At any point in time while the activity is open for work, its status can be reported. Certainly, the percentage of work completed will be of interest, but even more important will be an estimate of how much time is required to complete the task.

Each Activity Is Bounded

Each activity has clear starting and ending events. When these events occur, either work can begin on the activity or the activity is finished.

Each Activity Has a Deliverable

Something tangible is produced by the activity. That might be something you can hold in your hands, a signature, or a document.

Time and Cost Are Easily Estimated

"Easily" is a relative term. It may mean an estimate has been provided in an earlier project, or it may mean it is the simplest it can be and no further decomposition will make the estimate any easier to obtain.

Activity Duration Is within Acceptable Limits

This is an organizationally determined limit. Two weeks (80 hours) is a common choice in a TPM project, but the situation may dictate a smaller or larger limit. In an APF project, the cycle length might only be two weeks, so the limit for activity would be much shorter. Three days is probably about right for an activity within an APF cycle, but the limit is a judgment call in any case.

Work Assignments Are Independent

This is critical. It simply means that once work has begun on an activity it can continue without interruption because additional input is not needed. This has obvious scheduling implications.

Once an activity has all six of these properties, it is renamed a task. When this part of the WBS contains all tasks at the lowest level of decomposition it is the complete WBS, but for the coming cycle only. No further decomposition is needed or advised. For more details on these six completion criteria see Chapter 4 in *Effective Project Management*.[3] The WBS for this cycle is now complete, and a dependency-precedence diagram of the tasks can be constructed. This becomes the input into the partitioning of tasks into swim lanes. An example of a complete WBS for the coming cycle will be given in the case study discussion below.

Identify Resource Requirements

Estimating resources requirements for an APF cycle is very different than the process you would follow for a TPM project. In an APF project, you already know the resources available to you. They are assigned 100 percent to your APF project. In a TPM project, you have to estimate the people resources by skill level or position title. You won't know the specific person in each role until much later in the process. In the APF project, resource requirements are determined during the Version Scope phase, and are generally not reassessed during the project.

Who will be assigned to work on what is the major decision to be made here. As a first pass, I usually assign the best person to each task, and worry about any schedule conflicts this creates once duration estimates and the dependency network are built. The person who is initially assigned to specific work will provide the input needed to plan the cycle schedule. At that point, there may be some reassignment to reconcile scheduling conflicts.

Estimate Task Duration

For each task, you would usually estimate the clock time (duration) it would take with normal resources to complete it. Don't get heroic here. This estimate is nothing different than the traditionalist would do at this point.

---

[3] Robert K. Wysocki, Ph.D., *Effective Project Management: Traditional, Agile, Extreme, Fifth Edition* (New York: John Wiley & Sons, 2009).

In an APF project, however, you have the advantage of knowing who will be working on each task. That is not the case in a TPM project, where all you know is the skill level required. You don't know what you will get for TPM staff. You might get the skill level you need, but you might not. You might get one person to complete the task, but you might not. You will probably get the FTE count you need, but you might not. All you can plan for the TPM task duration estimate is that you will get the average-skilled person working on the task at a normal pace with all of the normal interruptions that will get in the way. You have the added burden of actually acquiring the staff when you need them. Resource managers have a lot of competing priorities, and you could be disappointed if a person is not available when the time comes to report to your TPM project.

For the APF project, the people who will be assigned to work on tasks are already 100-percent assigned to the team and participating in cycle planning. They can provide the estimated duration better than anyone else. Since they are assigned 100 percent to the project, you don't have to worry about outside scheduling conflicts. Hence, APF task-duration estimates are considerably more reliable than those from a TPM project, and are more likely to be achieved than their TPM counterparts.

I recognize that a 100-percent assignment to an APF project may be idealistic and not often possible. Know that to have a team member assigned less than 100 percent will add risk to the project. The project is already high risk because the solution is not known, so don't add to the risk if it can be helped. My best advice is to *adapt.* You have to do the best with what you have. Just keep the downside of increased risk in mind. In the final analysis, that is what APF is all about.

Establish Dependencies and Cycle Schedule

Now we are going to put all the pieces of the puzzle together for a first look at what we have. My low-tech approach is to arrange these tasks into a network diagram from left to right on the whiteboard, showing their dependencies using marking pens. You will eventually want to scale the display on a timeline so that you will know if you are meeting the cycle time-box constraint. The high-tech folks won't be able to resist the temptation and will go ahead and put these dependencies into a software tool. They will let the tool tell them about the critical path. That's fine; just remember that the cycle duration is only two to six weeks, so the task list will be short. Be careful not to create a monster in your software tool, because you will have to feed it throughout the cycle to get any return for your investment of time.

The tasks are few in number, and you know the availability of your team members. APF works best when the resources are assigned 100 percent to the cycle. If that is the case, you should have total control over their schedules. That means that you can create the cycle schedule with both dependencies and resources schedules taken into account. The traditionalist seldom has that luxury.

Once the low-level WBS for this cycle has been constructed and all task durations have been estimated, print the unique name of each task and its duration on a separate sticky note. To add to the intuitive nature of the display, you might color-code the sticky notes. Each function or feature in this cycle gets a different color. You will see the value of this later in the phase. If you choose to use project-management software to produce a tidier display, enter the name of each task and its duration into the package. Print the PERT diagram, which will produce a columnar display of task nodes because no dependencies have been specified. You can then cut out each task node and tape it to a sticky note. Adding the task number on the sticky note can help with task sequencing later.

By defining project tasks to be those activities that meet all six completion criteria, you should have reached a point of granularity with each task sufficient to make it familiar. You may have done the task or something very similar to it in a past project. That recollection, that historical information, gives you the basis for estimating the resources you will need to complete the tasks in the current project. In some cases, you may rely upon straightforward recollection; in others, you may refer to a historical file of similar tasks; in still others, you may obtain the advice of experts.

Dependency relations and the initial schedule generated are recorded using sticky notes, marking pens, and plenty of whiteboard space. If you really must have the comfort and assurance of software, go ahead and use it. Just remember that you created the monster, and you will be responsible for its care and feeding over the life of the cycle. Having planned and managed many APF cycles using nothing but sticky notes, marking pens, and whiteboards, I know that using a software package is non-value-added work. In other words, it is a waste of time, and APFists don't waste time! *(Sorry, project-management software providers. That's life in APF-land.)*

The steps for building the dependency diagram can be found in any good book on project management. See *Effective Project Management*[4] for a step-by-step process for generating the dependency diagram and calculating the schedule. An example of the dependency diagram and schedule for the coming cycle will be given in the case study that follows.

Generate Sub-team Plans

This is the first pass at building a staffed schedule for the coming cycle. Based on the dependencies between tasks that will be open for work in the coming cycle, we partition the tasks into sets of tasks such that within a set there are task dependencies, but between sets there are few task dependencies. To the extent this is possible, it will reduce the number of scheduling dependencies between your sub-teams. Once the partitioning is acceptable to the team and the client, you can begin to form sub-teams that will plan and implement the tasks in their partition.

Every task is assigned to one person who is responsible for getting the task done. This person is called a task manager. There might be others assigned to work on the task, but the task manager is ultimately responsible for completing the task. The case study below gives an example.

Minimize Cross-swim-lane Dependencies

If done properly, this step will minimize the risk of schedule and resource dependencies across swim lanes. As stated previously, the total elimination of these dependencies is highly unlikely, but you must make every effort to minimize them. The process for doing this consists of observing the dependency diagram and partitioning it into independent streams of work, then allocating those streams of work to different swim lanes. An example will help; see the case study later in this chapter.

---

[4] *Ibid.*

Work Packages

For every critical task in the cycle plan, it is a good insurance policy to have the person responsible for the task develop a brief step-by-step description of a plan to complete the task within the allotted time. If you lose that person or have to reassign the task, the person who takes over can continue with minimal loss of time.

Remember, these tasks are of short duration (only a few hours or days) and quite simple to understand. The description of each should be one or two sentences. Your concern here is to not add a lot of narrative, which may turn out to be lost effort and time. Don't waste time!

Work Packages are descriptions at the task level that tell how a task will be completed. They are often not much more than sequenced to-do-lists with names attached of those who will complete each to-do, and in some cases descriptions of how they will complete it. The purpose of the Work Package is to act like an insurance policy that protects the cycle against the loss of a task manager or development-team member. This is one area that we need to be very careful about, because it borders on micro-management. The writing of Work Packages will not be readily received by the development team, so you will need to introduce and justify them carefully. You have to be very careful about which tasks you ask the manager to prepare a Work Package. Figure 3.7 shows a template for Work Packages I developed and use extensively.

By inspection, you will be able to identify the critical tasks for which Work Packages will be needed. Aficionados will want to use a software tool to locate the critical path. That's fine, but don't let the tool do the thinking for you. I would rather have you reason your way to the decision than to default to the software tool. There is no substitute for thinking.

The critical-path tasks are only some of the tasks for which a Work Package will be written. The decision as to which tasks you finally decide to create Work Packages for is based not just on how those tasks fit into the cycle schedule, but also on who is working on them, what level of risk is associated with the task, whether or not the assigned resources are scarce, and a host of other factors.

Figure 3.7
Work Package
Template

WORK PACKAGE DESCRIPTION	Project Name		Project No.	Project Manager		
Work Package Name	Work Package No.		Work Package Manager	Contact Info	Date	

Start Date	End Date	Critical Path Y N	Predecessor Work Package(s)	Successor Work Package(s)

TASK

No.	Name	Description	Type (days)	Responsibility	Contact Info.

Prepared By	Date	Approved By	Date	
				Sheet 1 of 1

You might also want to create Work Packages for high-risk tasks or tasks with which there is little experience among the team members. I have requested Work Packages for tasks that require a scarce resource. If we lose that resource, perhaps we can replace it with less-skilled resources and depend on the Work Package to help them over the tough spots. If formatted correctly, the Work Package can be used by the task manager to post progress and record any other information that might be useful in the event that she is not able to continue with the cycle build.

Task Plan

The task schedule can be built on the whiteboard as a time-scaled matrix. One row of the matrix is devoted to each member of the task team, and the columns are all of the calendar days of the cycle. Each sticky note is a sub-task; all you have to do is lay them out in the matrix (remembering dependencies) and you have it. Later, when the cycle is underway, there may be a need to revise the schedule. Any changes that must be made due to slippages or other surprises are easily incorporated. Just move the appropriate sticky notes without violating any dependencies or over-allocating any task team member. Here is where sticky notes, marking pens, and whiteboards really show their value.

If you put the task team's work into perspective, you will see the reason for my recommended approach. The cycle is short—just a few weeks' duration. The task team works on a small set of sub-tasks—all of which must be completed within the duration of the cycle. If this cycle were the entire project, it probably wouldn't even meet the basic requirements to be called a project. For a two-to-four-week cycle time box, we don't need a high-tech solution.

I've successfully managed three-year APF projects using nothing more than the low-tech tools as described following. So here is your low-tech solution.

Step 1

Make a sticky note for each sub-task, and lay them out in a network diagram as shown in the upper portion of Figure 3.8. Note that the network diagram is time-scaled. Please excuse the variance from convention I have taken to show the time-scaled dependency diagram. This time scaling is important

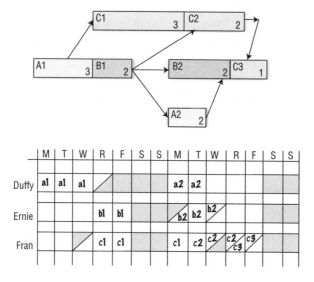

Figure 3.8
An Example
Micro-level
Schedule

because it is to replace what otherwise would have been a schedule produced by a project management software package.

Step 2

At another spot on the whiteboard (ideally below the network diagram and on the same time scale), lay out a grid that shows the timeline on a daily basis across the columns, and have one row allocated to each development-team member. The resources shown in this example are Duffy, Ernie, and Fran. Show all seven days of the week on this grid. For any workday or half workday in this cycle for which a resource will not be available for cycle-build work, enter an X or some other indicator of unavailability in the corresponding cell or half cell. (In Figure 3.8, we have used shading to indicate unavailability.) This grid is your resource calendar for this cycle.

Before finalizing the task plan, check whether the initial schedule and resource assignments allow the task team to complete its work within the allotted time box. You can do this by inspecting the scaled timeline you created in the Cycle Plan phase. If the current schedule doesn't meet the cycle time box, look for alternative resource assignments that bring the schedule back within the schedule. Resources that are not assigned for periods of time are the place to look. They can either take over sub-tasks or help other resources complete sub-tasks earlier than currently scheduled. What you are doing is manual resource leveling, in a way that makes more sense than the approach taken by most software tools.

Once you have met the cycle time-box constraint, you are ready to finalize the information on the grid. For each resource, simply transfer the information to the grid that shows what sub-task that resource is working on, what day the person expects to start it, and what day the person expects to end it. Every morning, have a 15-minute team status meeting, at which time you compare what was completed the previous day with what the grid had scheduled for the current day. Any adjustments to the plan are made on the grid. Resources can be moved to meet schedule delays. Because you still have the sticky-note network diagram on the whiteboard, you will be able to see whether schedule delays will cause any other delays downstream in the plan and adjust accordingly.

Let's look at a few important points with regard to Figure 3.8. First, when scheduling resources, try to keep them busy for consecutive days.

That makes things easier if you need to replace an individual on the team. Second, notice when a resource is not busy (for example, Figure 3.8 shows that Duffy is available for a half-day on Thursday of the first week). While this is early in the cycle, it may provide a resource that can help Ernie or Fran or the team recover from a slippage or a problem. Finally, note that in the second week Duffy and Ernie are available to perhaps help Fran complete C2 when Fran is unavailable on Wednesday afternoon. If that can be scheduled, C3 may be able to be completed early. This means that the cycle would be completed ahead of schedule. Alternatively, that staffing adjustment might provide a way to make up for earlier slippages.

This grid should be permanently displayed in the team war room. It becomes the focal point of daily team meetings. As status is being reported, the team can refer to this schedule and make any changes to later parts of the schedule. The most important benefit to having it displayed is that it is visible and accessible to the team. The only negative you have to worry about is that there is no backup for this approach. An electronic whiteboard or good digital camera would be a plus. Having the team war room reserved for the exclusive use of the team and securing it will mitigate most of the risk, but not all.

The reason why the use of sticky notes and the grid works is that the cycle length is short. The example cycle is only two weeks long, but even if it were three or four weeks long, the same approach would work. Just roll the grid forward at the end of each week. Though I have used project management software packages extensively, I still find this low-tech approach to be far more intuitive and efficient than any software display. The entire team can see what's going on and can see how to resolve scheduling problems in a very straightforward manner. Try it.

This approach would never do well in TPM, for the following reasons.

The network diagram would take up too much real estate and is generally not available from the software package—and not because it can't be generated. We know that it can, but the labor to format it so it is intelligible just doesn't justify the effort required. There are, of course, add-ons that make this task a bit easier. It's your choice.

Resource balancing is another function that benefits from the low-tech approach. On the whiteboard, this is easy. In a software package, who knows what happens when you try to level resources? Most popular project management software packages level resources using an algorithm that starts at the beginning of the project and works on the critical path, moving the task schedule out in time to remove any over-allocations of resources. That sounds all right, but in our experience it has produced some rather bizarre resource schedules that put the project completion date beyond what the client requires. Because we are working with a cycle of only a few weeks, we can easily represent the problem on our grid and create a workable resource schedule that meets client timeline requirements for this cycle. We want to *see* the problem, and the software package just doesn't measure up.

Use of Software Packages in Planning APF Projects

If you are an APFist and you still want to use project-management software, be my guest. Just remember that you have to feed and care for the monster that you will have created. Ask yourself whether the time spent doing that is really value-added time.

Cycle Scope Changes

In an APF project, the scope-change process does not exist in the forms we are used to seeing. That should come as good news to the traditional project manager. This may sound strange, given what we have already said about APF thriving on change. Scope change does not occur like it does in a TPM project. Rather, what we would call scope change happens in a very different way on an APF project. Any thought or idea that the client team or the development team has as to something different to do in the solution is captured and stored in what I have called a Scope Bank. The Scope Bank is the only repository of ideas for improving the solution. It may contain new functionality, new sub-functions, or new features to be considered for future cycles. The Scope Bank is the major input into the Client Checkpoint phase. Here all of these ideas for change are discussed and prioritized for future consideration in later Cycle Build phases. The major difference between TPM and APF scope change is that in TPM, scope-change requests are considered one at a time, on a first-come, first-served basis. Furthermore, in APF projects, scope changes become part of the project plan going forward, whereas in TPM they are an add-on to a project plan that already exists. It is easy to see that in a TPM project there is a lot of wasted time revising a plan to accommodate scope changes. That doesn't happen in APF because the plan going forward has not yet been prepared, so there is no wasted time processing scope changes. In an APF project, resources are used to best business advantage on value-added work, whereas in TPM there is no assurance that that is the case.

Issue Tracking and Resolution

Because of the short cycle durations, the early identification and quick resolution of issues is critical to the project. Some issues will need resolution in the cycle in which the issue is first identified. Others may be more systemic and not as urgent. Examples of issues requiring immediate resolution are the following:

- The client is no longer meaningfully involved.
- One or more team members are consistently behind schedule.
- One or more team members have a habit of missing or being late for team meetings.
- The vendor has shipped the wrong product.

Any one of these issues can bring a cycle to a dead stop, and until resolved put the cycle deliverables at risk. In an APF project, you always have the option of delaying a deliverable to a later cycle. You don't have that luxury in a TPM project.

Some issues are not as critical, and may be resolved at some later time. For example:

- A team member will be leaving the company or will be reassigned elsewhere and must be replaced.
- The major competitor has introduced a new product that will compete with the products being developed in this project.
- A new technology has just been introduced that impacts this project.

In both cases, an Issues Log must be created and maintained. The Issues Log is a dynamic document that contains all of the problems that have arisen during the course of the project and have not yet been resolved. The resolution of these problems is important to the successful continuation of the project. The Issues Log contains the following information.

- ID number
- Date logged
- Description of the problem
- Impact if not resolved
- The problem owner
- Action to be taken
- Status
- Outcome

If a Risk Log is maintained, it is often integrated into the Issues Log. At each project status or team meeting, the Issues Log is reviewed and updated.

Micromanaging an APF Cycle

Remember that every activity you define in the low-level WBS must be managed. That opens up the possibility of micromanagement and the addition of non-value-added work resulting from useless status reporting. We want to make sure that the final decomposition isn't at such a granular level that we are forcing ourselves to be micromanagers.

Best APF practices suggest that you manage an individual's work down to units of three days. For example, Harry is going to work on an activity that you and he agree requires 10 hours of effort. The activity is scheduled to begin first thing Monday morning, and the schedule requires that it be completed by close of business on Wednesday. Harry has agreed that he can accommodate the 10 hours within the three-day window, given his other project commitments. Now, Harry's development team manager could ask Harry to report exactly when during the three-day window he will be working on this 10-hour activity and then hold him to that plan. What a waste of everyone's time that would be, let alone an insult to Harry's abilities and commitment. Harry provided the 10-hour estimate, so why not give him credit for enough intelligence to make his commitments at the three-day level? No need to drill down into the window and burden Harry with a micro-plan, and his manager with the burden of managing that micro-plan. The net result of such micromanagement may, in fact, be to increase the actual time required to complete the activity, because Harry will have been burdened with the need to comply with unnecessary oversight by the development-team manager. The exemplary APF development team manager will have more confidence in the team member, knowing that the processes are in place to ensure plan attainment. Harry, being the good team player that he is, will report daily on status and let us know if there are any issues or concerns regarding his meeting his commitments for delivery. In other words, we manage Harry on an exception basis, we accept his open and honest attitude, and we accept his status reports.

It is more valuable to the project to have the APF development team manager spend time encouraging that behavior from Harry than it is to waste the time micromanaging Harry. If it should happen that Harry doesn't deliver against the commitment, there will certainly be a conversation between him and the development-team manager about future assignments and how progress will be managed. As you can see in this example, APF defines a structured framework, and within that framework, it gives maximum latitude to the team members.

I have always given my team members the benefit of the doubt and trusted their openness and commitment to the project. I call this my **long rope** management style. If, on the other hand, they have kept secrets and their estimates are not reliable, I use my **short rope** management style. The difference between the two styles is obvious.

Advice to Management

Understand at the outset that micromanagement is an easy trap to fall into in an APF project. APF is a creative approach. It seeks to discover a solution to a critical unsolved problem. This requires an environment that supports creativity rather than a tightly controlled management environment. Let the client and the development teams have plenty of encouragement, support, and flexibility to apply their creative energies.

Case Study: Try & Buy Department Stores

After some discussion with the Try & Buy client team, the following partial prioritized list of functionality was established. The known sub-functions and features, along with the functionality to which they are attached, are included. Sub-functions are prioritized within the functions to which they belong. There are two functions and several sub-functions that are prioritized. This is a partial list, but it's enough to serve our learning objectives.

1   Curriculum Design

   1.1   Establish curriculum learning objectives

   1.2   Define curriculum contents

      1.2.1   Group topics into six courses. The current prioritized topic list is:

         Project Management Models

         Agile Project Management

         Software Development Project Management

         Planning & Control

         Requirements Management

         Scope Change Management

         Risk Management

         Quality Management

         Communications

         Scheduling

         Team Organizational Structures

         Team Building

         Governance

Customer Relations

Vendor Relations

Supply Chain Management

Procurement & Contract Management

    1.2.2 Name each course

    1.2.3 Establish prerequisites for each course

    1.2.4 Define learning objectives for each course

  1.3 Establish format for each course

  1.4 Identify courses exercises

  1.5 Establish duration of each course

2 Course Development

  2.1 Course #1

  2.2 Course #2

  2.3 Course #3

  2.4 Course #4

  2.5 Course #5

  2.6 Course #6

3 Course Pilot Test

4 Course Revisions

5 Course Deployment

Sub-functions 1.1 to 1.2.4 and 1.5 will require 12 days' duration, and have been established as the contents of the first cycle. Don't be misled into thinking that this is a well-defined project. It is far from that. The learning objectives for the curriculum may not align with the topic list. Remember that the topic list came from interviews with the project managers. The grouping of the topics into six courses of 17 days' duration could be like putting five pounds of dirt in a three-pound bag. Topics low on the priority list might not make it into the final curriculum. Functions 2 through 5 cannot be further defined at this stage.

Case Study: Pizza Delivered Quickly

It has been decided that the first few cycles of the Pizza Delivered Quickly (PDQ) APF project will build an iconic prototype of the entire system. The project team includes the PDQ supervisors and their key staff as well as the development team. The development team includes Pepe and his staff and a contractor team which will do the systems development. Pepe, the co-manager of the client team, and the manager of the contractor's development team thought this was the best approach to the entire project for several reasons.

- PDQ supervisors and staff were not technically savvy and probably could not relate to how technology could play an integral role in the new business model. They needed to come to a basic understanding of where technology could improve their way of doing business.

- Whatever form the solution took, it was not at all obvious to the development team what the underlying business rules should or could be. More structure was needed.

- The new business model would have a lot of moving parts, and how those parts interacted operationally was not at all obvious.

Note

This may appear to be a pedestrian approach, but consider the reasoning. There is no reason to believe that the client group has any grasp of the business process or technical complexity of the as-yet undefined solution. PDQ is a family-owned business that has not leveraged technology to any meaningful degree. For all intents, PDQ is technically challenged. For any APF project to have a chance at success, everyone must be on the same page. A prototype serves that purpose in this case. Not only will it be useful in getting everyone on the same page, but it will also give the project team some insight into the requirements of the solution and the underlying business rules.

The solution will be very complex and consist of a number of dependent parts. It is hoped that the prototype will help answer several operational questions, such as:

- What factors will be used to evaluate a potential pizza-factory location?
- How will the PDQ market be defined and organized?
- What factors determine the production facility (store, factory, or van) that will be used to fulfill a specific order?
- How will these factors be used to make the decision as to which production facility to use?
- What factors determine which pizza van will deliver the order?
- How will these factors be used to make the decision as to which pizza van will deliver the order?
- What performance metrics can be used to measure solution effectiveness?

Figure 3.9 shows a high-level process flow of the six subsystems that make up the solution.

The prototype proved to be valuable in helping the client gain an understanding of what the solution might include. Following that exercise, the RBS was generated. It follows. Based on what you now know about the solution, you will next map out your strategy for approaching the cycles for this systems-development effort. This same strategy applies to any APF project.

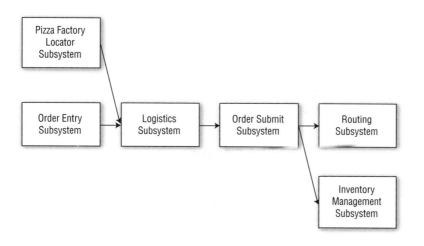

Figure 3.9
PDQ Subsystem
Process Flow

Subsystem #1: Pizza Factory Locator

This subsystem takes into account the current PDQ production and delivery facilities and primary, secondary, and tertiary markets to locate new sites for pizza factories. The model must take into account the impact of a new site on the success criteria.

Function 1.1: Aggregate sales data and order entry to order fulfillment time by census block

Function 1.2: Calculate market penetration by census block

Function 1.3: Analyze market area by census block

Function 1.4: Identify census blocks that are underserved

Function 1.5: Identify potential pizza-factory sites

Function 1.6: Analyze impact on success criteria of each potential pizza-factory site

Function 1.7: Update pizza factory locations

Subsystem #2: Order Entry

The customer enters an order into the system. This can be done by phone, Internet, or store visit.

Function 2.1: Identify customer

    Feature 2.1.1 Customer history

    Feature 2.1.2 Name, address, etc.

Function 2.2: Get order

    Feature 2.2.1 Products requested

    Feature 2.2.2 Quantity ordered

    Feature 2.2.3 Options selected

    Feature 2.2.4 Baked or unbaked

    Feature 2.2.5 Update order history

Function 2.3: Get delivery instructions

    Feature 2.3.1 Delivery location

Feature 2.3.2   Delivery options (pick-up, delivery, and so forth)

Feature 2.3.3   Delivery time requested

Function 2.4: Price order

Feature 2.4.1   Apply promotions

Feature 2.4.2   Calculate price

Feature 2.4.3   Maintain pricing table

Function 2.5: Confirm order

Feature 2.5.1   Payment type

Feature 2.5.2   Display order

Feature 2.5.3   Accept, cancel, or modify

Function 2.6: Submit order details to Logistics Subsystem

Feature 2.6.1   Submit order

Feature 2.6.2   Confirm order acceptance

Feature 2.6.3   *Unknown*

Subsystem #3: Logistics

This subsystem continuously monitors workloads across all preparation locations and all delivery alternatives. Based on current workloads, the system decides where to prepare the pizza and which van will deliver the order.

Function 3.1: Choose prep location

Feature 3.1.1   Get prep-location workload

Feature 3.1.2   Get next-order data

Feature 3.1.3   Estimate production and delivery time from each prep location

Feature 3.1.4   Assign prep location (business rule not clear)

Function 3.2: Transmit order to prep location

Feature 3.2.1   Submit order to prep location

Feature 3.2.2   Update prep-location workload

Function 3.3: Choose delivery van

Feature 3.3.1 Estimate location of each delivery van when order is ready to be delivered

Feature 3.3.2 Estimate pick-up and delivery time for each van to each location

Feature 3.3.3 Choose delivery van (business rule not clear)

Subsystem #4: Order Submission

Based on output from the Logistics Subsystem, the prep location receives the order for scheduling.

Function 4.1: Receive order detail from Logistics Subsystem

Feature 4.1.2 Retrieve order detail

Function 4.2: Schedule order for prep

Feature 4.2.1 Prioritize new order

Feature 4.2.2 Get into prep queue

Function 4.3: Check order status

Feature 4.3.1 When will order be ready?

Feature 4.3.2 When will order be delivered?

Feature 4.3.3 Notify delivery van driver of order pick-up time

Feature 4.3.4 Notify delivery van driver that order is complete

Feature 4.3.5 Update Inventory Management Subsystem

Function 4.4: Schedule order pick-up and delivery

Feature 4.4.1 Delivery-van driver confirms pick-up time

Feature 4.4.2 Get route from Routing Subsystem

Feature 4.4.3 Confirm order delivery

Feature 4.4.4 Confirm payment receipt

Feature 4.4.5 Update delivery-van location and time

Subsystem #5: Routing

This subsystem gives the driver the route from the prep location to the customer location. There should be a COTS application for this subsystem.

Function 5.1: Upload delivery-van location

Feature 5.1.1 *Unknown*

Function 5.2: Upload customer delivery address

Feature 5.2.1 *Unknown*

Function 5.3: Download driving directions

Feature 5.3.1 *Unknown*

Function 5.4: Confirm order delivery

Feature 5.4.1 *Unknown*

Subsystem #6: Inventory Management

This subsystem monitors real-time inventory levels at all preparation locations, automatically issues replenishment orders to the trucks to replenish preparation-location inventories, and automatically re-orders inventory from the vendor.

Function 6.1: Get inventory-use data

Feature 6.1.1 Collect inventory-depletion data by prep location

Feature 6.1.2 Update on-hand inventory by product

Function 6.2: Identify reorder needs

Feature 6.2.1 Send reorder automatically to vendor

Feature 6.2.2 Inform each prep location of reorder quantity and date for each product

Function 6.3: Receive reorder

Feature 6.3.1 Inspect and accept reorder shipment

Feature 6.3.2 Package orders for each prep location

Feature 6.3.3 Ship orders to each prep location

Putting It All Together

The APF Cycle Planning phase is a miniature version of the TPM Project Planning phase. The APF cycle-planning horizon is only a few weeks long. For this reason, the planning tools for the APF Cycle Planning phase are typically much less sophisticated than those used in a TPM Project Planning phase. Therefore, the APF Cycle Planning process is a stripped-down version of a TPM Project Planning phase.

Discussion Questions

The following questions are posed for your use. Use them to test your understanding and potential application of the materials presented in the chapter. If you are using this book for a course you are teaching, the questions will provoke good class discussion.

1. Suppose your team has one person who can't do without the support of a software tool and another who is vehemently opposed to using them. You are the project manager. How might you resolve this dilemma?

2. Make a list of the advantages and disadvantages of using or not using a project management software tool for the Cycle Planning phase of an APF project. Discuss your findings. Is either approach superior to the other? In what ways?

Chapter 4

How to Build the APF Cycle

Try several solutions at once. Maybe none of them, alone, would solve the problem, but in combination they do the job.

—*Ray Josephs, President, Ray Josephs Associates, Inc.*

People who produce good results feel good about themselves.

—*Kenneth H. Blanchard, Chairman,*
Blanchard Training and Development

The Cycle Build phase is similar to Traditional Project Management practices you are already familiar with. Work commences, scope changes are proposed, problems arise, and solutions are put in place. Time, cost, and resource availability are affected.

There are some noticeable differences from TPM, however. First, APF cycle duration is fixed, and almost never changes for any reason. Early termination of a cycle is not allowed unless all sub-teams finish ahead of schedule or a severe problem forces repurposing of the project (as discussed in the next section). Lengthening the time box is not allowed in APF under any circumstances. If something is scheduled to be completed during the cycle and time expires, the unfinished parts of that deliverable are put back into the Scope Bank and the deliverable's priority is reconsidered in a later cycle. Even though it had received high-enough priority to be included in the current cycle, there is no guarantee that it will be given a high-enough priority to be included among the deliverables of any future cycle.

The second, and most significant, difference is that there is no scope-change process in an APF cycle—at least not in the forms you are familiar with. Anything suggested by the client team or the development team that would be seen as a change request in a TPM project is temporarily placed in the Scope Bank for disposition during the next Client Checkpoint phase. All of these suggestions are treated as a group rather than one at a time. Made this way, decisions are more closely aligned with maximizing business value than when taken one at a time.

Overview of the Cycle Build Phase

Work is now underway to build and integrate the functionality prioritized for this cycle and to investigate the ideas represented in the probative swim lanes. Even though the cycle is short and the build not very complex, things will not all go according to plan. About this time, the APFist is thankful that not a lot of time has been spent planning, and takes the unexpected events in stride. And the unexpected is sure to happen. A person gets sick or leaves the company. A vendor is late in shipping or ships the wrong hardware or goes out of business. These are the same kinds of risks that traditionalists face, but for them the results are far more catastrophic than they are for the APFist. The APFist will simply return unfinished work to the Scope Bank. If the work didn't make it into the current cycle, perhaps it will still have high-enough priority to be included in a later cycle.

Depending on the severity of an unexpected event, the APFist either finishes the current cycle or, for really major problems, cancels the current cycle and immediately moves into the Client Checkpoint phase in preparation for repurposing the project. Terminating the current cycle early is the result of some catastrophic event that may render continuation of the project in its present form to not be in the best interest of the organization. In rare cases, canceling the version and starting the project again, with an entirely different approach to finding an acceptable solution, may be the best strategy. The criticality of finding a solution doesn't go away. The project team just hasn't found a fruitful direction for solution discovery yet.

In order to complete the build activities, the Cycle Build phase will utilize a number of tools—many of which you may already use in TPM projects. These tools include:

- Responsibility Matrix
- Micro-level Schedule
- Work Packages
- Issues Log
- Problem Solving
- Decision Making
- Conflict Resolution
- Consensus Building
- Team Meetings
- Ending a Cycle

In most cases, the APF project team will remain intact from cycle to cycle, and many of the above activities will be performed once as part of team formation during the first cycle plan. In other cases, many of them will be repeated, because team membership will have changed between cycles.

Let's take a detailed look at each activity. While we are doing that, you might want to reflect on similarities and differences in the ways they are used in APF as compared to how your organization uses them in TPM projects.

Responsibility Matrix

A very simple yet effective tool for assigning responsibilities across a project is the Responsible-Approve-Support-Coach-Inform (RASCI) matrix. As shown in Figure 4.1, its rows are any tasks or other activities that are significant parts of the project, and its columns are the team members. At the

Figure 4.1
The RASCI
Matrix

		Jack	Bob	Cheryl
T	Comfirm Customer Approval of Scope	R	S	
A	Choose Project Team	R	I	A
S	Plan Project	S	R	
K	Define Budget	C	R	I
S	Plan Kick-off Meeting	I		R

R = Responsible, Accountable for Successful Completion
A = Needs to Approve Decisions
S = Will Provide Support for the "R"
C = Available to Coach and Consult
I = Needs to be Kept Informed of Status

intersection of each row and column is one of the letters R, A, S, C, or I, denoting the responsibility of the team member to that task. Every task has one and only one R, and one A, in its row. The RASCI Matrix should be posted in the team room or other prominent place so everyone can see and remember it.

Certain responsibilities must be delegated in every APF project. Here is my list.

- Update and post the RBS.
- Update and post the Scope Bank contents.
- Update and post the RASCI matrix.
- Update and post the Issues Log.
- Maintain work packages.
- Maintain the cycle schedule.
- Schedule project reviews.
- Maintain the project notebook.
- Schedule and arrange meeting facilities.
- Maintain and post the team war room utilization schedule.
- Communicate project status to the sponsor.
- Communicate to the client team.
- Communicate to the development team.

In assigning these responsibilities, I defer to the project team and member preferences, as long as every responsibility is assigned at all times. That could mean changing responsibilities through the project. I've been surprised more than once by such preferences. I recall one project where keeping and distributing meeting minutes was a responsibility that no one on the team really liked. When we got to assigning that responsibility, I suggested that we rotate the responsibility among the project team so everyone had to bear some of the burden. Before I could go any further, a woman in the back of the room raised her hand and said that she loved taking and distributing minutes, and could she please have that responsibility for the entire project. You could feel the tension draining from the room!

Micro-level Schedule

To this point in the process, the sub-teams will have built a schedule at the task level and assigned tasks to individuals. As one further planning step, the team member responsible for each task creates a work plan based on definition and scheduling of the sub-tasks that make up the task. This is a very simple plan that may be nothing more than an ordered "to-do" list. Because the timeframe for completing a task within the cycle is so short, the project manager will want some assurances that the task can be completed on schedule and will not delay any successor tasks beyond their Late Start dates (defined in Chapter 3). There won't be much in the way of slack (also known as "float") available to recover from any schedule slippage.

Despite all of the team's due diligence in putting the micro-level schedule together, there will be problems. We don't need to enumerate what they might be—we all know them by now. The bigger issue for APF is how to handle them within the context of a learning-and-discovery framework. An APF team is conditioned to expect change. That applies to the cycle plan as well. APF accommodates changes by assessing their impact on business value and taking the action that best protects business value. Usually that means deferring the completion of the affected task or tasks to later cycles so that an informed decision can be made regarding the continued prioritization of those tasks compared to the remaining functions and features. In an APF project, it is not uncommon for priorities to change from cycle to cycle, so that a feature that was once thought to be part of the solution loses priority over the course of several cycles and is deemed unimportant after all.

Work Packages

Work Packages are used in all types of projects. They are a wonderful insurance policy against the unexpected absence or loss of a team member. The Work Package describes how the task leader intends to accomplish the subtasks that make up that person's task. This allows another member of the team to pick up the task and complete it with the aid of the Work Package, if something should happen to the task leader. In the interest of avoiding simply adding paperwork rather than value-added work, the project co-managers will want to be careful, and not request Work Packages for tasks that are not critical to the scheduled completion of the cycle. Work Packages should be written for Integrated Swim Lane tasks generally, and in rare cases for probative swim lane tasks. Tasks that are critical, high risk, or use resources that are difficult to replace are candidates for Work Packages. Figure 4.2, first presented in Chapter 3, is an example of a Work Package template I have used quite successfully for several years for all types of projects.

Figure 4.2
Work Package
Template

WORK PACKAGE DESCRIPTION	Project Name		Project No.	Project Manager	
Work Package Name	Work Package No.	Work Package Manager	Contact Info	Date	
Start Date	End Date	Critical Path Y N	Predecessor Work Package(s)	Successor Work Package(s)	

TASK					
No.	Name	Description	Type (days)	Responsibility	Contact Info.

Prepared By	Date	Approved By	Date	Sheet 1 of 1

The template can be used for any type of project, but is especially useful in an APF project. There is little time to be wasted, so anything within reason that can be done to protect that time should be considered. If you add a column that reports status, the Work Package becomes a status report. That makes the document even more valuable whenever the task has to be handed over to someone else.

Issues Log

The timely discovery and resolution of issues in an APF project is critical. An issue that arises in a cycle should, with few exceptions, be resolved in the same cycle. This requires immediate attention from the co-managers, because cycle length may be only a few weeks.

In some cases, an issue may be systemic to the project and require more than the cycle in which it arises for discovery and resolution. For example, if the client team is not participating to the extent expected, that is a systemic issue. A test facility being unavailable for the current cycle build would be an issue to be resolved in the current cycle. Table 4.1 presents a template I use for issue tracking.

Table 4.1   Issue Log Template

Issue ID	Date Posted	Posted by	Assigned to	Description	Planned Action	Status

Some notes regarding fields in the Issue Log template:

- Issue ID could be a brief title with perhaps the date of discovery. An entry like "Meeting Attendance" or "030109 Meetings" would be appropriate. The ID serves as a reference and a mental trigger.
- Who posted the Issue and who is responsible for taking action are important fields too. There is no reason to assume these will be the same people.
- The Description is brief and to the point. One or two brief sentences would be sufficient. An example: "Client Team Manager is usually late for project-team meetings."
- Assigned To is the project-team member who is responsible for resolving the issue. While that person may require the help of other team members or even people not on the team, she or he is the responsible party. In the example in the preceding bullet-point, the entry might be, "Development Team Manager." In some cases, this might even be the person responsible for creating the issue. In this example, that would be the "Client Team Manager."
- Planned Action is a brief statement of what is to be done to resolve the issue.
- Status is the current situation. It may simply be a statement of work underway against the Planned Action. A Status of "Completed" would indicate that the issue has been successfully resolved. These issues generally pertain to the current cycle and would be resolved in the current cycle, although on occasion a more-serious issue may require more than one cycle to resolve.

The Issues Log is posted in the team war room (on a whiteboard is best) and lists the problems and issues the team has encountered during the current cycle along with those issues still open from a previous cycle. Because the list is continually changing, I recommend that it be handwritten (I use non-permanent marking pens) in a convenient location on the whiteboard. This facilitates the updating and keeps it always visible to the team.

The Issues Log contains the information shown in the preceding bullet list, and is updated daily. The items in the Issues Log need resolution, and there should be a plan to resolve each. The person to whom the issue has been assigned is responsible for developing that plan and keeping the team informed by updating the Issue Log so it is visible at the daily team meetings. While there may be some discussion of an Issue Log entry at the daily team meetings, this is the exception, not the rule. An example that would require discussion is an issue that causes a task manager to fall behind schedule.

There will typically be a sense of urgency with an Issues Log entry. If it affects the current cycle, something must be done as soon as possible. Here is where the prioritized Scope Triangle constraints help us. The triangle helps us focus our efforts on finding a solution within the constraints that are available to us. These constraints will save us the needless wasting of time pursuing solutions that are not feasible in the minds of the stakeholders and sponsor. The prioritized Scope Triangle should also be posted in the team war room or otherwise visible to the entire project team.

Problem Solving

When a problem arises within an APF Cycle Build phase that must be solved within the cycle time box, you don't have time to form a committee and launch an exhaustive study of the problem. You need to have a problem-solving model that can be executed quickly. The best model I have found for this purpose is described by Daniel Couger.[1] The ideal application of Couger's model is a one-session solution identification and implementation process within the cycle time constraint. In most cases, I would expect the model to be executable in less than half a day. The attendees at the problem-solving meeting are only those team members who have direct involvement with the problem, knowledge of the problem or solution, or a vested interest in its solution. Don't waste the time of team members whose involvement is not needed. They already have full plates! Time is not on your side, so you have to act quickly

---

[1] J. Daniel Couger, *Creative Problem Solving and Opportunity Finding* (Danvers, MA: Boyd & Fraser Publishing, 1995).

The steps in Couger's model are as follows:

Couger's Creative Problem Solving Model

1. Define the problem and the owner.
2. Gather relevant data and analyze causes.
3. Generate ideas.
4. Evaluate and prioritize ideas.
5. Develop an action plan.

I would add:

6. Implement the action plan.
7. Evaluate the results.

These steps are explained in the following subsections.

1. Define the Problem and the Owner

Scoping the problem is basically a boundary-setting exercise. That is, what is in the scope of the problem space, and what is beyond the scope of the problem space? You are trying to solve the immediate problem only for this cycle, not for all time. Don't let scope-creep enter the picture! It is important to identify the owner, and the owner must agree that it is her or his problem. This may be quite difficult. If done publicly, it may be embarrassing. I've had the best results from one-on-one meetings to establish ownership, but more importantly to assure the owner that I will do whatever I can to help find and deploy a solution. With the owner identified, the project team commits to supporting that person to find and implement a solution.

2. Collect Relevant Data and Analyze Causes

The data at hand is the only relevant information for this step. It may be incomplete, but that is what you have to go by. Surveys and other time-consuming activities are nice, but out of place here. Stay within the scope defined in the first step. Some preliminary data should be collected by the team member who brought the problem to the attention of the project team. If the problem is process related, there might be some performance data at hand to measure current state and evaluate the effect of the proposed solution on the problem. Use the data you have, take an educated guess at the cause and move ahead.

3. Generate Ideas

This is a brainstorming exercise. Get all possible solutions or approaches to the problem on the table. Think outside the box: Look for creative and innovative ways to identify a solution. While building this list, do not enter into conversations about the quality of any idea. The only conversation that is allowed is for clarification purposes.

The brainstorming process I use is itemized below. For a more-detailed discussion, see the section on Brainstorming in Chapter 5: How to Manage the Client Checkpoint.

- Assemble individuals with knowledge of the problem area.
- Throw any and all ideas on the table.
- Continue until no new ideas are forthcoming.
- Discuss items on the list, combining them as appropriate.
- One or more solutions will begin to emerge.
- Test each solution with an open mind.

4. Evaluate and Prioritize Ideas

The brainstorming exercise will eventually slow, and no new ideas will be forthcoming. It's time to evaluate the list and form a set of possible solutions. Those may come about as combinations of ideas on the list, or as revisions of ideas on the list. In any case, a list of possible solutions emerges from the brainstorming exercise. Three to five possible solutions would be a good number to work with, and would not burden the team. The criteria for evaluation will be some kind of determination as to which solution is most likely to solve the problem in the available time. There are a variety of qualitative and quantitative prioritization approaches you can use. I have three to offer you that have worked well for me in APF projects. They are:

- MoSCow
- Forced Ranking
- Paired Comparisons

MoSCoW

MoSCoW is an acronym:

M stands for <u>m</u>ust do it

S stands for <u>s</u>hould do it

C stands for <u>c</u>ould do it

W stands for <u>w</u>on't do it, now or alternatively, <u>w</u>ouldn't it be nice if we could do it?

MoSCoW can be used by an individual or by the problem-solving team. If the team approach is used, there will be a discussion, with a prioritized list resulting. MoSCoW is not unlike the "A, B, and C" or "1, 2, and 3" prioritization schemes you are probably already familiar with. The advantage of MoSCoW over other two prioritization methods is that the name of each priority classification tells you what it means. The alternatives given an "M" priority are the ones for which an action plan should be developed.

Forced Ranking

In those situations where you want to get input from the problem-solving team, the Forced Ranking approach is my choice. This approach is best explained by way of an example. Suppose five solution ideas have been proposed. I've numbered them "1" through "5" so I can refer to them later. Suppose the APF project team has six members (we'll label them "A" through "F"), and each is asked to rank the five solution ideas from most likely to solve the problem (1) to least likely to solve the problem (5). Members may use any criteria they wish, and they do not have to describe the criteria they use. Let's say the results of their rankings are shown in Table 4.2.

Table 4.2 Forced Ranking

Solution Idea #	A	B	C	D	E	F	Rank Sum	Forced Rank
1	2	1	3	2	1	4	13	2
2	4	3	2	3	4	3	19	3
3	5	4	1	5	3	1	19	3
4	1	2	4	1	2	2	12	1
5	3	5	5	4	5	5	27	5

The individual rankings from each of the six members for a specific solution idea are added to produce the rank sum for each solution idea. Low numerical values for the rank sum are indicative of solution ideas that have been given greater priority by the members. In the example, solution idea #4 has the lowest rank sum, so among the five alternatives is the one most likely to solve the problem. Ties are possible. They can be broken in a number of ways. I prefer to use individual rankings to break ties. In the example solution ideas #2 and #3 both have rank sums of 19. The tie is broken by taking the tied solution idea that was given the least priority by any member and moving it to the next-lowest forced rank. That means solution idea #3, which was ranked "5" by two members (while the least priority given to solution idea #2 by any member is "4"), will move to the fourth forced-rank position.

Once the forced ranking is complete with no ties, the greatest-priority solution idea can be implemented. In the example, that would be solution idea #4. In some cases, it may add some protection to implement the two greatest-priority solution ideas. In the example, solution ideas #4 and #1 are rated almost the same, so implementing both solutions may be advisable.

Forced ranking works well for small numbers of solution ideas but it does not scale very well. Its advantage over the other two models is that it gathers the opinions of several people.

Paired Comparisons Model

The other scoring model that I often use is the Paired Comparisons model. In this model, every pair of solution ideas is compared. A single evaluator chooses which solution idea in the pair is most likely to resolve the problem and therefore is given the higher priority. The matrix in Table 4.3 illustrates the commonly used method for conducting and recording the results of a paired-comparisons exercise.

First, note that all five solution ideas are shown across the five columns as well as down the five rows. For five solution ideas, you have to make ten comparisons. The cells above the diagonal formed by shaded cells contain the comparisons you make. First, solution idea #1 is compared to solution idea #2. If solution idea #1 is more likely to solve the problem than solution idea #2, then a "1" is placed in cell (r1, c2) (the cell at row 1, column 2) and a "0" is placed in cell (r2, c1). If solution idea #2 had been given a higher priority than solution idea #1, then you would have placed a "0" in cell (r1, c2) and a "1" in cell (r2, c1). Next, solution idea #1 is compared to solution idea #3, and so on, until solution idea #1 has been compared to all other solution ideas. Then solution idea #2 is compared to solution idea #3, and so on. Continuing in this fashion, the remaining cells are completed. The final step is to add all the entries in each of the five rows, producing the row Sum for each solution idea. The higher the sum, the higher the rank. The rightmost column reflects the ranks resulting from those calculations. Note that solution idea #4 has the highest rank sum, and hence the greatest overall priority. The highest-prioritized solution idea can now be implemented. The Paired Comparisons model does not scale very well to evaluate large numbers of solution ideas.

5. Develop an Action Plan

For each solution idea that will be implemented, a plan is needed for that implementation. Don't expect to spend more than an hour developing that

Table 4.3   An Example of Paired Comparisons

	#1	#2	#3	#4	#5	SUM	RANK
#1		1	1	0	1	3	2
#2	0		0	0	1	1	3
#3	0	1		0	0	1	3
#4	1	1	1		1	4	1
#5	0	0	1	0		1	3

plan. In most cases, a few minutes will be sufficient. Whoever owns the problem should be charged with the responsibility of developing and managing the plan. If others will be involved in implementing the solution, they should also participate in developing the plan.

6. Implement the Action Plan

The highest-priority solution is implemented. Depending on the results of the solution-ranking exercise, the next highest priority solution might be implemented concurrently.

7. Evaluate the Results

The chosen action will have either solved the problem, partially solved the problem, or not worked at all. Additional action plans might be discovered and prioritized in an effort to find an acceptable solution.

Conflict Resolution

Conflicts arise when two or more parties have differing views on a given situation. Conflicts can be either good or bad. Lack of conflict might seem good at first brush, but actually, that is not always the case. Lack of conflict may be a signal that the project is dominated by a group-think mentality, and that is bad. Conflict is bad when it is an obstacle to progress. If it escalates to the level of combativeness, the team can become dysfunctional. The key to the effective use of conflict lies in the leadership abilities of the project co-managers.

Effectively managing conflict is the key to successfully managing the creative process. Creativity is driven by the synergy of the team and not by any single individual. Synergy implies mutual respect. Statements like, "That's a stupid idea" are personal attacks. A more appropriate statement might be, "The concern I have about this approach is that it does not address one important aspect of the situation." Attack the idea, not the messenger. Give the opposing parties an opportunity to work out their differences. If that fails, you will have to step in.

There are basically four conflict-resolution strategies that have been used in APF projects (see Figure 4.3).

Figure 4.3
Conflict-
resolution
Strategies

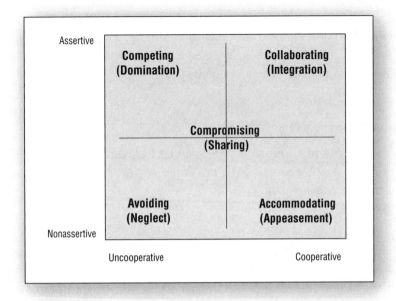

Avoiding

Some team members will be reluctant to participate in direct confrontation. They give in to opposing points of view. They reason that the issue is not important enough to create conflict. They make a concession now, but will use having done so to get their way at some later time.

In an APF project, it is critical that all ideas be heard. To assure everyone's input, I will often poll every participant in a conflict to express their opinions about the conflict and what they think should be done to resolve it. If done properly, this can prevent direct confrontation between the two individuals involved in the conflict.

Accommodating

If there is any doubt that your understanding of the situation is accurate, under an accommodating strategy you will be willing to give in to the opposing view. This is reasonable, and will build your reputation for further conflict situations. If the issue over which the conflict arose isn't that important to you, it might be an appropriate occasion for giving in.

Competing

You want to win at all costs, and your behavior makes that obvious. Sometimes a team member will use this strategy to intimidate another member with less stature on the project team. In other words, the individual pulls rank and gets her or his way. In emergency situations, this may be the appropriate strategy.

Playing devil's advocate is a common competing behavior pattern for many individuals. If done properly, this is good. If done poorly, it is an obstacle to progress and a waste of time.

Collaborating

This is the most productive of the conflict-resolution approaches. Here, the parties seek to identify common ground as the foundation for moving toward agreement. If collaboration is done well, there should be clear evidence that all parties are flexible in their thinking as their differences are mitigated, and solution convergence happens.

Compromising

This would seem to be the best way to resolve a conflict. Both parties give and take until an agreement is reached.

Consensus Building

In an APF project, arriving at a consensus might be the quickest way to decide what action to take, but it may not produce the best action. A typical consensus decision process might go something like this. Someone suggests the action to be taken, and if no one seriously objects, that becomes the team's decision. Depending on the credibility of the team member who makes the suggestion, the proposal might be taken or not.

I recall a team member on an APF project I was managing whose behaviors were such that his suggested action might be good or bad but it was never determined which was the case. His name was George, and if he is reading this book, he will know that I am referring to him. (That won't come as any surprise because he knows I have singled him out before, with his approval.) Anyway, George is probably the most intelligent person I have ever met. His mind operates at speeds I have never experienced with anyone else before. On many occasions when the team was assembled to solve a problem, before a team member could finish describing the problem, George would suggest a solution. He spoke first, and was very aggressive. He demonstrated a command of the situation and the relevant facts. The other team members were unwilling to challenge him because they would lose the argument, so most of George's suggestions were never challenged. They would appear to be the consensus opinion. Fortunately, George was usually correct.

In an attempt to bring some fairness to these sessions I asked George to be the second person to suggest a solution. He knew that he dominated these sessions and I showed him why it was so important to the team's morale that he do this. That worked—at least for a while. Old habits die hard!

Daily Team Meetings

In an APF project, team meetings are held daily, usually first thing in the morning. They last less than 30 minutes—15 minutes is my strong recommendation. There are no chairs to fall asleep on; there are no handouts; everyone who has a task open for work attends (even if by telephone), and meeting facilitation is rotated among the attending team members. These kinds of team meetings are not typical of TPM projects. In an APF project, these are no-nonsense meetings. Every morning before the meeting starts, each task leader with a task open for work posts its status on a whiteboard in the team room, and gives a verbal status report which includes: days (or hours) ahead of or behind schedule; whether there is or is not a corrective action plan in place to recover; what was completed yesterday, and what will be completed today. If task leaders need help getting back on schedule, they will ask for it, and take volunteers off line—say, right after the team meeting adjourns. Problem solving, decision making, conflict resolution, who wants to order pizza for lunch—none of these is part of a team meeting. The only open discussion that is allowed is for clarification purposes, and even that is very brief and controlled. When the team is new to these types of meetings, they tend to be clumsy at first, and they will usually run over schedule. With a little practice the team quickly settles into a pattern, and the 15-minute meeting becomes routine.

For larger APF projects, the team is often divided into sub-teams. Each sub-team is responsible for one or more activities. Sub-teams hold their own daily meetings. Less frequently, sub-team managers might meet to coordinate across sub-teams working on the same activity. Even less frequently, the entire team meets for general updates on the status of the APF project. The important thing to remember here is that you don't want to overload the team with meetings. The cycle is short, and every hour spent in meetings is one less hour spent in building deliverables.

Tip

While the project manager might be the first choice for leading the team meetings, this is not necessary or even advised in an APF project. Rotating the person who leads the team meeting is a good idea. It gives others a chance to develop that skill, and promotes team unification.

I have found it to be a good team-development strategy to rotate the facilitator of the daily team meeting. That gives you a chance to observe future team leaders in action, and to develop their leadership and team-management skills. Stepping back from meeting facilitation sometimes helps the project co-managers take an objective view of the project. The project status is always posted in the team war room and is updated daily. Anyone who has an interest or a need to know can always go there for details. Brief written status reports should be available for the sponsor at milestone events, and more lengthy reports to senior management at the end of each version. While the project is underway, we tend to place responsibility for status reporting outside of the extended project team, into the hands of the client. Placing it with the client maintains the core value of a client-focused and client-driven approach. Ownership is in the hands of the client, not in the hands of the project manager or project team. That is as it should be. The reason for this recommendation is that putting the client in a position of responsibility for reporting the status of their project to the sponsor and to senior management results in a business-type report, not a project-type report.

Status Reports

Written reports that circulate among the team members do not exist in APF projects. They are a waste of time in an APF project. All inter-team reporting is verbal, and everyone on the team who needs to know will know. There are reports that circulate outside the team, but these are the responsibility of the project co-managers. In many cases, these will be exception reports or escalations of open issues and problems that are outside the span of authority of the project co-managers, so are escalated to the appropriate senior manager or project sponsor. The project co-managers often use team meetings to quickly give the team the status of open issues that affect the project.

Monitoring and controlling functions pertain to the cycle-build tasks. As part of the control function, the team collects whatever learning and discovery has taken place and records it in the Scope Bank. All change requests go into the Scope Bank as well. No changes are implemented within a cycle. All changes and other learning and discovery are reviewed at the checkpoint. That review results in placing newly discovered functions and features into a priority list for consideration at some future cycle.

The Realities of the Swim Lane

There are some points to be aware of for each of the swim-lane types.

Integrative Swim Lanes

In the Cycle Build phase, these swim lanes are no different than the Build phase in the typical TPM project. A cycle build plan is in place for each integrative swim lane. Schedules slip, issues arise, and problems surface. These have differing impacts on the cycle, and must be resolved. For an APF project, there is an additional matter to consider—learning and discovery of changes to the current cycle deliverables. What should be done? Since the changes have not been subject to the rigors of prioritization, it would be a mistake and potential waste of time to employ the TPM scope change management process for this change. Without exception, put the scope change into the Scope Bank, and consider it along with other items already prioritized in the integrative swim lane queue for integration in a later cycle.

I can hear the argument from the development team: "We are already working on that part of the solution, and it would be so easy to just process the scope-change request and take the ensuing steps." Nice argument—but it is not in keeping with the spirit of an APF project. The business value of this scope-change request has not been prioritized relative to other items in the integrative swim lane queue. If you do allow such cycle-plan modifications, where do you draw the line? How many scope-change requests will you consider in the cycle time box? What about the relative priority of other scope-change requests from other integrative swim lanes in this cycle? In my mind, simple is best, and that means putting all such requests into the Scope Bank to be considered all at one time.

Probative Swim Lanes

Whereas integrative swim lanes are planned in detail using TPM tools, probative swim lanes are more like xPM projects and do not have such plans, but rather depend on the creative process for their completion. There really is no limit to the approaches that can be used in a probative swim lane. Prototyping, brainstorming, and problem solving have already been discussed, and are the three approaches I have used in past APF projects. The outputs from these three approaches fall into the categories discussed below.

Because of the volatile nature of probative swim lanes, be prepared to move resources to other cycle work as available.

Positive Results—More Investigation Advised

This idea looks like a promising direction to investigate, but more detail is needed. That detail should be left for development in a later probative swim lane, so its description should be placed into the Scope Bank for prioritization.

Negative Results—Looks Like a Dead End

This idea doesn't seem like it will produce any fruitful results. No further action on it is recommended. It should be returned to the Scope Bank for further idea generation.

New Ideas Have Surfaced

Probative swim lane ideas will often lead to other ideas for consideration. Depending on the extent of those new ideas, they might be considered within the context of the current swim lane or relegated to the Scope Bank for later prioritization and consideration.

Ending a Cycle

A cycle build can end normally or abnormally.

Normal End of Cycle

The normal end of a cycle occurs when the time box expires, and has nothing to do with the swim lanes being completed. Any planned work that is not finished is returned to the Scope Bank for re-prioritization and consideration in a later cycle. If the deliverables within the cycle build plan have been scheduled for development based on their positions in the prioritized list, then nothing is lost. The work not completed had a lower priority, and can be rescheduled as long as its new position on the prioritized list has placed it out of reach for a future cycle.

Swim Lane Scheduling

To the extent possible, I would advise you to schedule the tasks in a swim lane in priority order. That priority order should be based on expected business value. Technical dependencies may affect the prioritization. Prioritizing in this way gets the most business value into the solution if for some reason the swim-lane tasks are not completed. Any incomplete tasks will be low-priority items and can be returned to the Scope Bank for re-prioritization for a later cycle.

Abnormal End of Cycle

The abnormal end of a cycle can occur in one of two ways.

Ahead of Schedule

The first way a cycle can end abnormally is that all deliverables can be completed ahead of schedule. If so, end the Cycle Build phase and proceed to the Client Checkpoint. For each of the swim-lane teams, this means finishing their work as quickly as possible. If you see you can finish early, it doesn't mean you should stretch out the work to fill the available time. Parkinson's Law has no place in an APF project!

External Events

The second way a cycle can end abnormally is when a significant external event renders continuing the current cycle a waste of time or money (or both). A major competitor makes an unexpected announcement of the latest version of its product or introduces a new product, giving the client reason to rethink this project. An internal reorganization affects the process interfaces of your business process design project. That might be good reason to postpone your project until the dust has settled from the reorganization.

Several options may be considered when deciding to end a cycle due to external events. Ask:

- Should it continue as scoped?
- Should it continue with significant revisions?
- Should it be postponed?
- Should it be abandoned, and restarted in another direction?

Let's look at the implications of each of these choices.

Should It Continue as Scoped?   Upon further analysis, the client may decide that the external event will not compromise the current project to such an extent that postponement or termination is warranted. Rather, the current project will continue, with a view toward using the next version to correct any anomalies caused by the external event.

Should It Continue with Significant Revision?   If enough of the product-design solution is in place, you might want to salvage the work already completed by revising the project goal. That will have an impact on the solution objectives of the now significantly revised project.

Should It Be Postponed?   For process-design or -improvement projects, the best strategy will usually be to postpone the project, and restart it when the reorganization is complete and stabilized.

Should It Be Abandoned and Restarted in Another Direction?   If the external event was catastrophic for this project, continuing would be a waste of time and money. Once the impact of the external event has been evaluated, the project can be restarted, taking that impact into account. Note that there may be some residual business value in the aborted project.

Extending Cycle Length

Suppose it's the end of the workday on Thursday, and the current cycle is scheduled to end on Friday afternoon. Harry is managing an integrative swim lane, and he comes to you asking for a two-day extension so he can finish his scheduled integration testing. It would be nice to get the functionality integrated into the solution. Should you grant the extension? The answer is a qualified "no."

Cycle length is sacred for several reasons. If you were to say "yes," should the rest of the project team just make work to fill the two days? That's a waste of time, and APFists don't waste time. Should the rest of the project team work on another project? You might lose them. Then what would you do?

The unfinished work from a cycle can be returned to the Scope Bank for re-prioritization for a later cycle—perhaps the next cycle.

Cycle Build Variations

Remember that project management is organized common sense. That extends to the Cycle Build phase. Adapt the cycle build to meet the needs of the project team and of the solution. There are some variations that I want you to be aware of, because they have occurred quite frequently in the APF projects I have participated in.

Single Swim Lanes

In those projects where it was obvious that the client was having trouble envisioning any solution, I began the project by building an iconic prototype of how the solution might look. A single-swim-lane approach is the only approach that makes sense for these kinds of situations, at least for the first few cycles, as both probative and integrative swim lanes are premature. The first priorities in this situation are to make sure the client (and maybe even the development team) can relate to the problem, and to ensure that entire team is on the same page. Exploit the Client Checkpoint phase by having lengthy conversations with the entire team present. Your objective is to get a defined starting point for the project. Once that is in hand, you can begin the introduce probative and integrative swim lanes into the cycles.

In some projects, the size of the team is the operative constraint. If the development team is very small (three to four members), a single-swim-lane approach may be all that is possible. In these situations, you will have to carefully consider when to plan a cycle as a probative cycle versus an integrative cycle. Remember that probative swim lanes are what will help the client envision other additions to the solution, and integrative swim lanes are what give the client a solution richer in functions and features, upon which to build even further additions to the solution. In the small-team situation, determining the type of cycle will present the project co-managers with a delicate balancing act as they seek to provide the best mix of swim lanes from cycle to cycle, so be careful.

Finally, in some projects it simply makes sense to take the one-lane approach. Sometimes your gut will just tell you to take a single-swim-lane approach. Assuming you and your project co-manager are an experienced team, go with your gut feelings.

Concurrent Swim Lanes

The preferred approach for me has been to plan two parallel sets of swim lanes in each cycle. In the interest of limiting total project duration and from a management perspective, it makes sense to simultaneously pursue solution discovery and solution building. That means having a mix of probative and integrative swim lanes within a cycle. The mix will change depending on the understanding the project team has of the solution and the degree to which the progress to date has converged on the complete solution. Obviously, team size and the cycle time box will be constraining factors in determining how much of this concurrent activity can occur.

Because probative swim lanes can be very speculative, I have often seen situations where one idea expands into other ideas that can be investigated concurrently within the same cycle. The situation where a single probative swim lane can spawn several other concurrent swim lanes is quite common in the early cycles of an APF project. I caution not to dig too deeply into a purely speculative idea at first. Make sure the idea is feasible before you spend too many team resources on it. The Client Checkpoint phase is the only place to test feasibility. Unless it has been planned, do not use the Cycle Build phase as the place to test feasibility. If a new idea that arises during a Cycle Build phase seems feasible, put it into the Scope Bank and leave it for discussion in the Client Checkpoint phase, to get concurrence from the project team about its feasibility and relative priority among competing probative swim lane ideas. The decision to continue a particular line of investigation should be made on an informed basis, not because the item is someone's pet project.

Case Study: Kamikazi Software Systems

The current project management process documentation had never been a favorite of the development teams and their managers. Their complaints were:

- They had to read too many pages to get to the information they needed.
- Best practices were not useful, and often didn't apply.
- Information was hard to find.
- There was very little "how-to" information.

Before any meaningful process design work was planned, Crash dePlane, the project manager, prepared and circulated a prototype documentation system for review by the developers. His idea came from a Web site he had stumbled onto, and he thought it would find favor with the Kamikazi developers. Crash's idea was to create three levels of documentation, with each level having multiple links to more detail on topics at the next-lower level. Level 1 was for the executive or client manager. Level 2 was for the project team, and gave a high-level definition of a tool, template, or process for someone who had the detail knowledge and experience and just needed a memory jogger. Level 3 provided the lowest level of detail, and described a tool, template, or process for anyone who had forgotten the how-to's. Level 3 would have links to the best-practices file and the names of those who have agreed to provide advice on the best practices. With this format, Crash thought an individual could read whatever level of detail that person needed without having to read unnecessary lengthy text.

Putting It All Together

With a few exceptions, the Cycle Build phase looks just like the traditionalist approach, although very limited in scope. Note, however, that the cycle plan and functionality are not tampered with. Whatever doesn't get done within the cycle is reconsidered for some future cycle. Change management, which is a big issue for the traditionalist, doesn't even come up in an APF Cycle Build phase. It is embedded in the Client Checkpoint phase as a routine activity.

In the next chapter, we spend some time on the Client Checkpoint phase. It is the critical piece that makes or breaks an APF project.

Discussion Questions

The following questions are posed for your use. Use them to test your understanding and potential application of the materials presented in the

chapter. If you are using this book for a course you are teaching, the questions will provoke good class discussion.

1. Make a list of the advantages and disadvantages of using a high-tech versus a low-tech approach in this phase of the project. Discuss your findings. Does one approach win out over the other? In what ways?

2. Clearly, this phase is very dependent upon the people on your team. APF gives team members great discretion in completing their work. If you were managing an APF project, how would you balance your need to know against the need to empower team members to do their work? Be specific.

3. Compare what happens to a TPM project versus an APF project when a team member is taken off of the team and no longer available. What are the impacts on each approach? Which approach is least affected by such a change?

Chapter 5

How to Manage the
Client Checkpoint

Nothing is more dangerous than an idea when it is the only one you have.

—*Emile Charter (Alain), French philosopher and essayist*

The most beautiful thing in the world is precisely the conjunction of learning and inspiration. Oh, the passion for research and the joy of discovery.

—*Wanda Landowska, Polish harpsichordist and music critic*

The Client Checkpoint phase is the critical junction between the project's past and its future. The past is defined by the updated solution from the just-completed cycle along with the current contents of the Scope Bank. The future is defined by the learning and discovery from the just-completed cycle regarding possible directions the following cycles might take. In this phase, the client team and the development team review everything that has been done and everything that has been discovered to craft the contents of the next cycle. This exercise must be done correctly if the project has any hope of reaching an effective solution. In this chapter, I discuss exactly how to do this.

One of the real advantages of APF over other agile approaches is that the client is involved as a principal and as a decision maker at all critical junctures in the project. The role of the client in the Client Checkpoint phase is not unlike the role of the Product Owner in a Scrum project. Because APF cycle length is so short and so controlled, there is little that can go wrong that is not immediately known and easily corrected. Within the cycle itself, not even a day goes by when the team doesn't take stock of where it is compared to where it had planned to be and adjust accordingly. Little can go wrong that cannot be corrected. Few dollars and little time are wasted because of the structure of APF.

The Client Checkpoint phase is really the heart of APF. It is here that the team and the client spend valuable time looking at what was done, reflecting on what was discovered and learned since the last checkpoint, prioritizing the functionalities that might be built in the next cycle, and initiating probative swim lanes to discover new functions and features to be incorporated into the solution.

Together, the client and the development team will analyze what has happened in the project so far and jointly decide what will be considered in the next cycle. This is a very creative and challenging part of an APF project. Deliverables from the just-completed cycle are discussed with the full participation of all. This is a characteristic of what I mean in describing the APF approach as **client-facing**. These discussions focus on what has to be done to maximize business value within the time and cost constraints established by the client (client-driven constraints). I've often observed how the client and the team interact at these checkpoints. From those observations, it has become obvious whether or not the project had been moving along according to the principles and core values of APF.

An Overview of the APF Client Checkpoint Phase

The Client Checkpoint phase in its totality is the unique part of APF: It has no equal in either Traditional Project Management or any other APM approaches. Certain parts of the Client Checkpoint phase, such as a review of what has been done, are common to all APM approaches.

The Client Checkpoint phase is the closing phase in an APF cycle, as highlighted in Figure 5.1. This is where the rubber meets the road in APF, for it is in this phase that the project team and the client team jointly conduct a number of analyses. Those analyses address eight very serious questions that they must answer. These are discussed in detail in the Client Checkpoint Questions section below. This is not the time to be politically nice or correct. It is time for the client team and the development team to put all of their cards on the table and make some hard business decisions. The decisions they make now will set the tone and direction of the project for the next and all remaining cycles. These decisions will put creativity at the forefront. The teams will have to muster all of their creative skills as they deliberate the contents of the upcoming probative swim lanes. I can't stress enough the importance of the Client Checkpoint phase. The team may be

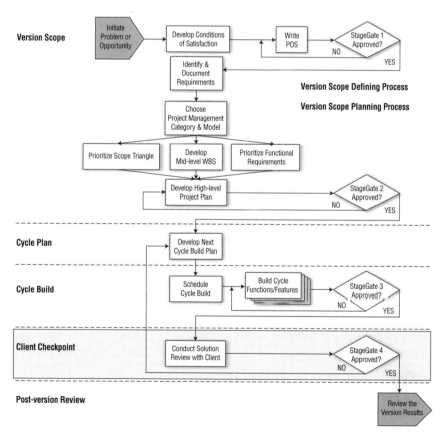

Figure 5.1
APF Project Management Life Cycle with the Client Checkpoint Phase Highlighted

taking the project into uncharted waters, and the outcome is by no means guaranteed.

I have always felt that by observing the interaction between the client team and the development team during a Client Checkpoint phase, you can determine how well the total project team is functioning. Do members act openly and honestly with one another, or do you get the feeling that some are harboring thoughts they are not willing to share with the entire team? Do they seem to be protecting turf? Can you identify any reasons for their hesitancy? Conversely, are discussions lively, and ideas presented without regard for turf issues? Are members treating each other as equals, or is there some undefined pecking order? All of these are clues to how well the participants are functioning as a team rather than as just a group of people thrown together to pursue a common purpose.

Inputs to the Client Checkpoint Phase

There are five major inputs to the Client Checkpoint phase needed to answer the eight questions discussed in the next section. These five inputs are discussed in this section.

Planned versus Actual Functions and Features Added

For the cycle just completed, the cycle plan called for a specific list of functions and features to be added to the deliverables through one or more integrative swim lanes. No schedule or scope changes were allowed during the cycle, yet it is possible that not all the planned functions and features actually made it into the deliverables. There are several reasons for this, which we will not discuss. They are obvious (for example, schedule slippages that could not be recovered from, a discovery that rendered the functionality unnecessary) and occur in all kinds of projects. APF accommodates these anomalies without skipping a beat. Any functions or features not completed in the just-finished cycle are returned to the Scope Bank and prioritized for consideration in a future cycle.

I have often seen unfinished deliverables that never get high-enough priority to be completed in a later cycle. This is quite common, especially when you consider that the work of the cycle build plan should be completed in order of priority. If that has been done, any incomplete work will have low priority in the cycle plan. The question is then what its priority is with respect to other functions and features waiting in the integrative swim lane list within the Scope Bank. The answer determines whether or not those incomplete functions and features will ever make it into the solution.

Learning and Discovery Results

Using probative swim lanes to search for new functions and features is the most creative part of an APF cycle. The less you know about the solution, the more challenging is the identification of probative swim lanes, and the higher the risk that you won't find that solution at all. Because the project team is journeying into the unknown, don't be too discouraged by limited short-term results. Sometimes it will take several false starts before a promising direction is discovered. Even then it may take several additional probative swim lanes to fully explore a discovery that can then be implemented through one or more integrative swim lanes.

As work proceeds, a probative swim lane's results may suggest that the question explored in that swim lane doesn't seem like a fruitful direction to pursue. The less is known about the solution, the more likely that will be the result. From experience, my best advice is not to throw the baby out with the bathwater too soon. I have experienced situations in which a past probative swim lane didn't produce any immediate insight, but later led to an idea that did. So just remember to put all probative swim lane results (both good and bad) into the Scope Bank for future reference.

The APF Scope Bank

The Scope Bank is the cumulative repository of all functions, features, ideas, and proposed changes generated during all previous cycles that have not yet been completely acted upon. It is owned by the project team. Anyone on the project team can add items to the Scope Bank at any time during the Cycle Build phase. Except for the new additions to the Scope Bank from the just-completed cycle, all entries will have been prioritized during the previous Client Checkpoint phase. Those that became part of the solution and were incorporated into integrative swim lanes in the previous cycle can be safely removed from the Scope Bank. Those parts of the solution that have been identified but not yet completely integrated into the solution remain in the Scope Bank in the integrative swim lane queue. In any case, the current contents comprise all of the items not previously acted upon. There may be cases where ideas suggested earlier that didn't seem relevant at the time and so were not incorporated may now be viable. That is the reason why the Scope Bank is cumulative.

The Scope Bank is the primary input into the Client Checkpoint. Its contents are updated at the completion of each cycle. The contents are of two kinds—future integrative swim lanes and ideas for future probative swim lanes. Since there are fixed resources for the next cycle, the contents of these two types of swim lanes must be jointly prioritized. Depending on the degree to which the solution is complete, there will be a healthy mix of the two types of swim lanes, as discussed in Chapter 3: How to Plan an APF cycle.

The Scope Bank is posted on the whiteboard in the team war room and kept up-to-date by the entire project team. At the completion of a Cycle Build phase, the Scope Bank becomes input into the next phase, the Client Checkpoint phase.

The process of discovery and learning by the team is continuous throughout the cycle. Any new ideas or thoughts on functionality are simply recorded in the Scope Bank and saved for the Client Checkpoint phase. The Scope Bank can be a physical list posted in the team war room, or may take some electronic form (such as a spreadsheet or a word-processing document). Whichever form you decide to use, make sure it is always visible to the team.

Changes to scope are never made during a cycle. The cycle plan is adhered to religiously. There are no schedule extensions or additions of resources within a cycle. Whatever can get done gets done. All unfinished items are taken up in the Client Checkpoint phase.

The following fields are used to describe an item in the Scope Bank:

- ID
- Date Posted
- Posted By

- Brief Description of the Item
- Projected Business Value, If Appropriate
- Estimated Duration to Complete the Item
- Resource Requirements to Complete the Item
- Team Comments on the Item
- Prioritization in Appropriate Swim Lane

The Scope Bank is posted in the team war room. An ID is assigned. The next three items are completed by the person who initiated the item. The brief description helps the rest of the project team put the idea in context and gives them a reference for later discussion. During the next Client Checkpoint phase, the project team will review and further discuss all ideas in the Scope Bank. Business value, duration, and resource requirements may be of some help in the prioritization decisions. Each idea will be prioritized in the appropriate swim lane.

Scope Change Process Is Not Part of the APF PMLC Model

Note that the usual scope change control process is not part of the APF process. Instead, it is replaced by the team discussion and resulting prioritization. All of the non-value-added work of administering a scope-change process is avoided via the team discussion and prioritization process. This results in a significant reduction in non-value-added work time in an APF Project Management Life Cycle (PMLC) project as compared to a Traditional Project Management (TPM) project.

Scope Bank Status Reporting

A cumulative history of project performance metrics should be maintained. These metrics should inform the project team about the rate at which convergence toward an acceptable solution is occurring. Frequency of changes, severity of changes, and similar metrics can help. One metric I have found useful to track is the size of the Scope Bank over the cycles. Figure 5.2 shows three trends in Scope Bank size that I have seen in my client engagements.

Figure 5.2
Tracking Scope
Bank Size

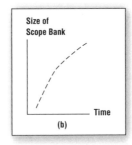

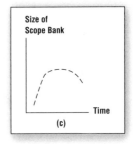

Increasing at an Increasing Rate

This is the trend displayed in Figure 5.2(a). It is evidence of a client whose involvement has increased over time, and it probably indicates that the process is diverging from instead of converging upon a solution. Changes beget changes, and those beget even more changes. Sometimes a change reverses an earlier change! Although it is good to have increased client involvement, it may have come too late for this example. If you see a pattern like this, it may be too late for any corrective action to be taken. Your intervention should have come much earlier when you would have had a chance to work with the client to increase involvement earlier in the project. The solution would have been to put some tripwires in place as early-warning signs that client involvement is below expectations. If this increasing-at-an-increasing-rate pattern is what you are experiencing, you may have a runaway project. Whatever the case, you have a problem that needs immediate attention. Further analysis of the underlying causes is needed.

Increasing at a Decreasing Rate

Figure 5.2(b) shows that the size of the Scope Bank is increasing at a decreasing rate. That may be a good sign, and the size of the Scope Bank may eventually actually decrease. The fact that it is still increasing this far into the process is not good. Like panel (a), it might be indicative that the path toward solution is diverging. I would wonder whether it weren't too late to rescue the process.

Decreasing at an Increasing Rate

Figure 5.2(c) is the desired trend. It implies an exemplary level of client involvement early in the project and shows good solution convergence. The

Scope Bank size should increase for awhile, then sooner or later, as the solution-seeking begins to converge on the ultimate solution, the size of the Scope Bank should start to decrease, then continue decreasing until the project has ended.

Tracking the Size of Probative Swim Lanes and Integrative Swim Lanes

The overall size of the Scope Bank is a good indicator of project performance, but it does not tell the whole story. The ultimate measure of progress is, of course, the incremental business value delivered by the just-completed cycle. In most cases, that will be a subjective assessment by the client team.

I don't know of any metric that can objectively measure incremental business value at the completion of a cycle. The metric I have found most useful for helping with this assessment is the relative sizes of the two swim lanes over time. At the next level of detail, I like to track the relationship between the probative and the integrative swim lanes over the history of the project. Figure 5.3 is an example of this type of report. It shows all four possible relationships between the two swim lanes: one is increasing and one is decreasing [Figure 5.3(a) and Figure 5.3(d)]; both are increasing [Figure 5.3(c)]; or both are decreasing [Figure 5.3(b)]. Each pattern lends itself to at least one interpretation.

The relative size of the two lists is a simple concept, but there is a lot of information here, and a lot of guidance for future cycle planning. As the project progresses, the relationship between the sizes of the two prioritized swim lane lists changes. Depending on those relative changes, the project can be in trouble, or converging as expected toward an acceptable solution.

Figure 5.3(a) generally connotes a successful project. The number of probative swim lanes is decreasing while the number of the integrative swim lanes is increasing. In other words, ideas are being translated into actual solution components. This is the ideal situation. The size of the probative swim lane list will continue to decrease as the process is nearing as complete a solution as is possible for this version. It remains to see whether the success criteria will have been met and business value achieved. There are still a number of integrative swim lanes prioritized for inclusion in future cycles. At some point, these should begin to decrease, and continue to decrease until the project ends. A project displaying this profile has all the earmarks of success.

Figure 5.3
Size of Probative versus Integrative Swim Lanes

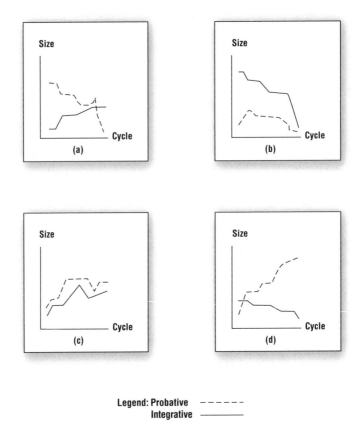

Legend: Probative ------
Integrative ————

Figure 5.3(b) paints a different picture, and can be interpreted as follows. Both swim-lane quantities are decreasing. The number of probative swim lanes is decreasing, and they are not producing usable solution parts, as reflected by the decreasing number of integrative swim lanes. Nearly all integrative swim lanes are complete. If the project is early in its history, the situation is not good, but may be the best that can be achieved. Either the solution is acceptable for now, or more work needs to be done. This project is essentially complete, and the current solution may or may not be acceptable. If not, then the project should be terminated and the resources transferred to a more encouraging solution approach. As is the case with Figure 5.3(a), a more-detailed investigation is needed to determine which situation is operative. If the situation is positive, the solution is nearly complete, and that is the reason for the decrease in the number of probative swim lanes. The remaining question is the business value delivered by the identified solution.

This is similar to the interpretation of Figure 5.3(a). The only difference is that this pattern reflects a project that is much closer to completion than is illustrated in Figure 5.3(a). It is unlikely that the few remaining probative swim lanes will introduce new solution features. This project is essentially complete.

Figure 5.3(c) shows both swim lanes increasing in size. This is the pattern you would expect to see during the early stages of a healthy project. The list of functions and features to be integrated is growing, as is the list of ideas for future function and feature exploration. The probative swim lanes are producing good results. If it is early in the project, the project appears to be healthy and should continue. As the project moves into the later stages, both swim lanes should begin to decrease in numbers.

Figure 5.3(c) can also indicate a runaway project. When the size of both prioritized lists is increasing, an appropriate question is regarding solution convergence. Is the solution converging to something that will achieve the expected business value? If this pattern continues later in the project, that is a strong signal of solution divergence. If the number of each type of swim lane begins to decrease, the project is healthy. A serious check on the Conditions of Satisfaction and project scope is in order in any case.

Figure 5.3(d) shows an increasing number of probative swim lanes and a decreasing number of integrative swim lanes, leading to the following interpretation. The solution is about as complete as it is going to be for the approach taken. Missing parts of the solution continue to be elusive. The increasing number of ideas is not producing any meaningful additions to the solution. This project may be spinning out of control; another approach might have been more productive. You also have to admit that the solution has not been discovered. Either the problem is unsolvable, or you may be looking for a solution in the wrong places. In either case, the project should be terminated.

Updated Requirements Breakdown Structure

The Requirements Breakdown Structure (RBS) is defined before any project work is done, and is the primary input into the choice of best fit PMLC model. At each Client Checkpoint, the RBS is updated with the deliverables from the just-completed integrative swim lanes. The degree to which the updated RBS is considered complete is a clue to what type of PMLC model makes sense to use going forward. While changing the PMLC model may be suggested because of increased solution clarity, there are costs of abandonment to consider. Those costs are discussed below.

Redefining Development Team Membership

Generally, a PMLC model change will be to a PMLC model more appropriate to a project with greater goal or solution clarity (or both). That means a relaxation in the skills, competencies, and experiences required of team members. This often makes project staffing a lot easier, but you still have to bear the cost (often indirect) of re-staffing the development team.

Briefing New Team Members

New team members need to be brought up to speed with the status of solution implementation. This will impact the project budget, whether the costs it generates are direct or indirect. Don't forget to include the time needed to bring new team members up to speed.

Developing the Project Plan

Whatever PMLC model you adopt will require you to take the time to develop a new project plan. If the project has changed from an Extreme Project Management (xPM) to an APM project, the new planning will be minimal. If the project has changed from an APM to a TPM project, a complete project plan will have to be generated. That will impact both the schedule and resource requirements going forward.

Probative Swim Lane Results

Integrative swim lanes are well-defined and the development and the cycle build plan established. Probative swim lanes are very different. They can be very speculative, and can change depth and direction of investigation at any time. A good probative swim lane investigation needs to be as adaptable as the situation dictates. The best return will be from a hands-off management style. Let the creative process unfold without any constraints except the cycle time box.

Probative swim lanes are designed to expand the depth and breadth of the solution, so the major question in evaluating their outcomes is whether anything has been learned about further enhancements to the solution.

A probative swim lane may have three possible results, as described below.

An Enhancement to the Solution Has Been Identified

Another piece to the solution puzzle has been discovered! It may have taken several probative swim lanes spread over several cycles to reach that conclusion. The discovery may be so significant that a celebration is in order, but don't order the pizza just yet! The solution piece needs to be documented and placed into the integrative swim lane queue for prioritization and consideration in a future integrative swim lane.

This Direction May Produce Results and Should Be Continued

The idea shows promise. Continuing in the same direction or some other discovered direction will be appropriate. This outcome needs to be documented and placed on the priority list for consideration in an upcoming probative swim lane.

Nothing New Has Been Identified and this Direction Should Be Abandoned for the Time Being

No idea is ever removed from the Scope Bank. What doesn't seem like a fruitful direction now may turn out to be valuable later in the project.

Client Checkpoint Questions

Once the five inputs are available, the following eight questions can be answered during the Client Checkpoint phase:

1. What was planned?
2. What was done?
3. What was learned about the solution?
4. Is the version scope still valid?
5. What was learned about the project team and APF?

6. Is the development team working as expected?

7. Is the client team working as expected?

8. What was learned about the APF process?

These questions are discussed in the following subsections.

1. What Was Planned?

The answer to this question is nothing more than a list of the objectives and functionalities that were planned to be completed during the just-completed cycle.

2. What Was Done?

This answer is nothing more than a check-off of the objectives and functionalities completed. There are often comments accompanying the check-off, because some items may not have been completed as planned. Sub-functions may have been left undeveloped, and there may be good reasons for that. In such cases, the Scope Bank should reflect the situation.

The only questions to be answered here are these: Did the cycle meet its objectives? Did the cycle meet its planned functional requirements? If not, where are the variances? The answers will provide input into planning for the objectives of the next cycle and the functionality to be built in that cycle. Remember, you may have already specified objectives and functionality at a high level for the next cycle in the Version Scope phase, so you have the original scope and potentially a revised scope to consider in deciding what the next cycle will contain.

> **NOTE**
> TPM defines a formal change-management process that can be invoked at any time in the project. In APF, a formal change process does not exist. The essence of a scope-change process is the identification and prioritization of functions and features to be built or investigated in the next cycle. All of this takes place in the Client Checkpoint and Cycle Planning phases.

3. What Was Learned about the Solution?

The client will need some time to evaluate the most-recent contributions to the solution. That evaluation has two aspects. First will be experimentation with the newly expanded solution, paying particular attention to the functions and features added in the just-completed integrative swim lanes. Are other changes suggested based on what was just produced? The aspect second is the results from the probative swim lanes. Did you learn about any new functions or features? Are there any clues about other parts of the solution yet to be built? Will additional probative swim lanes be needed to further define these discoveries, or can they be planned for inclusion in the solution through future integrative swim lanes?

4. Is the Version Scope Still Valid?

Armed with the information developed by exploring the two preceding questions, we now can ask a very basic question: "Is the version scope still valid?" A review of the COS and the Project Overview Statement (POS) can help answer this question. If the answer is "yes," we are on the right track. If not, we need to revise accordingly.

Revisions to version scope can be significant. In some cases, they may be so significant that the correct business decision is to kill the current project, go back to the drawing board, and start over again. You can see that the cost of killing an APF project will always be less than the cost of killing a TPM project. The reason is that TPM spends money and time on functionality that may not remain in the solution. APF, on the other hand, almost guarantees that all functionality that is built will remain in the application. Further to the point, TPM projects are often killed, if at all, very late in the game, when all the money is spent. APF projects are killed at the point when it becomes obvious that the solution is not converging and will not be acceptable. That will generally happen while there is still money and time left in the budget. Cut your losses and allocate the time, money, and team to a more-fruitful direction.

Canceling an APF project for this reason is not a sign of project failure. That is important. Terminating an APF project because of lack of convergence is nothing more than the realization that the current line of pursuit is not going to find that elusive solution. Resources need to be redirected.

5. What Was Learned about the Project Team and APF?

This question is perhaps the most important one of all. Here is where the process will be reviewed to provide more value to the client. In an APF project, an effective process is a prerequisite to an effective solution. The new ideas that are generated via APF could not come about through a TPM approach. This point in the process is where APF (and xPM, in all fairness) really shine. Both APF and xPM take their value from learning by doing.

> **Observation about the APF Process**
> In an APF project, having an effective process is a prerequisite to finding an effective solution.

6. Is the Development Team Working as Expected?

Real teamwork is a critical success factor in APF. A lot of worker empowerment is threaded throughout APF. If you count the frequency of use of the word "I" as compared to "we," you will have a pretty good metric for measuring team strength.

> **Team Strength Metric**
> Team Strength = number of We's ÷ (number of I's plus number of We's)

You would like to see this number hovering around 1. The APF team needs to work in an open and honest environment for this to happen. That means all team members must be forthright in stating the actual status of their project work. To operate otherwise would be to violate the trust that must exist among team members. The project co-managers must ensure that the working environment on the project is such that all team members are unafraid to raise their hands, say they are having trouble, and ask for help. To do otherwise would be to let the teammates down.

Is the team nothing more than a group of professionals thrown together on the same project, or have they morphed into a cohesive team with clear unity of purpose and effort? At one extreme they are like a herd of cats (you can't manage a herd of cats), and at the other extreme they are like a school of fish (you don't need to manage a school of fish). If either team manager sees a problem in either team, it is incumbent upon that manager to bring the issue out into the open on the Issues Log and do whatever it takes to get it fixed.

7. Is the Client Team Working as Expected?

Clients range from those who maintain some distance from the project to those who are fully engaged. Expect everything in-between. The extremes are not good. We have discussed the risks to the project when the client doesn't meaningfully engage in an APF project; but there are also risks when the client is too engaged. Not being meaningfully engaged means the necessary questioning and introspection won't take place, and an acceptable solution won't be produced. Being too engaged has its risks too. The over-engaged client is always in your face, suggesting changes and using valuable development-team resources on work that doesn't add business value. The too-engaged client will have you chasing windmills rather than adding business value to the solution. That is why the Scope Bank field "expected business value" is so critical to the decision-making process.

8. What Was Learned about the APF Process?

The refinement of APF is an APF project! I don't see this project as ever ending. The project landscape will continue to change, and APF will have to change with it. If you think of APF as a thought process rather than a fixed procedure, you will understand why APF must continually change. In every project, you should be looking for ways to improve APF. Discover and learn about the solution to the problem, "How do we create an improved APF?"

Observation

If every project is unique and will never be repeated under the same set of circumstances, then the management approach to each project must also be unique.

Major Inputs to the Next Cycle Planning Activity

Once the answers have been given to the eight questions discussed in the preceding section, it is time for the client team and the development team to look forward to the next cycle. The inputs to the next cycle planning activity are:

- The answers to the above eight questions
- Any functionality and features planned and integrated during the previous cycle
- Any functionality and features planned but not integrated during the previous cycle
- Learning and discovery from all previous cycles (stored in the Scope Bank)
- Functionality and features identified for all remaining cycles (stored in the Scope Bank)
- Any items still remaining on the Issues Log
- Team members available for the next cycle
- Any changes that took place in the business environment during the previous cycles

Any Functionality and Features Planned and Integrated during the Previous Cycle

These are the deliverables from all previous integrative swim lanes. In other words, they comprise the current solution. What was delivered will be used to update the solution through the RBS. Therefore, the RBS serves as a hierarchical map of the current solution. It should be posted in the team war room. Through experience, I know that the updated RBS is one of the most intuitive artifacts produced in an APF project. I have also seen it used as an idea generator for planning probative swim lane contents.

Any Functionality and Features Planned but Not Integrated during the Previous Cycle

What was planned in the integrative swim lanes may not have been implemented, for a variety of reasons. It is not unusual for what's planned to differ from what's actually integrated—not as a result of change, but as a result of running out of time or experiencing some other event that prevents the orderly completion of the cycle plan. This happens all of the time in TPM projects; expect it to occur in APF projects too. Since the cycle time box is fixed, any schedule delays that cannot be recovered will result in some integrative swim lane deliverables not being integrated into the solution. These deliverables will be returned to the Scope Bank for reprioritization and consideration in some later cycle.

Learning and Discovery from All Previous Cycles (Stored in the Scope Bank)

The Scope Bank is the nerve center of every APF project. Everything that is related to a function or feature is stored in the Scope Bank. Nothing is ever removed from the Scope Bank except completed deliverables from the integrative swim lanes.

Functionality and Features Identified for All Remaining Cycles (Stored in the Scope Bank)

We started this whole process with the Conditions of Satisfaction, and it is to the COS that we now return. The only question to be answered here is this: Is the COS still valid? If it is, continue on. If not, revise accordingly. These revisions will help identify the functionality to be pursued in the next cycle.

The client team and the development team should spend most of a day in frank and honest conversation, considering all of these factors and then agreeing on the functionality that will be planned for the next cycle. Do not underestimate the value that can come from the sharing of learning and discovery. That will be your most-important information, because it helps both parties understand what this solution is really all about and what should be offered as the ultimate solution. This part of the process is no trivial task.

The process that was used in the first cycle to prioritize functionality can be repeated here. The criteria used to determine priority may be the same or different. Again, take advantage of all the learning and discovery from the previous cycles.

Any Items Still Remaining on the Issues Log

There will be issues that must be resolved before the next cycle begins. For example, a team member might not be available for the next cycle and may therefore need to be temporarily replaced. If you have known about that before now, you may have been able to get the replacement up to speed in time for the next cycle. If you have just found out about it, you have a few alternatives to consider. Maybe an equally skilled and experienced person is available and could substitute for one cycle. That's the first thing someone more experienced in the TPM world might think of; but in the APF world you have another alternative. Simply postpone the work that the lost team member would have done. Replace that person on the team with an individual properly skilled and experienced for the work of the next cycle. This may actually be a blessing in disguise. You might be able to take advantage of the replacement's timely skills, whereas the missing team member might not have had those skills. Whatever decision you make, you will probably still have to adjust both integrative and probative swim lane priorities to work around the missing team member.

Team Members Available for the Next Cycle

In a situation where you lose several team members for the next cycle or two, you will need to adjust your cycle plans going forward. Furthermore, there may be a need to create handoff documentation in the event of the loss of team members between cycles.

Any Changes that Took Place in the Business Environment during the Previous Cycles

Changes happen that are outside the control of the project team. Suppose, for example, a competitor introduces a new or upgraded product that competes directly with the deliverables you expect to produce in your project. This brings a TPM project to a screeching halt in almost every case, but that is not what happens on an APF project. Like good athletes, the APF project co-managers are prepared for such changes and can adjust accordingly. Whatever solution existed at the completion of the previous cycle may have sufficient business value to complete now. If not, all is not lost, because the APF project can adjust deliverables going forward and produce solutions that come into the market at a later time with expanded functionality and features.

Artifacts of the Client Checkpoint Phase

Using the answers to the eight Client Checkpoint questions and the inputs discussed in the preceding section, the project team generates the following outputs from the Client Checkpoint phase:

- Reprioritized list of functionality and features to be integrated in the solution
- Reprioritized list of probative swim lane ideas
- Next cycle length

Using Brainstorming to Identify Next Cycle Swim Lane Contents

Brainstorming is a tool you will use frequently in APF projects. It is the best mechanism I know for generating the creative input needed to successfully plan and execute an APF project. You will use it throughout every phase of the APF project. It is simple and quick, which is why it is the preferred tool of choice.

A brainstorming session is simple to conduct and does not require any special training of either the facilitator or the attendees. All you need is an environment where no one is hesitant to contribute and no one is critical of the ideas expressed by others. There have been times when I felt that I didn't have that environment. When that has been the case, team-building workshops have been helpful. The project co-managers both are responsible for creating the open and honest environment needed here.

Brainstorming sessions should be lively with lots of involvement, and therefore are excellent team-building experiences.

The rules of the engagement for identifying the solution to a problem using brainstorming are simple:

1. Assemble any individuals, whether they are team members, consultants, or others who may have some knowledge of the subject. They don't need to be experts. In fact, it may be better if they are not. You need people to think creatively and outside the box. Experts tend to think inside the box, using their own experiences.

2. The session begins with everyone throwing any idea out on the table. No discussion (except clarification) is permitted. This continues until no new ideas are forthcoming. Silence and pauses are fine.

3. After all the ideas are on the table, discuss the items. Try to combine or revise ideas based on each member's perspective.

4. In time, some solutions will begin to emerge. Don't rush the process, and by all means test each idea with an open mind. Remember that you are looking for a solution that the responsible individual could not identify, but that you hope the collective wisdom and creativity of the group is able to identify.

5. List and prioritize the feasible solution ideas using either the Forced Ranking or Paired Comparisons model. (These are explained in Chapter 4.)

Brainstorming is invaluable to the project team as part of the discussion regarding what to investigate through probative swim lanes. The more complex and incomplete the solution, the more the team will benefit from brainstorming. I use these sessions at every Client Checkpoint.

Reprioritized List of Functionality and Features to Be Integrated into the Solution

Any functions or features planned for integration in the previous cycle but not integrated at that time must be added back into the Scope Bank list and reprioritized with all other functions and features not yet integrated. This is not unusual. Just remember that the functions and features not integrated in the previous cycle should have been the lowest-priority items for that cycle. Considering what was learned in the previous cycle about the importance of functions and features to be added, those functions and features not integrated in the previous cycle may be given lower priority than new candidates for integration. Therefore, the failure to complete them in the previous cycle may not be a failure after all.

Reprioritized List of Probative Swim Lane Ideas

The discovery and learning from the previous cycle suggest further probative swim lane ideas. These are integrated with the current list of probative swim lane ideas, and the combined list is reprioritized. The criteria used to prioritize the list have to address the likelihood a discovery or learning will actually result in an addition to the current solution.

Next Cycle Length

The decision as to length for the next cycle is based on two prioritized lists: the functionalities to be integrated into the current solution, and ideas to be investigated in the next cycle. The actual contents of the two prioritized lists have to be evaluated subjectively to decide on cycle length. Remember to be true to the overall time-box decision made during the Version Scope phase if possible.

The following are the major analyses conducted at each Client Checkpoint:

- Assess the quality of what has cumulatively been produced to date, with particular emphasis on the just-completed cycle.
- Decide whether the project should continue.

- Combine items from the Scope Bank with the functionalities not completed and the functionalities that were previously assigned to the coming cycle, and reprioritize everything.
- Determine the functionality to be built in the next cycle.
- Determine the ideas to be investigated in the next cycle.

The outcomes of these analyses lead to answers to five questions that the team and the client must jointly formulate before the project can proceed. These are:

1. Do the cumulative deliverables meet expectations?
2. Should the project continue to the next cycle?
3. What is the priority order of the remaining functionalities?
4. What should be built in the next cycle?
5. Does the project start over?

These are discussed in the following subsections.

Do the Cumulative Deliverables Meet Expectations?

Two characteristics speak to the viability of the progress the project has made to date. The metrics to measure these characteristics do not exist at this writing; I am just starting to work on their quantification.

The first characteristic is **tempo** (also called **velocity**). Because the development team and the client team have partnered throughout the completed cycles, they should have already sensed whether the project is gaining momentum as they discover and learn about the solution and integrate the results. Morale should be running high. The entire project team should be excited about the progress to date. There should be visible signs of commitment on the part of all team members. The client team should be eager to be involved in the ongoing affairs of the project. That extends to solving problems and making decisions with the team. Those are good signs, and will instill confidence that the project is a success waiting to happen. On the other hand, if the project seems to be wandering aimlessly, morale is down, or the client team is not really involved but rather is just being courteous, those are not good signs. The project's future is in question. The answers to the five questions discussed in the preceding subsection will provide the input for determining how solution discovery is proceeding.

My expectation is that some variant of a burn chart may provide the metric.

The second characteristic is **convergence**. Because of their close working relationship, the development and client teams should know whether the project is converging on an acceptable solution. That will be evidenced by a growing sense of clarity regarding functionalities remaining to be developed. The end is coming into focus. If the frequency of change requests is diminishing, that is one possible indicator of convergence. These are good signs that the project is healthy and should be continued. On the other hand, the deliverables from each cycle may not give any indication that the project is approaching the end.

My expectation is that some variant of earned value may provide the metric.

Should the Project Continue to the Next Cycle?

If the team and the client have done their due diligence in the analyses described above, their decision should be a no-brainer. If the tempo is increasing and there is sound evidence that the project is converging upon an acceptable solution (and therefore will deliver acceptable business value) within the time and resource constraints, by all means the project should continue. On the other hand, if the opposite seems to be true—the project doesn't engender such confidence—maybe it's time to pull the plug. Even if the current project is cancelled, there may be sufficient evidence that a new project with the same goal but approached along very different lines shows promise of producing the missing solution. Out of the ashes comes a new beginning.

The deliverables from the probative swim lanes should provide some clues to an alternate approach. This is more of a research-and-development situation, which may be entirely appropriate for some projects. Be advised that many R&D projects straddle APF and xPM. It's all a question of goal clarity, as we discussed in Chapter 1.

All agile PMLC models are structured so that a termination decision can be made at any Client Checkpoint phase. The metrics that have been tracked since the first cycle, along with the client team's and the development team's comfort with the project, are input into that decision. If the project is not showing steady progress in converging toward an acceptable solution, it may be time to get out and cut any further losses. The changing contents of the Scope Bank may also provide clues to aid in that decision.

What Is the Priority Order of the Remaining Functionalities?

There are several inputs into this reprioritization exercise. Included are all of the new functionality requests that have collected in the Scope Bank during all previous cycles. There are the functionalities that was planned for the last cycle but not completed. Finally, there are the functionalities that were identified earlier but not yet prioritized for any cycle. The same prioritization exercise that was done in the Version Scope phase is repeated here. The difference is that the development team and the client team are much smarter today than they were back on day one of the project. The prioritization is much more informed now, because a solution is emerging from the efforts of the previous cycles.

What Should Be Built in the Next Cycle?

Now that the next cycle's length is known and a new prioritized list of functionalities is available, the team assesses how far down the two swim lane lists it can expect to get within the next cycle. There may be some give-and-take between next-cycle deliverables and the cycle time box, but this should be minimal and easily resolved.

I previously cautioned you not to be too aggressive in the early cycles. As the team gets to the performance stage and the client team becomes more comfortable working with the development team, the list of deliverables for the next cycle can be allowed to become a bit more aggressive. APF allows the luxury of returning undone functionality to the Scope Bank for consideration in a later cycle. It is still worth reining in the tendency of technical professionals to have steak appetites on bologna budgets. Don't set the client up for results that cannot be achieved. That would put a serious dent in a relationship that had been hard-earned.

Does the Project Start Over?

The success of this project is critical to the organization, so the project should not be abandoned. If the experiences with the approach taken so far haven't proved fruitful, some other approach is needed. Don't fall into the "hope creep" trap by expecting things to get well in some later cycle. In my experience, that is not very likely. APF is a creative process, and by its nature self-corrects. The collective efforts of the entire project team are what it takes to find the solution. Termination is a tough business decision, but it has to be made without the emotion and attachment some project team members will surely have.

Based on what was known at the beginning of the project, the project team made the best decision it could as to the direction for the project. Now that you and the client have learned a bit more about the solution, you might see that a different direction is called for. That is not failure. That is the nature of creative problem-solving. Making the decision to terminate is not easy, and must be done in full collaboration with the client and with full disclosure of all the facts.

Decision-making Styles

The preceding are some of the many decisions required in every Cycle Build phase. A brief discussion of decision-making styles is useful here.

Most decisions are related to the next cycle's Swim Lane contents. Since team membership is already determined, one of the major decisions will be the allocation of resources between the two Swim Lanes.

There are basically three approaches to decision making that apply in an APF project.

Directive

There will be emergency situations when the development-team manager or the client-team manager must make decisions without any input other than what the manager already knows. If the enemy is charging, you don't convene a meeting to decide whether and how to retaliate. The leader makes a decision on the spot based on the information at hand.

There are two considerations when using a directive approach.

Do you feel that you correctly understand the situation? Do you have correct and complete information on which to base your decision? If there is any doubt and if there is time, one of the other approaches might be more appropriate.

What will be the reaction of the other team members, especially the other co-manager, to your decision? Are there points of view that perhaps differ from yours? Will any of the other team members be offended because they weren't consulted? If they weren't even asked for input, will they be hesitant to support your decision? Again, if there is time, you might want to use one of the other approaches.

Participative

At the other extreme is the participative approach. Here, everyone has an opportunity to contribute opinions. All opinions are carefully weighed, and the decision is reached through group discussion. Since all are participating and all are heard, it is more likely that everyone will be much more committed to the chosen decision and more likely to support it during implementation. In this approach, the co-managers make a decision consistent with the input and advice of the participants. They collect and weigh the input and make the best decision possible. In most cases they will use some, but not all, input given.

A participative approach is the best way to decide on Swim Lane contents for the coming cycle.

Consultative

The middle ground between these two approaches is the consultative approach. Here, the decision maker gathers input from all affected or involved parties and then makes a decision. There is no discussion among those who are consulted. Their input may or may not be considered in making that decision. If time is of the essence, the decision maker can gather input from some of those who are most knowledgeable of the situation and then make the decision.

Next Cycle

The next cycle will contain some combination of probative and integrative swim lanes. The exact allocation of team resources to each type of swim lane is a subjective decision. The only clues you have are documented in the cumulative history of the Scope Bank.

Integrative Swim Lanes for the Next Cycle

Integrative swim lanes will be planned based on an updated and prioritized list of the functions and features that have been identified as part of the solution but not yet integrated into it. The more of the solution you can present to the client team, the better; so some priority should be given to integrative swim lanes over probative swim lanes.

Probative Swim Lanes for the Next Cycle

This will be an updated and prioritized list of all ideas that have been identified but not yet investigated. If the solution is mostly unknown and the integrative swim lane list is sparse, some priority should be given to probative swim lanes over integrative swim lanes. The tie-breaker will always be the capability of the project team to accommodate the specified mix.

Cycle Length

While keeping cycle duration at a fixed length throughout the project is generally advised, there will be occasions when that is not appropriate. Just as a TPM project manager would estimate task duration and define task dependencies in order to establish a schedule, so do the APF project co-managers estimate the duration of each swim lane and compare that to the cycle time box. One of the swim lanes will be the longest. Is it too long? Is it too short? (That is rarely the case.) If so, adjustments to cycle length will be needed. Keep in mind the balance between the number of probative swim lanes and the number of integrative swim lanes. The typical pattern for a given cycle depends on the status of the solution.

Client Checkpoint Variations

APF Project Reviews

Project reviews have been used quite extensively in TPM projects and have a place in some APF projects. APF projects that are particularly complex or uncertain, or are critical to the business, are good candidates for project reviews.

During a typical project review, the project co-managers appear before a panel of peers to present an in-depth review of the project status. The review can take place at quarterly or semi-annual points in time, or at milestone events. Obviously, reviews should be scheduled at the completion of some APF cycles, but not after every cycle. They might also be scheduled when one-quarter of the time or the budget has been expended. If problems and their resolution have been discussed at previous reviews, subsequent reviews might be scheduled at shorter intervals to check on the status of recommended corrective actions.

APF project reviews should be more prescriptive than punitive. The problem/opportunity being addressed is critical and complex. All help is welcomed, and sometimes it helps to have people from outside the project offer their perspectives and ideas. The strategy here is that the more eyes that can review the project and offer suggestions for improvement, the better the chance of project success.

COS & POS Reviews

As the project progresses from cycle to cycle, these two documents must be included in the decision making and planning for the next cycle. Is the project still aligned with these documents, or has reason for change emerged?

Case Study: PDQ

Pepe and the project team received the following memo from Dee at a time when the project was already well along. Have you anticipated the kinds of changes Dee brought into the project? What provisions have you made to handle such events?

MEMORANDUM

DATE: September 5, 2009

FROM: Dee Livery

TO: All PDQ Employees

SUBJECT: Status Report

I just wanted to update you on the company-wide business improvement project. As you know, we hired Hype, Hype, and Morehype, a local marketing research and planning company, to ascertain our situation in the marketplace and our business processes. I have seen the draft of their report, and wanted you to be aware of certain steps I feel are necessary and must be implemented without further delay.

Their final report will be distributed next week, but I wanted you to hear from me before copies of that report begin to circulate. First of all, they have done an admirable job in addressing all of our major issues. They were a good choice. Here are the salient points from their report:

1. From their interviews, competitor surveys, and analyses, they have verified that we do have the best pizza in our market area. We ranked higher than the competition in all categories (taste, variety, appearance, price, and quality of ingredients). The survey also suggested that we add a selection of oven-baked sandwiches to our menus.

2. In the same market survey, we were ranked second only to our major competitor in our home-delivery service. The survey pointed out that our time to deliver and pizza temperature at delivery were the only areas needing improvement.

3. The market survey also asked about delivery of unbaked pizzas. The results were:

We would definitely use the service	28%
We would probably use the service	31%
Not sure if we would use the service	20%
We probably would not use the service	10%
We definitely would not use the service	11%

   The unbaked pizza market is not served by our competitor, and we should move immediately to take advantage of this opportunity.

4. From analysis of our sales data over the past 30 months, we learned that our home-delivery sales began to drop a few months after our competitor moved

into the market, and have continued to drop at a fairly steady rate. Over the past 18 months, we have lost more than 30 percent of our revenues in the home-delivery business. That has hit all four of our stores about equally. Our eat-in and carry-out sales have remained steady over the same period.

The summary-level data are as follows.

Store	2007	2007	2008	2008	2009
	Jan/June	July/Dec	Jan/June	July/Dec	Jan/June
#1 (opened in 1999)					
In	1.2M	1.3M	1.3M	1.2M	1.3M
Del	0.7M	0.5M	0.5M	0.4M	0.3M
#2 (opened in 1992)					
In	1.2M	1.1M	1.1M	1.1M	1.0M
Del	0.8M	0.6M	0.5M	0.5M	0.4M
#3 (opened in 1975)					
In	1.1M	1.0M	1.0M	0.9M	1.0M
Del	0.7M	0.9M	0.8M	0.7M	0.6M
#4 (opened in 1984)					
In	0.7M	0.7M	0.8M	0.9M	0.9M
Del	0.7M	0.8M	0.8M	0.6M	0.5M
All					
In	4.2M	4.1M	4.2M	4.1M	4.2M
Del	2.9M	2.8M	2.6M	2.2M	1.8M
Total	7.1M	6.9M	6.8M	6.3M	6.0M

Our major competitor began opening stores at the rate of one per month beginning in January 2007. They now have 20 stores. Every PDQ store has lost home-delivery sales over the past 30-month period and continues to lose sales. In-store sales, which include take-out, have held fairly steady over the past 30 months.

Solutions proposed by HH&M include the following.

1. Our marketing consultants have shown how an advertising campaign would boost sales. They also suggest a discount-coupon program to introduce our new home-delivery services. I like their ideas and recommend we try them out.

2. The business process improvement program has identified two problems. First, we need to implement a preparation area where pizza ingredients are sliced, chopped, diced, and otherwise prepared for the production line. As you know, our kitchens are already cramped for space and so I am going to use the four pizza vans as that staging area. They will service all four stores' inventory needs from the two pizza factories. The pizza factories will have the main inventory to supply the pizza vans. The pizza vans will carry inventory destined for the stores and for their own production needs. This is expected to be a continuous service. Second, in order to make room for growth, we need to replace the ovens in all four stores. The new ovens will be rotary ovens that occupy the same footprint as our current ovens but can handle 50% more volume. I've had several of our regular customers sample the pizzas baked in these new ovens. As long as we baked the pizzas on pizza stones, they didn't notice any differences. Customers who order unbaked pizzas will be given complementary pizza stones for their future orders of unbaked pizza. The ovens are on order and will be delivered in one month.

3. Our major competitor has just introduced a 30-minute order-entry-to-delivery time. We do not have any details on how it expects to meet that goal, but we must counter its program with one of our own.

Based on all of this information and on my 30 years of successful experience in this business, I have made an executive decision as to how we are going to proceed. The details will follow, but here is a summary of the actions we are going to take:

1. We will open two pizza factories to add capacity to our home-delivery line of business. The four existing stores will continue to offer home delivery. Two take-out businesses have recently closed, and their fully equipped properties were put on the market with five-year renewable leases and an option to buy at any time. One was the German store Schnitzels-R-Us, and the other was the Cambodian store Sprouts-To-Go. They are very strategically located in our growing market areas. I have signed leasing agreements for both of those properties. They are available immediately.

2. I have been informed by our long-time supplier that it is outfitting trucks to bake pizzas for a small chain on the west coast. I talked with the owner of

that chain who said that the early sales figures exceeded their forecasts. I have asked our vendor to customize four of these pizza vans for us. They will be delivered in six weeks. Two of them will operate out of our existing four stores, and the other two out of our new pizza factories. We'll continue to use the four vans that now service our four stores. At this time they will not be retrofitted to bake pizzas, but that option is open to us if it is deemed to be a good business decision. This will be the pilot for further expansion of pizza factories and/or pizza vans.

3. We have been studying our telephone system. It needs to be replaced with a system that receives all orders via a single number and routes each to the appropriate store, factory, or pizza van for processing.

4. We need a POS system to handle all data collection (in-store, pick-up, and home-delivery) and analyze the collected data to help us make further decisions about pizza-factory locations and pizza vans. The network that will service our business going forward must link all information and physical systems into a single system. We haven't used information technology to our advantage in the past, but we must do so in the future if we intend to succeed in this highly competitive business. I need your teams to be limited only by their own creativity.

5. Since each order is routed to either a store, a pizza factory, or a pizza van, we need a hardware/software/communications/data system to handle all scheduling and routing in real time.

6. Inventory-replenishment orders must be routed from the store to the appropriate pizza van for fulfillment. Each such order should be initiated by the POS system, since that system will be constantly monitoring store inventory levels that change as a result of orders.

7. We will also announce a 30-minute order-entry-to-delivery service for unbaked pizzas, 45 minutes for baked, as soon as we get our new pizza factories and pizza vans into operation. This will be announced through a major advertising blitz in our markets.

I recognize that this plan preempts the work you are now doing. Please be assured that your work to date with the marketing consultants has been exemplary, solidifying my thinking and making these decisions possible. Your work is far from done, and we will need to closely monitor our sales and performance to make sure we can reach our goal of recouping and surpassing the revenues lost over the past 18 months.

As always, my door is open to all of you, and I welcome your input. We have a significant challenge ahead of us, and the business needs all of us pulling together as a team.

Putting It All Together

In this chapter, I have given you an understanding of how important the Client Checkpoint phase is to the success of an APF project. As we have discussed, APF embraces change, for it is through change that we can converge on a solution that delivers maximum business value for the time and money invested. All of the change that occurs in APF occurs in the Client Checkpoint phase. There is no separate change-management process as there is in the traditional approach. Make the Client Checkpoint phase the high spot of your APF experience, and you won't go wrong.

The Client Checkpoint phase is the last phase in a loop that returns back to the Cycle Plan phase. The plan → cycle build → client checkpoint loop repeats itself for as many cycles as have been planned within the version time box.

By now, you should be getting a good sense of the dynamics in an APF project. You should also begin to appreciate the value of a solid team-client partnership, and how valuable the client is in an APF project.

APF is client-facing and client-driven. That is perhaps the most important of the core values that underlie the APF approach. As APF is introduced into an organization, senior project management must be proactive in establishing the environment in which the bond between client and project manager can grow and mature. It is up to the project manager to carry that bond forward to the team, so that the team will begin to appreciate the value of that relationship. This will happen just because we ask our managers and staff to make it happen. It requires encouragement and support from the entire organization.

> **Advice**
> The pathway to finding the solution to your problem is paved with the openness and candor you and the client have nurtured with one another. It is essential that you are always frank with one another; otherwise, you are just wasting each other's time.

Discussion Questions

The following questions are posed for your use. Use them to test your understanding and potential application of the materials presented in the chapter. If you are using this book for a course you are teaching, the questions will provoke good class discussion.

1. You are the development team manager. You aren't comfortable with the way your client team manager interacts with you during the Client Checkpoint phase. If there is a problem here, you need to get it out in the open and resolve it. What do you do? Be specific.

2. A member of your team is a systems analyst from the "old school," and just cannot adjust to APF. Her problem is that the client has decision-making authority over the direction your software development project is taking and the client is, shall we say, technically challenged. How do you handle this dilemma?

3. You are the project manager over one of your company's first APF projects. You are having trouble getting the client's involvement. What do you do?

Chapter 6

How to Conduct the
Post-version Review

Out of intense complexities intense simplicities emerge.

—Winston Churchill, English Prime Minister

*[Very successful] projects that entrepreneurs initiated and carried
through had one essential quality. All had been thoroughly
contemplated by the regnant experts and dominant companies, with
their large research staffs and financial resources, and had been
judged too difficult, untimely, risky, expensive and unprofitable.*

—George Gilder, Economist

After more than 40 years practicing project management and 20 years
of business consulting in project management, I can honestly say that
while everyone extols the value of the post-implementation audit, only a
small percentage of companies actually conduct a post-project or post-
implementation review. People are too busy, and are already behind on
their next projects. It just doesn't seem important. As many senior managers and sponsors have told me, "the project is over. What difference
does it make?"

In the APF world, this attitude has to change. There is far too much valuable information to be gathered from a completed APF project—not only in terms of the additional business value that could be delivered by the next version of the solution, but also in terms of improving the APF process itself. The chef will always be looking for ways to improve and adapt recipes!

Just as the traditionalist might conduct a post-implementation audit at the end of a project, so does the APFist always conduct a Post-version Review at the end of the current version. There are a number of similarities between a traditional post-implementation audit and an APF Post-version Review, but there are differences too. The traditionalist is looking for final closure on the project, while the APFist is looking for ways to further increase the business value of the solution. In other words, the APFist is never looking for final closure; instead, he or she is always looking for more business value. The version just completed is just another step toward increasing business value. In that sense, APF is quite like a production prototype, because it consists of a never-ending cycle of repeated solution improvements. The only final ending to an APF solution is to retire the solution altogether and replace it totally with a different solution. So an APF project is one more step in a never-ending journey, not a final destination.

I have no expectation of changing your attitude toward the post-implementation audit. If you don't routinely use them for your TPM projects, you aren't likely to use them for your APF projects either. My objective in this chapter is to share my thoughts on the Post-version Review phase.

The completion of the Post-version Review phase marks the formal close to the work on the current version of the solution. It is here that assessments are made of actual business value achieved versus planned business value. If there is a gap between those two values, there may be reason to commission another APF project to create a next-generation solution that closes the gap. The contents of the Scope Bank at the end of the project are the best evidence available on the potential value of another version. The analysis of the Scope Bank relevant to another version is clearly the domain of the client team. If another version is commissioned, the same project team should be assigned to work on it. The learning curve-effect and the team formation from the previous version are invaluable.

The Post-version Review phase also collects lessons learned and best practices. This is especially important because APF will always be a work-in-process. There is still a lot to be learned about APF, and it can only be learned from the experiences of teams using APF. At this writing, APF is ten years old and at a point in its development where change in the approach is still expected. Establishing a sound APF infrastructure is an APF project! Only by using APF and producing constructive feedback can we hope to evolve APF to a complete and comprehensive approach. Eventually, I hope to evolve APF into a more-comprehensive agile approach that can accommodate the APM and xPM projects a project manager is likely to encounter.

Overview of the APF Post-version Review Phase

The Post-version Review phase marks the end of the work on the current version. It also leaves open the possibility that additional versions might gain even further business value. Indeed, the final client checkpoint may have ended with functions and features that have not yet been considered still in the two swim-lane lists in the Scope Bank. Remember that functionalities not yet addressed are lower priority and may not have the potential for adding measurable business value to the current solution.

The APF Post-version Review phase is the closing phase of an APF project, as shown in Figure 6.1.

Let's look at the questions that must be answered in this final phase of an APF project.

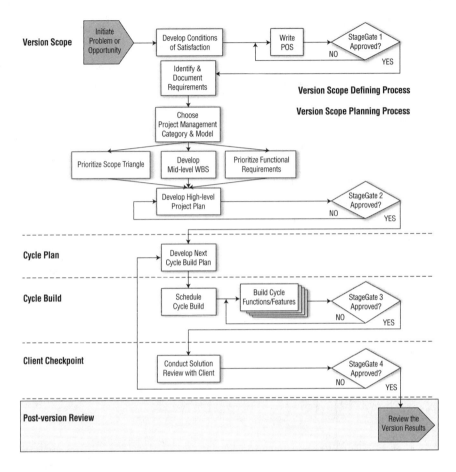

Figure 6.1
The Adaptive Project Framework: Post-version Review

Major Questions for the Post-version Review Phase

Answers to the following questions provide a complete analysis of the solution delivered by the APF project.

Did the Team Find an Acceptable Solution?

The project team includes both the client and the developers, and both bear responsibility for a favorable answer to the question.

There are really two parts to this question. The first is whether or not a solution was found. Remember that the distinguishing feature of an APF project compared to other types is that the goal is clearly understood, but the solution is not. The first part of our answer is that we either did or did not find a solution. Because of the structure of an APF project, the likelihood is very high that some type of solution was found. Had that not been the case, the project would have been terminated based on the absence of tempo or convergence or both.

The second part of our answer is whether or not the solution was acceptable. This is the more-significant of the two questions. The solution is acceptable if it solves the problem. The business value of that solution depends on the cause-and-effect relationship between the problem and the solution. If the solution addresses the cause, it is acceptable.

Were the Success Criteria Achieved?

The next question deals with the value of the solution. Except for mandated projects, every project is justified on the basis of the business value it is expected to deliver. APF projects are no exception. Even though the business value may not be demonstrable for some time, it is an important consideration in assessing the degree to which the project was successful. If it is determined that the expected business value was not attained or cannot be attained, the results may suggest that a second project built on the results of the just-ended project may deliver the remaining business value. If the expected business value was attained, or it is clear that it will be attained at some future date in the normal course of events, that is reason to celebrate.

Remember from the Project Overview Statement that the success criteria are specific quantitative metric(s) on which success is to be determined. They are the basis for justification for doing the project in the first place. They either were achieved or were not.

The Post-version Review phase is the time to check whether the project has achieved these outcomes. Oftentimes, however, these outcomes cannot be measured until weeks, months, or even quarters have passed since the version was put into production status. This part of the review is no different than in the traditional approach. The project has finished, and the team will be disbanded for reassignment to other projects. Waiting on the validation of a business outcome is related to the business reason for doing the project and in no way affects the team. Depending on that business outcome, another project focused on the same application may be commissioned and a new team assembled to do that work.

I have had many managers from my client organizations say, "The project is done. What difference does it make if we met our expected business outcomes? I've got three projects waiting to be staffed and two of them are already behind schedule. I simply don't have the time to do post-project analyses."

Somebody has to own the validation of business outcomes. The bottom line is that unless someone owns the validation, it simply won't happen.

Is a Second Version Recommended?

We know that learning and discovery are important parts of the Client Checkpoint phase because that phase leads the client team and the development team to adjust the cycle plans going forward in pursuit of that elusive solution. Similarly, in the Post-version Review phase, the client team and the development team consider the contents of the Scope Bank at the close of the last cycle. By design, the contents remaining in the Scope Bank should be the lower-priority deliverables that would be the starting point for the next version. The analysis of this information becomes the major part of the business validation for that next version.

Part of that analysis will include observing the performance of the just-deployed solution over time. Keep in mind that several partial solutions will have been in place only briefly as part of the process of defining the end result. Metrics should have been defined to track the performance of even the partial solutions. In that sense, the final outcome is itself an interim solution, and time will tell whether it holds up to the rigors of changing conditions.

The initial solution should be viewed in the same context as a continuous process-improvement program whose purpose is improving the business value of the solution. The question is, "Will the expected improvement in the solution be worth more than the cost of implementing that improvement?"

That process-improvement program is an APF project too. Each cycle of an APF Process Improvement project will include both integrative and probative swim lanes, just as in the original solution-development project.

Lessons Learned

So far, the lessons learned focus on the solution (that is, the *product*) from the just-completed version. The other type of lessons learned focuses on the *process* that was followed to create the solution, and asks such questions as, "How well did APF work?" and "How well did the client and the team follow APF?" In answering these questions, the client and the team offer suggestions for improvement of the process and the practice of the process. As you can see, APF has a built-in, continuous quality-improvement process.

How Well Did APF Work?

The further development of APF is an APF project! APF must fit the enterprise culture and integrate with other business processes, so every rendition of APF will be unique to the enterprise. Within the enterprise, APF will even be unique to the business unit within which it is implemented.

Every project follows some type of approach. Completed projects are the best source of information on how well the approach matched the needs of the project. That question should be answered for every completed or abandoned project. If the project failed due to some shortcoming in the approach, that information needs to be ferreted out and analyzed. Some corrective action is certainly needed. For APF, which is a work-in-process, that information is critical to its continued growth and development. I would appreciate any feedback you can provide on your experiences using APF.

How Well Did the Project Team Use APF?

Apart from having a fully documented and integrated APF approach is the question of its usability. Projects have so many variations and subtleties that an approach must be adaptive in order to effectively support the project team. That is why **adaptive** appears in the title Adaptive Project Framework.

There are a number of opportunities for feedback and evaluation during the course of an APF project. At each Client Checkpoint, both the client team and the development team should honestly and openly reflect on what happened during the last cycle. This is no time to be shy. If there is true team spirit, that should not be a problem. Members should be looking for lessons learned. What went well and why? What did the project team do that worked, and why? What did the project team do that didn't work, and why? What didn't the project team do that it should have done, and why? The answers to all of these questions provide valuable information for future versions of this project and for other APF projects as well. For any of this to be a valuable exercise, the team members must approach the exercise with open minds and with the intent of improving the business value of APF. Personalities and egos must be put aside in order for this to be a worthwhile experience.

Feedback, evaluation, and corrective action should be part of every Client Checkpoint phase. Waiting until the project has been completed to conduct such an evaluation doesn't make sense in an APF project. That would be a waste of learning opportunities, and is not consistent with the adaptable nature of the APF Project Management Life Cycle (PMLC) model.

A Job Well Done

To be able to look back and honestly say that you and your client gave it your best is the mark of great APF project co-managers.

How Well Did the Development Team Use APF?

For developers new to the APF approach, it can be a major shock to their way of doing business. For example, in systems-development projects, the database architect is very uncomfortable having only a partial description of the data and its structure with which to begin the process of database design. Knowing that whatever they produce will likely be modified through the cycles of the project is frustrating to purists. The mindset of the development-team member must adjust to the fact that every APF project is high risk and is a journey of learning and discovery into the solution space.

How Well Did the Client Team Use APF?

For clients, the transition to APF requires a significant change in the way they relate and interact with development teams, as compared to traditional approaches to project management. The client's role changes from passive to very active. They are the Subject Matter Experts (SMEs) on the project team and an essential part of the learning and discovery effort. Their leadership in this effort is critical to the success of the project. As project co-manager, the leader of the client team is equally responsible and accountable for the success or failure of the project. The bond between the client-team manager and the development-team manager is far more intimate than in any traditional project. This bond will grow and be strengthened through experience gained from repeated involvement in APF projects. It is a learned behavior.

The APF PMLC model is tailored to the client, and can be somewhat different from client to client. In my experience, some clients will naturally take more-proactive roles and need only be pointed in the right direction. At the other extreme will be clients who are very passive and will need to learn their role and proper behavior. That may translate to an APF approach that includes training components running concurrently with the project. The client will learn by doing.

Improvement Opportunities

I think APF will always be a process in transition. There is so much to learn about the interaction among client team, development team, and process.

Process

As the use of APF grows and matures in an organization, its business impact will be more significant. Just as we learn and discover a solution by doing a project, so also will we learn and discover how to improve APF by doing APF.

The so-called "best practices" that are discovered during project execution need to be archived and easily retrievable. For some reason, not too many organizations have been successful with this effort. Many reasons are given:

- My project is different.
- I don't manage that way.
- I wasn't aware of that.
- It's too difficult to adapt to my project.
- The documentation is too complex and lengthy.
- I couldn't find it.
- I'm not sure why that would work better than our current practice.
- We have our own way of dealing with that situation.

The most effective best-practices documentation I have seen is simple. One client took this to the extreme. For example, if you have a problem with estimating testing time, the "best practices estimation of testing time" entry simply says not much more than, "Talk to Ed at ext23." The adoption of a best practice is difficult. There are a number of conditions that each situation requires, and only someone very familiar with the practice can help adapt it.

Client Team

At some point, every client team will get involved in an APF project for the first time. They will discover that their meaningful involvement is the most-important factor in the success of an APF project. Expect that this role will be uncomfortable at first. You will need to provide the necessary training and orientation. Meaningful client involvement was reported as a success factor in *Chaos Report 2007*.[1] For the first time, lack of client involvement was reported as the primary reason for project failure. I've added **meaningful** to the factor because, for an APF project, if client involvement isn't meaningful, the project will surely fail. In fact, that statement probably holds true for every Agile Project Management methodology. The client is the content expert, and without the client's meaningful involvement, an agile project cannot succeed.

There will be practices that worked and didn't work for the project's client, and these should be recorded for the next project with this client. There will be practices that worked and didn't work for this client that should be recorded for use in projects with other clients. Recording for posterity and for public use things you tried that didn't work is tantamount to documenting failure, and that has never been a comfortable exercise for us. Stop and think that recording what doesn't work may prevent another team from going down that same path. You will have saved them time, and time is the most precious asset of an APF project.

Development Team

For the APF development team, the transition from a traditional PMLC model to an agile PMLC model is challenging. In the traditional project, change is not welcome because it upsets the orderly plan and takes away from value-added work. In the agile project, change is expected and needed. The mentalities and attitudes are so very different. The stark difference between these two environments requires a major cultural change for the developer. The APF project would seem to be under the control of the client, whereas the TPM project is more under the control of the development team. In fact, the APF project should be under the joint control of the client team manager and the development-team manager. They share equal responsibility.

---

[1] Standish Group, *Chaos Report 2007: The Laws of CHAOS* (Boston: Standish Group International, December 2007).

Post-version Final Report

The final APF project report is a reflection of the history of the project. The purpose of an APF project is learning and discovery, and the final report should be consistent with that purpose. It is the document others can study to learn about APF as executed in a real project. Many formats can be used for a final report, but the content should include comments relative to the following points.

Overall Success of the Project

Taking into account all of the measures of success that you used, can you consider this project successful? These measures of success should relate to both the product produced and the process that produced it. As to the product produced, the focus is on business value delivered by the product. The major question addresses planned business value versus delivered business value, and the reasons for any gap between the two. The process measures of success will revolve around the effectiveness of the project team. Over the course of the project, did it in fact evolve into an APF team, or did it remain a group of individuals with a common purpose but without strong team cohesion?

Organization of the Project

Hindsight is always perfect. Now that you are finished with the project, did you organize it in the best way possible? If not, what might that organization have looked like? The focus here should be on how project organization affected the interaction between the client-team members and the development-team members. Did it foster an environment of openness and honesty? If not, why not, and how should the organization have been designed?

Techniques Used to Get Results

By referring to the project history, you can determine what specific things you did that helped to get the results. Start this list at the beginning of the project. The focus should be on measures that relate to team effectiveness, on the relationship between client and development teams, and on factors that improved their performance.

Project Strengths and Weaknesses

Again, the project history can help you determine which features, practices, and processes proved to be strengths and which were weaknesses. Do you have any advice to pass on to future project teams regarding these strengths and weaknesses? Start this list at the beginning of the project.

Project Team Recommendations

Throughout the life of the project, there will have been a number of insights and suggestions. This is the place to record them for posterity. The client team should submit its report and the development team its report. They should do this independently of each other. Start this list at the beginning of the project.

Case Study: Snacks Fifth Avenue— Kiosk Design

Most of the effort in this project was focused on kiosk design. Several non-production prototypes were built over the course of six months. Each prototype was the deliverable of a single cycle. Most cycles were four weeks long. Every Client Checkpoint phase included a focus group of actual customers. They offered input on kiosk design, and on functions and features to be offered through the kiosk. Their input was used to produce the next prototype. Six prototypes were built. A production version of the kiosk was built over the next three months using a traditional systems development life cycle. A focus group tested the new production version. A few minor revisions were made to the user interface, and the project was completed one month later. More than 200 kiosks were deployed.

Case Study: Kamikazi Software Systems—Systems Development Project Management Process Design

The major challenge in this project was that the 35-person development team was spread over 12 time zones in China, India, Germany, England, and the U.S. The interesting feature of the project was that the client group and the development group were one and the same. That resulted in great simplification for a project that presented significant challenges due to the geographic distribution of team members. With few exceptions, the team members would never meet face to face, but would rely instead on teleconferencing for daily team meetings. Obviously, this was not the ideal situation. It did add considerable management overhead, so a program management office was established to relieve the project manager from most administrative responsibilities. The project manager was hired from the outside. He was an expert in designing integrated project management life cycles and systems development life cycles.

The first few cycles were focused on how to document the Systems Development Project Management (SDPM) process. It was decided to use a three-level design. The first level would document a process phase at the highest level. The target audience included executives and other non-project management staff who simply had a need to know what the process steps involved. Embedded in that document were links to the next-level documentation, which was designed for project managers and teams. At this level, they could get an overview of the details involved in a process step. This level was for staff already familiar with the process but needing a quick review. Embedded in this level of the document were several links to the details of exactly how to execute each process step. The third level of documentation comprised those detailed explanations of how to execute the tools, templates, and processes associated with each process step.

Once the design of the documentation was complete, the actual SDPM could be designed and the three levels of documentation could be populated. The initial high-level APF Process Flow is shown in Figure 6.2.

It was obvious from the outset that the SDPM would have to be an iterative process. The continual scope-change requests from the client would

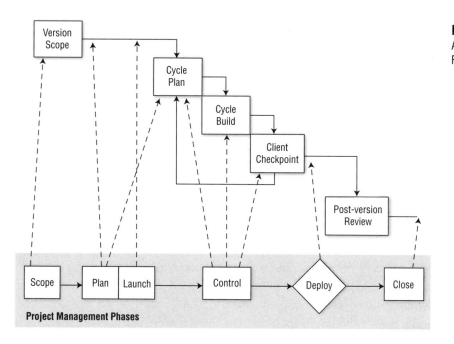

Figure 6.2
APF Process Flow

have to be accommodated, which is why an iterative SDPM would be required. The final SDPM, whatever form it took, would have to fit the initial APF Process Flow diagram shown in Figure 6.2. The team agreed, and the details could be developed.

Case Study: Pizza Delivered Quickly—Order Entry and Home Delivery Process Design

This project is a complete business process re-engineering project designed to leverage technology in a business that had depended on technology for only the most basic of business processes. PDQ did not have any inside expertise, so the project would depend heavily on the use of outside consultants. The consultant team quickly defined the project as consisting of six subsystems, and classified the subsystems into the following project types shown in Table 6.1.

Table 6.1 Subsystems and Corresponding Project Types

Subsystem	Project Type
Pizza Factory Locator Subsystem	APF
Order Entry Subsystem	Commercial off-the-shelf software
Logistics Subsystem	APF
Order Submit Subsystem	APF
Inventory Management Subsystem	Commercial off-the-shelf software
Routing Subsystem	Commercial GPS software

Three subsystems were built using a straightforward application of APF with minimal problems. The continued success of PDQ was on everyone's mind, so commitment was not a problem. PDQ staff was fully involved in solution discovery and implementation. The initial solution was deployed, and a number of system-performance metrics were put in place to monitor the achievement of the success criteria.

Case Study: Try & Buy Department Stores—Curriculum Design, Development, and Delivery

The first few cycles of this project involved requirements gathering. In these two cycles, more than 125 project managers, at all levels from junior project managers to program directors, were interviewed in small groups of two to four. Since there were 184 customer groups, not all of them could be represented in the 125-person sample. The purpose of the interviews was to scope out the needs for the training programs. Complete requirements could not be gathered from the interviews, so it was assumed that changes would be made as part of the initial offerings of the courses. APF was chosen as the PMLC model.

Each stage of the training program design, development, and deployment was done in several cycles. Each cycle deliverable was circulated as broadly as possible to solicit input from customer groups that were not included in the initial requirements interviews. As expected, a number of changes were recommended and incorporated.

Putting It All Together

Clearly, the Post-version Review is focused on the business value of what has just been completed and on the business value of any future versions that might follow, which is as it should be. A guiding principle of APF is to deliver maximum business value. We have shown how this applies to the critique of the solution just delivered and to preparation for any version that might follow.

Next, in Chapter 7: Adapting APF, we consider some variations that might be encountered and how APF can be adapted to fit.

We have now seen all five phases of APF. The seasoned project managers among you should see a number of similarities to TPM and xPM approaches. Both of these approaches have sets of effective tools and processes. In designing and developing APF, I have used as many of those as makes sense. I'm not going to ignore the more-traditional tools and templates that have been used productively. If they can be adapted to APF, I will use them. At the same time, I have not force-fed these tools and processes into APF. APF is a tub standing on its own bottom. I have seen good results from the few uses I have been privileged to be associated with. Much remains to be done to complete APF, but APF has already demonstrated that it does add business value above and beyond our experiences with TPM and xPM.

Discussion Questions

The following questions are posed for your use. Use them to test your understanding and potential application of the materials presented in the

chapter. If you are using this book for a course you are teaching, the questions will provoke good class discussion.

1. You have completed your first APF project. Compare and contrast the traditional and APF approaches when both of them have reached the completion point.

2. What differences might you see if it were possible to do the same project twice—once using the traditional approach and once using APF? Be specific. How might the differences in implementation affect your comparison of the approaches? Again, be specific.

Chapter 7

Adapting APF

We weren't forced to follow the old ideas.

> —J. Georg Bednorz, IBM researcher and Nobel laureate

*Few ideas are in themselves practical. It is for want of imagination
in applying them, rather than in acquiring them that they fail. The
creative process does not end with an idea—it only starts with an idea.*

> —John Arnold, MIT

APF is truly adaptive in that it can be used, and has been used, in a variety of
different situations. As its name implies, it will work well in a number of situations other than those we have discussed so far. We'll explore the more
popular variations in this chapter.

APF Is Flexible and Adaptive

We have seen how APF not only anticipates adaptations but also expects
them. We have already discussed that APF is not a recipe to be blindly
followed. Rather, APF offers a structured framework—a strategy—for
thinking about how best to manage a project. However, APF is far more
adaptable than even the situations in the preceding chapters have indicated.
There are three additional adaptations I want you to be aware of, and these
are the topic of this short chapter. The first two are brief topics that demonstrate how APF can be used as a proof-of-concept tool and in revising a

version plan. These are discussed first. Then we draw a comparison between APF and Extreme Project Management (xPM). The two are closely related approaches to managing projects—when the solution is not known (APF), and when neither the solution nor the goal is known (xPM).

> **Note**
> You will probably find other reasons to adapt APF. Feel free to do that. APF is not a rigid structure to be followed without question. For me, the bottom line has always been to do what is right for the client. If that flies in the face of some established process or procedure, you need to take a serious look at the process or procedure. It may not be serving your needs.

Variations

In this section, we explore the many variations and applications of the APF Project Management Life Cycle (PMLC) model.

Evolutionary Development APF

Similar to a prototyping approach, an Evolutionary Development APF PMLC model begins by building a production version of the entire known solution. This becomes the foundation for further learning and discovery of missing parts of the solution, first using probative swim lanes and then following up with integrative swim lanes as appropriate. This variation works best when most of the solution is known.

The Evolutionary Development Waterfall model is the underlying model in the Evolutionary Development APF PMLC variant. In the Evolutionary Development Waterfall model, the development team builds as complete a prototype of the solution as is known, and then shows the client how various alternatives with added functionality and features might look. The client chooses from among the alternatives, and a new prototype solution is presented. This evolutionary approach continues until the client is satisfied that the prototype reflects what the client needs. A production version is then built.

That's the standard Evolutionary Development Waterfall model. The APF variation differs in two respects.

Every Version of the Solution Is Production Ready

One of the major advantages of APF over most other agile models is that at the end of every cycle, you deliver a production version of the then-known solution. Scrum and XP (eXtreme Programming) are two APM approaches that produce production-ready code at the end of every cycle. Releasing that code to the end user will always be an option in those approaches too. At the end of a given cycle, the product may have enough business value to be released, but that is not necessary. Organizational velocity with respect to change and the support capabilities of the project team are major determinants of the release decision. At any time, the process can stop and the then-solution can be deployed.

APF Always Uses Probative Swim Lanes

The standard evolutionary model presents alternatives for the client to choose among. While there is some creativity involved in defining those alternatives, that creative effort is much less challenging than the creative effort demanded in the typical probative swim lane. As you know, these swim lanes are designed to learn and discover missing functions and features. The probative swim lanes in an Evolutionary Development APF PMLC model will be of two types. The simple type will present the client team with alternatives for a given function or feature. The client decides which alternative to use, and then the appropriate probative or integrative swim lanes, or both, follow. The more complex type is the probative swim lane approach we have discussed in previous chapters.

Proof of Concept

There will be situations where the business case has not been sufficiently made to get approval to build even the first version. In much the same way we have used prototyping to help with client definition of functionality, we can use the same concept in the first APF cycle, making it a proof-of-concept cycle. That proof of concept could entail any of the following.

- The creation of an iconic prototype
- A feasibility study
- The writing of use cases
- Storyboarding
- Cash flow, breakeven analysis, ROI, and other financial analyses
- Any other activity to demonstrate business value

The choice of which of these to use will be based on familiarity, experience, and other factors. There is no best choice. However, it is very important that you not drag this activity out too long. Client interest and the interest of the approving manager for your idea will wane. You need to strike quickly while the iron is hot.

Revising the Version Plan

There will be situations where the initial version scope misses the mark. You will see evidence of this via a significant number of discoveries and lessons learned in the first few cycles. These discoveries and lessons can create a big disconnect between the original direction of the project and the corrected direction that is now indicated. In other words, it becomes clear that continuing on the course suggested by the current version scope is a waste of time and money. Remember that you have previously built a mid-level Work Breakdown Structure (WBS) and are now making your cycle plans around that WBS. Too many changes brought on by learning and discovery may render much of the WBS out of sync.

Whether to revise the version plan is clearly a subjective decision. I would err on the side of revision rather than sticking with a plan that may be heading in the wrong direction. The APFist is hard-pressed to do anything that may be a waste of the client's time or money. The APFist would conclude that the plan is off course and should be abandoned immediately. The correct action is to revise (or even replace) the current version plan and basically start over.

> **Note**
> At this early point in the project, do not be afraid to kill the plan. In almost every case we can think of, you will be making the correct decision. Abandonment is costly, but not as costly as continuing a project that is going nowhere. Don't let "hope creep" get in the way of a clear decision.

Embedding APF in Traditional Project Management (TPM)

So far, we have considered only applications of APF for the entire project. APF is more adaptive than that. Figure 7.1 illustrates an example that has come up several times in APF's short history.

In this example, we have a project that meets the goal through six solution requirements. With one exception, the six requirements are clear and complete. If it weren't for that single requirement's lack of clarity, TPM would be a perfect fit. Well, in this case you can have your cake and eat it too, as you will see in the discussion that follows.

Requirements A through D are clearly defined and documented. Requirement E, the requirement associated with the APF activity, is not. For the purposes of this example, the unclear requirement will temporarily be treated as a task in the precedence diagram shown in Figure 7.2. The example is very simple, but it illustrates the point.

Under the condition that the unclear APF activity is a task, Figure 7.2 is a complete precedence diagram for the project and can be treated as such. Since the APF activity is a high-level task, it will have several predecessors

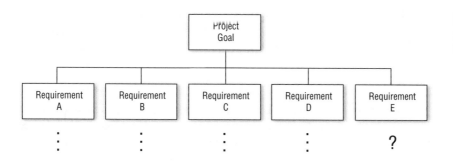

Figure 7.1
APF-TPM
Hybrid

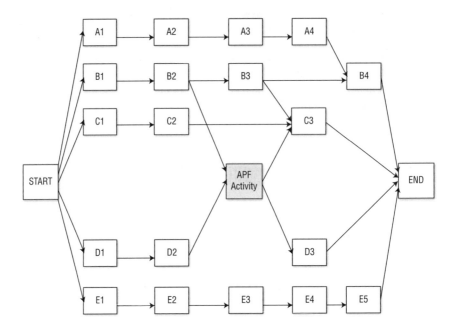

Figure 7.2
Precedence
Diagram for an
APF-TPM
Hybrid

and several successors, but it can be inserted in a precedence diagram and a schedule can be developed. Depending on how much task duration can be assigned to the APF activity, a complete project schedule can be established. In practice, you can calculate the Early Start Date and Late Finish Date[1] of the APF activity so that the project completion date would not be compromised. The Early Start for the APF activity is the latest date of the Early Finish Dates of tasks B2 and D2. The Late Finish for the APF activity is the earliest of the Late Starts for tasks C3 and D3. Using these calculated Early Start Dates and Late Finish Dates as the actual scheduled start and end dates for the APF activity means it is on the critical path.

The APF activity is an APF project. Its start and end date are determined. The client can set the budget for finding the solution to be delivered by the APF activity. All of the parameters are now set for the APF activity to be performed using an APF approach. We now have an APF project embedded in a TPM project.

---

[1] The Late Finish Date for an item is the latest date when it can be finished without delaying completion of the cycle. For more about Late Start Dates and Late Finish Dates, see the Swim Lanes subsection under Overview in Chapter 3: How to Plan an APF Cycle.

Actually, APF can be embedded in any Linear or Incremental PMLC model. For example, in a Staged Delivery Waterfall PMLC model, one of the swim lanes could be an APF project. Barring any constraining dependencies between the APF swim lane and any other swim lane, the APF project begins as soon as the first swim lane begins and ends when the last swim lane is complete.

Business Justification for Using APF

By nature, an APF project leaves a lot of holes in the deliverables, and many senior managers will have problems justifying these types of projects. If the successful completion of the project is critical to the business, and if the solution has in fact been elusive, then there is no alternative but to approach the project as an APF project. That doesn't eliminate the need to justify the project to senior management. They will want to know that the project isn't just jousting at windmills, and that it isn't an effort that will produce nothing of business value. If that is the reality, maybe the problem will just have to remain unsolved!

Design Cycles

I have used APF in the design phase of an Internet-based thin client software system and followed it with the development, testing, and deployment phases using an Incremental PMLC model. In this variation, APF design was accomplished using an iconic prototype. The application was extremely complex, and included a number of decision-support systems whose logic was not at all obvious. The design phase included design of the user views as well as the algorithms to drive the underlying decision-support systems.

Example of an APF Design Project Embedded in a Real Project

Early in the history of APF, I proposed and managed an APF project in which the first prototype was generated overnight. It was an iconic prototype, not a production prototype, and showed how a Web-based solution might work. The application was a thin client Web-based career planning and development system. The prototype consisted of several screens with no logic driving them. It helped the client visualize what a solution might look like and how the end user would interact with the various functions in the system. It became the basis for several discussions that led to further prototypes of the solution. In this case, a picture was worth more than a thousand words of documentation.

Several versions of the prototype were completed in the first two weeks of the project. While the client was reviewing prototypes, the development team was busy designing the architecture for the system. These two weeks constituted the first cycle of the project. At the completion of the two-week cycle, the prototype had reached a level of detail to the satisfaction of the client that it could be the foundation from which the solution would be further defined and built.

Two graphics described the high-level parts of the prototype. They are shown as Figures 7.3 and 7.4.

One of the core requirements of the solution was that it be intuitive. To the project team, that meant it would be driven by graphics. A second core requirement, which flowed from the first, was that no user manual would be allowed.

Career and professional development was a never-ending journey, so a roadmap was chosen as the theme. Figure 7.3 is the final vision of that roadmap. It shows in graphic form the journey from Jobsville to Career

Figure 7.3
CareerAgent
Systems
Roadmap

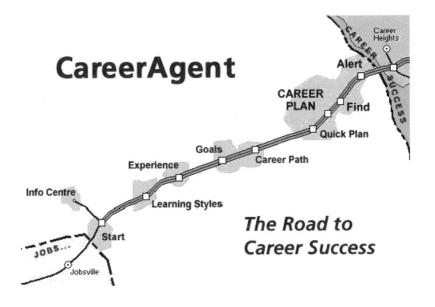

Heights and the ten major functions that CareerAgent must provide to guide the user on the journey. They were:

1. Authentication (Start)
2. Info Centre (CareerAgent Overview)
3. Learning Styles (a Web-based assessment)
4. Experience (a résumé that is kept up-to-date by the system)
5. Goals (what do you want to be when you grow up?)
6. Career Path (a system-generated sequence of positions to get you to your goal)
7. Career Plan (how will you get there?)
8. Quick Plan (what are the next few steps?)
9. Find (experience acquisition, on-the-job training, off-the-job training, professional activities)
10. Alert (things of interest to your plan)

The roadmap of the CareerAgent System shown in Figure 7.3 made the ten major functions visible to the project team and gave them a reference for discussion purposes.

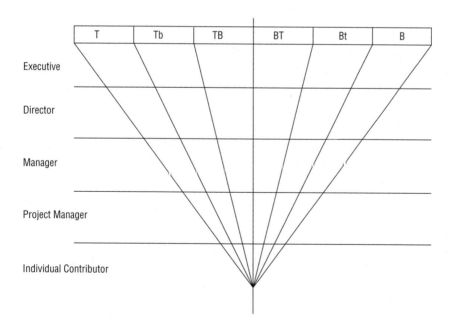

Figure 7.4
CareerAgent
Landscape

The landscape shown in Figure 7.4 captures all positions at all levels that require some combination of technical skill and experience and business skill and experience. It is a robust model, which I have used in a variety of position situations that combine two general position types. A recent application uses the landscape for project management and business analysis. The landscape in Figure 7.4 covers positions ranging from technology only (T) to technology with minimal business (Tb) to technology positions that are strong in both business and technology (TB). The right side is the mirror image of the left side, with the positions oriented toward business with progressive levels of technology skill added. For comparative purposes, the TB and BT sectors require equivalent skills and experiences. The only difference is that the TB positions are located in the IT function, while the BT positions are located in the business departments. See the Appendix for a more-detailed description of the CareerAgent System.

In a sense, the prototype and the two graphics showed the client team what was to be done, but not how. The prototype also put the client team and the development team on the same page. I could see very effective synergies emerging. Everyone was clearly on the same page! Both teams were able to work together more openly and effectively as a result of having the prototype, since they had an agreed upon solution to work toward. In this project, a vague idea of what the solution might look like was transformed into a tangible vision that turned out to be feasible.

In keeping with the client's then-current project-sizing process, the project was budgeted at $5 million over three years. It was the first time APF had been used in the client company, and the project was completed in 27 months at a little over $3 million. Within six months of implementation, CareerAgent had more than 18,000 registered users. I credit the success of this project to APF and the entire team! Senior management was thrilled, and immediately commissioned a project to make APF a major part of the company's project-management methodologies.

There is nothing new about prototyping. It has been around since the days of the Pharaohs, and is one of the most valuable weapons in the APF arsenal. Prototyping is an example of the Iterative PMLC model, which was discussed in Chapter 1: Overview of the Adaptive Project Framework. If you choose this approach, my advice is to use a software tool that can quickly generate the next-version prototype. In the CareerAgent example, a home-grown prototyping tool was used. In the team war room, two technographers (developers skilled in the use of the prototyping tool) captured all agreements in the tool and displayed them graphically in real time.

You will never get better participation and buy-in from the client team than at the early stage. Take advantage of the client members' early enthusiasm. Don't miss this one-time opportunity.

Business Process Improvement

I have used APF in business process improvement projects. This adaptation is quite straightforward. Most of the swim lanes are probative. Following the completion of a cycle, the client implements the prioritized process changes from those probative swim lanes that appear to give feasible results. Metrics are gathered to measure the performance impact of the most-recent changes to the process. This may take some time. Once those metrics have been collected, a Client Checkpoint phase is performed. If successful, some or all of the changes are permanently integrated into the process. If there has been no process improvement, the changes might be backed out and further probative swim lanes planned and executed.

There may be cases where the feasible process changes may require significant changes on the part of the affected personnel. It is not uncommon for business rules to be changed to accommodate the process improvements. In those cases, the impact of the changes might be measured using simulation models before changing real-world processes.

Prototyping

When little of the solution is known, you can use a prototyping variation to APF. Prototyping is generally applied when most of the solution is known and all that remains to complete the solution is to choose from among a number of alternatives. But prototyping can also be used when the client is having trouble envisioning any solution. A quickly built iconic model is created. Discussions with the client are held in the hopes that the prototype will give the client better insight into a solution. Several cycles may be needed before a clearer picture of the solution emerges so that the standard integrative and probative swim lanes can be planned and executed.

Research & Development

While R&D projects generally use Extreme PMLC models, APF can also be used quite effectively with many R&D projects. As long as part of the solution is defined, APF can be used. If none of the solution is known, Extreme PMLC models are the better choice.

If the APF PMLC model is used, there are some minor variations that you can expect. The goal will remain fixed, but the solution may address only part of the goal. However, that part of the goal that the solution addresses will be the best that can be done within the time and budget constraints placed on the project. The question of whether or not the partial solution delivers acceptable business value must be answered.

Putting It All Together

One noticeable difference between the TPM approach and the APF approach is that APF is a thinking person's approach, whereas the TPM approach often tends to be the blind following of a recipe with the expectation that everything will be all right. For example, APF requires continuous and meaningful involvement on the part of the client. Clear joint ownership by the client and the team is built into APF. That is not the case with TPM approaches. The TPM approach can be followed with little or no involvement from the client.

APF is an exciting and invigorating approach to those projects that don't quite fit the mold of the traditional approach. We hope the brief introduction to APF presented to this point will encourage our colleagues to ponder what we have said and add their own take on APF. It is an idea whose time has come, and it should be taken seriously by the project-management community.

When it comes to starting an extreme project, you have learned that the good habits formed in TPM and APF carry over into xPM. There is no need to learn anything new in order to get an extreme project underway. The Project Overview Statement will be used here just as it is used in TPM and APF. You want to get approval to work on your project, and you have a selling job to do. You are armed with the POS as your best weapon regardless of the type of project to be undertaken.

Finally, the best advice we can give you when you are doing an extreme project is to be open-minded. The habits that you formed in traditional project management may have great application in extreme projects, but they might not. You will be called upon to be adaptive. Keep the goal of your extreme project in mind, and use or adapt whatever you can from your earlier experiences with traditional or adaptive projects.

You should now have a better understanding of how this unstructured xPM approach can, in fact, converge on the goal. The learning and discovery that take place in a cycle gives the client and the project team the information needed to rethink how to move forward in the next cycle. The decision to move forward is a collective decision made by the client with the advice of the project team.

The ability of the team and the client to decide how to move forward is heavily dependent upon their ability to reconsider the prioritization of functionalities. The learning that has taken place is the major contributor to their ability to reprioritize. That learning brings clarity to the final goal specification, and that clarity helps the client and the team to eliminate functionality that is out of scope with that now-clearer goal, as well as to identify functionality that is critical to the more clearly defined goal.

Discussion Questions

The following questions are posed for your use. Use them to test your understanding and potential application of the materials presented in the

chapter. If you are using this book for a course you are teaching, the questions will provoke good class discussion.

1. Suppose a project should have used a TPM approach, but used APF instead. Comment on what might be different. Would the TPM approach have produced a better outcome? Why or why not? Be specific.

2. Referring to the PDQ case study described in earlier chapters, what situation would allow you to embed an APF approach into a TPM approach? In other words, what conditions would you expect to see for that approach to be feasible? Give an example and be specific.

3. How does xPM differ from APF? Discuss their differentiating characteristics.

4. Can APF be used on an extreme project? Why, or why not? Be specific.

5. In the formation stages of a project, are there any distinct disadvantages to using APF over xPM for an extreme project? If so, identify them. In considering your answer, think about what is really known versus what may be only speculation, and how speculating might create problems.

6. Is APF or xPM more likely to waste less of the client's money and the team's time if the project is killed prior to completion? To answer the question, you have to consider when the decision to kill the project is made in APF versus in xPM projects, and what is known at the time the decision is made. Defend your position with specifics.

Chapter 8

APF in the Extreme

An extreme project is a complex, self-correcting venture in search of a desirable result.

—Doug DeCarlo, *ProjectWorld, Boston, 2000*

Extreme Project Management (xPM) projects are the most speculative and high-risk projects one could expect to undertake. At the start, the goal of an xPM project is only vaguely defined, so to talk about a solution is premature. What is needed is a flexible model that simultaneously discovers the specific goal and the solution to that goal. Stated another way, we are looking for a more definitive statement of a goal for which there is a feasible solution. This matched pair will be found through an iterative approach.

APF adapts to this type of project. The xPM version of APF is known as **INSPIRE**, which stands for **IN**itiate, **SP**eculate, **I**ncubate, and **RE**view. In this chapter, we will discuss just how APF adapts to xPM projects.

xPM and APF originated at about the same time, so it is difficult to say which is a variation of the other from a chronological point of view. In any case, xPM handles the situation where the goal is not clearly defined and therefore the solution cannot be defined either. On the continuum of project-management approaches, the traditional approach occupies the structured end, where there is the most clarity with respect to both the goal and the solution, while xPM is at the unstructured end, where there is the least clarity with respect to the goal and the solution. APF occupies the middle ground.

This chapter defines the extreme project, and gives a high-level overview of the four phases that constitute the xPM approach. It is a good starting point for the executive or manager who simply needs to become familiar with the xPM approach.

Defining an Extreme Project

Doug DeCarlo offers the following definition of an extreme project: "An extreme project is a complex, self-correcting venture in search of a desirable result."[1]

What does this definition tell us about extreme projects? Here are a few thoughts.

Extreme Projects Are Processes of Discovery

Rather than specifying a planned result at the outset of the project, these projects entail discovering a desirable result in the course of the project. In other words, the goal of the project is defined within the process of doing the project. Obviously, planning, whatever that means in the extreme-project situation, takes on a meaning quite different than in the traditional-project situation.

Extreme Projects Are Complex

Many business-to-business (B2B) and business-to-consumer (B2C) Web-development projects are best attempts to get the attention of customers, whether they are other companies or end users of the product or service. By their nature, these projects are characterized by speed and rapid change.

---

[1] Doug DeCarlo, presentation at ProjectWorld (Boston, 2000).

Extreme Projects Require a Creative Mindset and Approach

The traditional project manager would ask us to maintain focus and stay riveted to the plan in place to reach the goal of the project. The extreme project manager would ask us to maintain focus but to think outside the box.

Extreme Projects Are Learning Projects

Change is expected in the extreme project. In fact, change is embraced. Without it, the whole venture comes to a standstill. Along with change comes the process of discovery and learning. These are the hallmarks of the extreme project.

Extreme Projects Do Not Have Specified End Dates

At the highest level of definition, extreme projects are made up of continuous streams of versions. The completion of one version leads to the beginning of the next. Each version delivers value and meets the then-defined customer needs, but must quickly be replaced with the next version, which meets yet another set of needs discovered as a result of changing market conditions. In other words, they really never end. Within a particular version, an extreme project looks a lot like a prototyping project. It consists of an unspecified number of cycles, many of which are performed concurrently and independently of one another. Neither the number of cycles nor their lengths can be determined at planning time. To the traditional project manager, this looks like one big mess.

Extreme Projects Do Not Have Well-defined Goals

In fact, the extreme project does not have a goal in the sense that the traditional project manager expects. This isn't the result of ignorance on the part of the customer or the project manager. It is simply a statement of fact. While customers may have some vague notion of what they want, they do not know what it looks like and may not even recognize it if they see it. Defining extreme projects may not be much more than a guessing game between the seller and the buyer. The seller takes a best guess at what buyers will buy and builds and deploys, say, an online-based product or service to the Internet. If it works, that's great. If not, it's back to the drawing board for yet another version of the extreme project. The game is one of rapid response. Get it done and get it on the 'Net! Conventional wisdom and good risk management don't carry much weight in the e-business world in which we are trying to practice project management.

Extreme Projects Do Not Have Specified Task Lists

With no end date and no clear statement of the goal, it is no wonder that there is no task list from which to develop a network schedule, plan resources, and do all of those things we are used to as project managers.

Extreme Projects Do Not Follow Accepted Practices of Change Management

Forget about a formal change-management process in which the change request is documented, reviewed by the portfolio committee, and referred to the project manager for an impact statement and recommendations for action. Extreme projects can't wait that long. Another approach is needed.

Another Way to Think about Extreme Projects

These characteristics would seem to render the traditional approaches to project management largely ineffective. And, in fact, they do.

Before proceeding to tinker with or completely overhaul project management, a word of caution is required. It is clear that extreme projects are creative projects. The minute we start putting process and procedure in place to manage such ventures, we risk destroying any opportunity for creativity. That would totally undermine the nature of these projects. The litmus test will be whether we have put an extreme project management process in place while preserving the creative spirit in such projects.

Another way to envision extreme projects is given in the following sections.

High Speed

The types of projects that are suited to xPM are groundbreaking, innovative, critical to an organization's future, and otherwise very important to their sponsors. That means the results are wanted as soon as possible. Fast is good, and if you can perform quickly you will be around tomorrow to talk about it. Slow is bad, and if you are slow, you will be looking for something else to do with the rest of your life. Fast-to-market is a critical success factor in every extreme-project endeavor.

High Change

The uncertainty about the goal or the solution means that as the project is underway, learning and discovery will happen, just as in APF projects. However, it will happen with more regularity and frequency in xPM than in APF projects. The changes in an extreme project may completely reverse the direction of the project. We can envision cases where the changes might be to cancel the current project and start two or more projects based on the learning and discovery to date from the now-canceled project. For example, R&D projects are extreme projects, as a discovery in one cycle may cause the team and the client to move in a totally different direction in the next and later cycles. APF changes can be thought of as minor in comparison.

High Uncertainty

Because an xPM project is innovative and research-oriented, no one really knows what lies ahead. The direction chosen by the client team and the development team might be 180 degrees out of phase with what they should be doing, but no one knows that at the beginning of the project. Everyone is simply taking their best guesses. After all, that is the most anyone could reasonably expect. Furthermore, the time to complete an extreme project is not known. The cost to complete an extreme project is not known either. There will be a lot of trial and error. There will be a lot of false starts and killed projects. That is the nature of a world of high-uncertainty projects.

These characteristics will strike fear into the hearts of most, if not all, project managers. Some will shy away from such assignments. Make no mistake: Extreme projects are extremely challenging. Their failure rate is high. Many will be canceled before they are completed. For those that are successful, what they deliver may not at all reflect what it was originally thought they would deliver. In other words, the actual goal achieved may be quite different from the goal that was originally envisioned. That is the reality associated with extreme projects—and that is where we begin our investigation of how APF applies to them.

> **Note**
>
> The acid test for APF has been its successful application to even the most complex and poorly defined projects.

Extreme Project Life Cycle

By its nature, xPM is unstructured xPM (see Figure 8.1), and APF is a variation on the same theme—that learning and discovery moves the project forward. The idea here is an adaptation of the Flexible Project model introduced in 2000 by Doug DeCarlo in his eXtreme Project Management Workshop.[2] Recall that the difference between xPM and APF is that APF requires a clearly defined goal, whereas xPM does not. As Figure 8.1 illustrates, xPM consists of four phases that we call **IN**itiate, **SP**eculate, **I**ncubate, and **RE**view (INSPIRE).

xPM, like APF, is an iterative approach. xPM iterates in an unspecified number of short cycles (one- to four-week cycle lengths are typical) in search

---

[2] The Doug DeCarlo Group, http://www.dougdecarlo.com. See also Doug DeCarlo, *eXtreme Project Management: Using Leadership, Principles, and Tools to Deliver Value in the Face of Volatility* (San Francisco: Jossey-Bass, 2004).

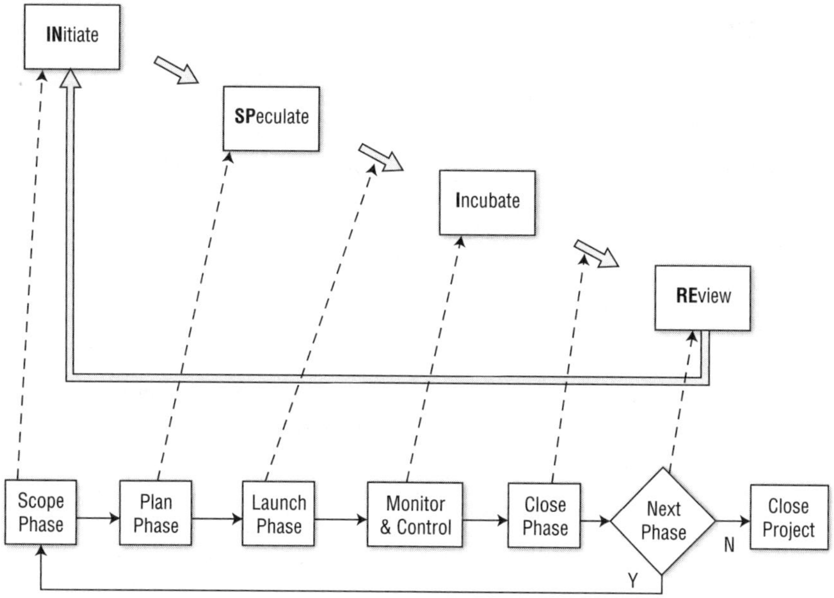

Figure 8.1
Extreme Project Management

of a solution that supports some form of a goal. The final goal will be some compromised statement of the original unclear goal statement. For example, "cure cancer" may have been the original goal statement, but the final goal statement might be "cure breast cancer," because the final xPM solution covers only that situation. It may find an acceptable solution, or it may be canceled before any solution is reached. It is distinguished from APF in that the goal is unknown, or at most, someone has a vague but unspecified notion of what the goal comprises. Such a client might say, "I'll know it when I see it." This isn't a new revelation to experienced project managers; they have heard such statements many times before. Nevertheless, it is their job to find the solution (with the client's help, of course).

Figure 8.1 is a graphical representation of the Project Management Life Cycle that we suggest defines the extreme project. The first thing to note in the bottom of the figure is that it is made up of cycles; there is an unspecified number of them. If you remove the feedback to the next version and consider the word "project" to be a replacement for "version," you will see the similarity to the linear PMLC.

There are four phases to this model: INitiate, SPeculate, Incubate and REview. The capitalization spells out **INSPIRE**, which is the name of the model. Following is a description of the four phases.

INitiate

The INitiate phase is a mixture of selling the idea, establishing the business value of the project, brainstorming possible approaches, forming the team, and getting everyone on board and excited about what they are about to undertake. It is definitely a time for team-building and creating a strong working relationship with the client.

Someone has an idea for a product or service and is proposing that a project be commissioned to investigate and produce it. Before any project will be launched, management must be convinced that it is an idea worth pursuing. The burden of proof is on the requestor. He or she must document and demonstrate that there is business value in the undertaking. The POS, which we used in both Traditional Project Management (TPM) and APF, is the documentation I recommend to sell the idea. There are some differences in the xPM version of the POS.

Defining the Project Goal

Unlike the goal of an APF project, the goal of an extreme project is not much more than a vision of some future state. Often, "I'll know it when I see it" is about the only statement of the project goal that can be made, given the vague nature of the goal as envisioned at the outset of the project. The xPM project has all the characteristics of an adventure where the destination is only vaguely defined. You have to understand that the goal of an extreme project unfolds along the journey. It is not something that you can plan to achieve; it is something that you and the client discover along the way. That process of discovery is exciting. It calls upon all of the creative juices the team and the client can muster. Contrast this to the project goal in an APF project. In APF, the goal is known; it's the solution that evolves as the project unfolds. In general, the client is more directive in xPM, while the team is relatively more directive in APF.

At this early stage, any definition of the project goal should take the form of that vision of the future. It would be good at this point to discuss how the user or customer of the deliverables will use the product or service. Don't be too restrictive, either. Keep your options open—or keep your powder dry, as one of my colleagues would say. Forming a vision of the end state is as much a brainstorming exercise as it is anything else. Don't close out any ideas that may prove useful later on.

xPM Project Overview Statement

An example will help ground some of these new ideas. Suppose the project is to find a way to prevent the common cold.

As discussed in earlier chapters, the OS is a critical document in both the TPM and APF approaches, and so it is as well in xPM projects. However, because the goal is known at the outset of TPM and APF projects but not at the start of xPM projects, there are some differences in the POS. These differences are best illustrated by way of example. Figure 8.2 presents the POS for a project to find a preventative for the common cold.

PROJECT OVERVIEW STATEMENT	Project Name Common Cold Prevention Project	Project No. 02-01	Project Manager Carrie deCure
Problem/Opportunity There does not exist a preventative for the common cold.			
Goal Find a way to prevent the occurrence of the common cold.			
Objectives 1. Find a food additive that will prevent the occurrence of the common cold. 2. Alter the immune system to prevent the occurrence of the common cold. 3. Define a program of diet and exercise that will prevent the occurrence of the common cold.			
Success Criteria The solution must be effective for persons of any age. The solution must not introduce any harmful side effects. The solution must be affordable. The solution must be acceptable to the FDA. The solution must be easily obtained. The solution must create a profitable business opportunity.			
Assumptions, Risks, Obstacles The common cold can be prevented. The solution will have harmful side effects.			
Prepared By Earnest Effort	**Date** 2-14-2009	**Approved By** Hy Podermick	**Date** 02-16-09

Figure 8.2
POS for the Project to Find a Preventative for the Common Cold

The following bulleted list looks at each of the elements of this xPM POS to illustrate the differences between this sort of POS and that used in a TPM or APF approach.

- **Problem/Opportunity.** Nothing unusual here. This is a very simple statement of a problem that has plagued health-care providers and moms since the dawn of civilization.

- **Goal.** This particular project is taking a calculated (or maybe wild) guess that a preventative for the occurrence of the common cold can be found. Unlike the goal statements in TPM and APF projects, there is no timeframe specified. That would make no sense for such a research project.

- **Objectives.** These objective statements identify broad directions the research effort will take. Notice that the format does not fit the S.M.A.R.T. characteristics defined in Chapter 3. In most cases, these objective statements provide some early guidance on the directions the team intends to pursue. Unlike in TPM and APF projects, these objective statements do not make up a necessary and sufficient set of objectives. Their successful completion does not assure goal attainment. In fact, some of them may be discarded based on learning and discovery in early cycles. Think of them as guideposts only. They set an initial direction for the project. Because the goal is not clearly defined, the objective statements cannot be expected to play the role they do in TPM and APF projects.

- **Success Criteria.** The goal statement might do just as well as any success criteria, so this part of the POS could be left blank. In this case, we have set bounds around the characteristics of an acceptable preventative.

- **Assumptions, Risks, Obstacles.** There is no difference between xPM, TPM, and APF when it comes to this section. The statements given in the example lean heavily toward assumptions. Having to make such assumptions happens to be the nature of this project.

Establishing a Project Time Box and Cost

As opposed to an APF project, an extreme project is not constrained by a fixed timeframe or cost limit. It is best to think of the xPM time and cost parameters as factors giving the project team guidance on what the client expectations are. This is much like having the client say, "I would like to see some results within X months, and I am willing to invest as much as $Y to have you deliver." The reality is that at each REview phase, a decision is made to continue or abort. That decision isn't necessarily tied to the time and cost parameters given earlier by the client. In fact, if there is exceptional progress toward a solution, the client may relax either or both of the parameters. Put another way, if the progress to date is promising, more time, money, or both may be put at the team's disposal.

Establishing the Number of Cycles and Cycle Length

In the beginning, short cycles are advisable. In the early cycles, new ideas are tested, and many will be rejected; proof of concept may be part of the first few cycles. The team should not be committing to complex activities and tasks early on. As the team gains a better sense of direction, cycle length may be increased. Specifying cycle length and the number of cycles up-front merely sets expectations as to when and how frequently the REview phases will take place. At each occurrence of a REview phase, cycle length and perhaps the number of cycles remaining may be changed to suit the situation. In an exploratory project, it would be a mistake to bind the team and the client to cycles that do not relate to the realities of the project. Remember that flexibility is the key to a successful xPM project.

Tradeoffs in the Scope Triangle

Despite the fact that xPM is unstructured, it is important that the priorities of the variables in the Scope Triangle be set. As project work commences and problems arise, which variables are the client and the team willing to compromise? As is discussed in Chapter 1, the five variables in a project are as follows:

- Scope
  - Quality
  - Cost
  - Time
- Resource availability

Which of these is least likely to be compromised? Which would you choose to compromise first, if the situation warranted? The answers depend on the type of project. For example, if the project involves conducting research to find a way to prevent the common cold, quality is the least likely to be compromised, and time might be the first to be compromised. But what if you knew that a competitor was working on the same project? Would time still be the first variable to compromise? Probably not. Cost might take its place, because time-to-market would be a critical success factor.

Scope is an interesting variable in extreme projects. Consider the common-cold example again. Hypothetically, what if you knew that the competition was also looking for a way to prevent the common cold and that being first to market would be very important? In an earlier cycle, suppose the team had discovered not a way to prevent colds, but a food additive that arrests the cold at whatever stage of development it happens to be at. In other words, the cold will not get worse than it is at the time the additive is taken. This early discovery also holds great promise to morph into the preventative that you are looking for, but you need time to explore it. You feel that getting the early result to market now may give your client a strategic barrier to entry, give the competition reason to pause, and buy you some time to continue toward the original goal. Therefore, scope is reduced in the current project, and the project is brought to a successful completion. A new project is commissioned to continue on the path discovered in the earlier project.

SPeculate

This phase defines the beginning of a new cycle, and always starts with a brainstorming session. The input will be either a blank slate or output from the preceding INitiate-SPeculate-Incubate-REview cycle. In any case, the project team, the client, and the final user of the product or service should participate in the brainstorming session. The objective of this session is to explore ideas and identify alternative directions for the next Incubate phase. Because an extreme project has a strong exploratory nature about it, no idea should be neglected. Several directions may eventually be pursued in parallel in the next cycle. Cycle length, deliverables, and other planning artifacts are defined in the SPeculate phase as well.

The word **speculate** in this context implies deep thinking, carrying out due diligence on several alternatives, choosing one or more of those alternatives, and then simply taking your chances. You should hear yourself saying, "I wonder if this would work?" That is what the SPeculate phase of xPM is all about.

Defining How the Project Will Be Done

The possibilities for an initial sense of direction for the team to take in the first cycle of an extreme project vary considerably. A good approach is to use the POS objective statements as a guide. The POS can be continuously updated to reflect the current view of the project, and its objective statements can serve as a guide to what will be done. In later cycles, the team and the client have the benefit of learning and discovery from the prior cycles. For the sake of discussion, let's treat those two situations separately. In this section, assume you are planning the first cycle. In some of the following sections, you will look at the SPeculate phase for the second and subsequent cycles.

Conditions of Satisfaction

We discussed the Conditions of Satisfaction in detail in Chapter 3 and will not repeat that discussion here. While the COS is a tool that produces a required deliverable in TPM and APF, its use in xPM is optional. COS loses its value as the goal becomes more and more elusive. If the client has only a vague idea of the goal, no amount of discussion around needs and deliverables will clarify the situation for either party. The other planning artifacts described in the text that follows may be more useful in the initial SPeculate phase.

If you choose to use the COS in your xPM project, think of it as more of a brainstorming tool. The project team and the client can investigate ideas en route to creating a list of what will be done in this cycle.

Scenarios, Stories, and Use Cases

The technical perfectionist would probably define these terms differently from one another, but for our purposes, they are synonymous. All three can be defined as descriptions of how a person might use the application. Because the application may be feature-rich, there can be, and usually will be, several such descriptions. If developed correctly, these descriptions will be exhaustive of how the application can be used. The descriptions can then be prioritized and assigned to the appropriate development cycles. There is no practical limit to the number of such descriptions that can be documented. In technology projects such as Web-site development, clients may be more comfortable telling you how they envision someone using the deliverable and what users can do at the Web site than they would be in trying to help you write functional specifications. The advantage of using scenarios, stories, and use cases is that the view you are building is from the user side, not from the technology side.

Prioritizing Requirements

Prioritization is the next step in the SPeculate phase. The collection of scenarios, stories, and use cases provides insight into the requirements the deliverable should meet. For the client, it is far easier to prioritize this collection than it is to prioritize the requirements themselves.

There are several ways to produce a prioritized list of the items in the collection. In Chapter 2, we discussed three such methods: forced ranking; must-haves/should-haves/nice-to-haves; and the Q-Sort. See Chapter 2 for details on those methods.

Following are approaches points to be considered when prioritizing.

1. There can be a great number of items in the collection; so many, in fact, that approaches like forced ranking are not practical. Forced ranking doesn't scale very well. A compromise approach might involve grouping the items based on their relationships to specific functions and then prioritizing between and within these groupings. The strategy here would be to assign all of the items that relate to a specific function to a sub-team for its consideration and development. Several sub-teams could be active in any given cycle.

2. Depending on how well the goal is understood, it might be wise to plan the initial SPeculate phase so that as many options and alternatives as possible can be investigated. The strategy here is to eliminate

those alternatives that show little promise earlier rather than later in the project. That allows more resources to be brought to bear on approaches that have higher probabilities of success.

3. Finally, where appropriate, prototypes might be considered as part or all of the first-cycle deliverables. Here the strategy is to prioritize items in the collection of functions without spending too much time developing the real deliverables. Getting the client familiar with the prototype may give sufficient information to allow not only a reduction in the number of items in the collection, but also prioritization of those items or functions that show promise. A good example is the typical B2C application. A prototype will show various ways a customer can interact with the application. Upon examination, clients will add to that list or delete from that list as they experience what the customer would experience when interacting with the application.

Think of the first cycle or two as exploratory in nature. The purpose is to discover directions that show promise so as to focus later cycles on them.

Identifying the First Cycle's Deliverables

Once the prioritization is done, it is time to decide how much of that prioritized list to bite off for the initial cycle. Remembering that you want shorter cycles in the early part of the project, limit the first cycle's deliverables to what you can reasonably accomplish in a week or two.

> **Note**
> By taking a limited-scope approach in the early cycle(s), you keep the client's interest up. That is important. APF follows the same strategy. Once the client has been fully engaged in the project, later cycles can be lengthened.

Because your team resources are limited, you have to face the question of depth versus breadth of deliverables. In other words, it might be better to extend the breadth to accommodate more functions by not delving deeply into any one function. Produce enough detail for each function in this initial cycle to get a sense of further direction for that function. You may learn from a shallow look at a function that it isn't going to be part of the end result. Taking a shallow look allows you to save labor that would have been spent on thoroughly examining a function that would later be discarded and to spend that effort on more-important work.

Making a Go/No-go Decision

Because the initial cycle can be exploratory, the sponsor must have an opportunity to judge the soundness of the initial cycle plan and decide whether it makes sense to proceed. It is entirely possible that the original idea of the client cannot be delivered with the approach taken in the first cycle, and thus the first cycle leads the client to a decision that the idea doesn't make sense after all. Some other approach may need to be taken, and that approach is not known at this time. A go/no-go decision point will occur at the end of each cycle. Decisions to stop a project are more likely to occur in the early cycles than in later cycles. One should expect later cycles to have the benefit of earlier results that suggest the project direction is feasible and should be continued.

Planning for Later Cycles

Later cycles will have the benefit of output from the previous REview phase to inform the planning activities that will take place in the SPeculate phase to follow. Each REview phase will produce a clearer vision and definition of the goal. That clearer vision translates into a redirection of the project, and in turn to a new prioritized list of deliverables for the coming Incubate phase. The newly prioritized deliverables list may contain deliverables from previous cycles that were not completed, deliverables that have not yet been part of an Incubate phase, and deliverables that are new to the project as a result of learning and discovery that occurred in the most recently completed Incubate phase. In any case, the revised prioritized deliverables list is taken into consideration as the team plans what it will do in the coming Incubate phase. It is now in the same position as it was in the very first SPeculate phase. What follows then is the assignment of deliverables to sub-teams, and the scheduling of the work that will be done and who will do it.

Incubate

The Incubate phase is the xPM version of the Cycle Build phase in APF. There are several similarities between the phases and some differences as well. Consider the following points:

- Even though the Incubate phase has a prioritized list of deliverables that are to be produced in this cycle, xPM still must maintain the spirit of exploration. It is a learning and discovery experience, and mid-cycle corrections may arise from that exploration.

- APF also benefits from learning and discovery as it proceeds with the cycle plan, but it does not vary from the plan. The learning and discovery are inputs into the client checkpoint; that is where plan revisions take place.

These points are an important distinction between xPM and APF.

Sub-teams, working in parallel, execute the plan developed in the previous SPeculate phase. The environment has to be very open and collaborative for this phase to be successful. Teams should be sharing ideas and cross-fertilizing discoveries and learnings. This is not a time to just execute a plan; it is a time for exploration and dynamic interchange. Mid-phase corrections with the collaboration of the client are likely as the sub-teams learn and discover together. New ideas and redirection or clarification of the goal are likely to come from these learning and discovery experiences as well.

Assigning Resources

The Incubate cycle begins with assignment of team members to each of the deliverables prioritized for this cycle. The assignment should take place as a team exercise. That team involvement is important because of the exploratory nature of xPM cycles. Team members need to express their interest in one or more deliverables and also share their ideas with their fellow team members. The assignment process can also be an opportunity for team members to recruit others who share their interests and would like to develop a deliverable with them. The project manager should not pass up the opportunity to create synergy among team members with similar interests, as well as between sub-teams that will be working in parallel on different deliverables. Any opportunity to create a collaborative work environment only increases the team's chances of success.

Establishing a Cycle Plan

With the sub-teams in place and with their assignments made, the sub-teams can plan how they will produce the deliverables assigned to them. Deciding how a team produces the deliverables is done in exactly the same manner as was discussed in Chapter 3: How to Plan an APF Cycle. In fact, many of the same tools discussed in Chapter 3 can be used to help establish a cycle plan here with equal effectiveness. For example, Chapter 3 presents the cycle plan as a time-sequenced whiteboard diagram showing a day-by-day schedule of what is going to be done and who is going to do it. The same type of plan can be used in xPM.

However ...

Never forget that there are some differences to a cycle plan in xPM. In xPM, the team has to be ready for changes at any time. Exploration will often bring the team to a point where a change of direction makes sense. When these situations arise, the team needs to collaborate with the client and decide how to go forward.

Collaboratively Producing Deliverables

Collaboration is the very essence of xPM. Collaboration among sub-teams must occur. I wrote earlier in the chapter about the exploratory nature of the xPM project. Because the project is exploratory, no one has a lock on the solution. Even the goal is somewhat elusive. That means the goal and the solution can be attained only through a solid team effort—a collaborative effort. There is a great deal of similarity between xPM projects and brainstorming. One idea may not be of much value when taken individually. However, combine it with one or more other ideas, and suddenly there is value. A statement from Estill I. Green, vice president of Bell Telephone Laboratories, is relevant here: "Clearly no group can as an entity create ideas. Only individuals can do this.

A group of individuals may, however, stimulate one another in the creation of ideas."[3]

REview

The REview phase is very similar to the Client Checkpoint phase in APF. All the learning and discovery from the just-completed Incubate phase are brought together in another brainstorming session, where these types of questions are answered:

- What did we learn?
  - What can we do to enhance goal attainment?
  - What new ideas arose that should be pursued?
- What should we do in the next cycle?

The most important decision is whether or not the project will continue. This is a client decision. Have the results to date met expectations? Is the project moving toward an acceptable solution? These answers will determine whether the project will continue to the next cycle or be cancelled. APF and xPM share this go/no-go decision point at the completion of each cycle. APF is less likely to result in a cancellation because so much more is known about the solution. xPM, on the other hand, is so exploratory and research-based that cancellations are far more likely.

Each cycle of an xPM project ends with a review of the just-completed Incubate phase. This takes place in a meeting attended by the client and the project team. The purpose of the REview phase is to reflect on what has just happened and what learning and discovery have taken place. The output is a definition of the next cycle's activities.

Applying Learning and Discovery from the Previous Cycle

Early in the sequence of cycles, the client and the team should expect significant findings and major redirection of further efforts. As the project moves

---

[3] Quoted in Lewis D. Eigen and Jonathan P. Siegel, *The Manager's Book of Quotations* (New York: Amacom, 1989).

into later cycles, the changes should diminish in scope, because the project team should be converging on a more clearly defined goal and an acceptable solution to reach it.

Note

This part of the xPM process differs from APF because in APF the goal has always been clearly defined; it is the solution that becomes clearer with each passing APF cycle.

Revising the Project Goal

The first order of business is for the client and the project team to revisit the goal statement from the prior REview phase. Ask the following questions:

- What has happened in the just-completed Incubate phase?
  - What new information do we have?
  - What approaches have we eliminated?
  - What new discoveries suggest changes in goal direction and definition?
- Are we converging on a more clearly defined goal?

Revision of the project goal is an important step and must not be treated lightly. The client and the team need to come to consensus on the new goal statement, then update the POS with the new goal statement.

Reprioritizing Requirements

The second order of business is for the client and the project team to revisit deliverables and requirements. The following questions should be asked here:

- How does the new goal statement impact the deliverables list?
  - Should some items be removed?
  - Should new items be added?
- How is the functionality embedded within the new goal statement impacted?

The answers to these questions guide the client and the project team in reprioritizing the new requirements. They then update the POS to reflect the changes in the objective statements.

Making the Go/No-go Decision for Next Cycle

Will there be a next SPeculate-Incubate-REview cycle? The question leading to that answer could be: Are we converging at an acceptable rate on a clearly defined goal and an acceptable solution? The client will consider this question in the context of the money and time already spent. Does it make business sense to continue this project? The updated POS is input into this decision.

A Variation of an Extreme Project: The Emertxe Project

On the project landscape (Figure I.4 in the Introduction), this is the quadrant where the goal is not known but a solution is. While that may sound like nonsense, it is a legitimate type of project, and these projects do in fact occur quite frequently. Let me explain by way of a few examples.

First is the application of Radio Frequency IDentification (RFID) technology. Early in the product-development history of RFID, Wal-Mart asked its technology people whether there was an application of RFID technology for its warehousing operations. RFID was the solution; its application was the goal. It turned out that RFID could be used in the Wal-Mart warehousing operation, but the reliability of the technology was not yet accurate enough to be of business value. Wal-Mart was the driving force in the further development of RFID, which now is used routinely in all types of warehousing operations.

Second, and among the simplest of Emertxe project types, is the evaluation of applying software systems to business problems. Say a new Human Resource Management System (HRMS) is introduced into the market. The question for your company is, "Can this HRMS solve our professional and career-development problems and support our resource constrained portfolio management process needs?" HRMS is the solution; meeting your HR needs is the goal.

Third, and among the most complex of Emertxe project types, is the area of drug research and development. Suppose a team of researchers travels to the Himalayas to investigate a claim that people there have the longest average lifespans of any people on earth, despite the harsh conditions in which they live. On reaching their destination, the scientists are greeted by a village elder who claims to be 112 years old and attributes his longevity to the juice and pulpy extract from a plant that grows only at these elevations. That juice is a major part of his morning meal, and has been since he was a toddler. Many others in the village make the same claim. So we have this mysterious juice (the solution), and the question of whether it has medicinal value that can be successfully produced and marketed back home. The entire field of drug research and development is populated with these types of very high risk projects.

For all of these example projects, the ultimate question is business value. No matter what goal can be defined to which the solution can be effectively applied, that solution must deliver some level of business value. If the project delivers a $1,000 solution to a $100 problem, you haven't produced any business value. Obviously, an Emertxe project can be a very high risk project. When you start with a solution and have to find a problem it solves, the solution must deliver business value in solving the problem.

Comparing xPM and MPx PMLC Models

xPM and MPx projects are quite different and quite similar too. I like to think of their major difference as a reversal of the timeline. An xPM project proceeds from goal to solution discovery; an MPx project proceeds from solution to goal discovery, so the timelines are the reverse of one another. So, if you haven't already guessed, their names are the reverse of one another. (Please pardon my liberties with the language.)

MPx and xPM projects also share some remarkable similarities. Both models are iterative. With each iteration, the hope is that the projects are converging on a goal-solution combination that will deliver business value.

In the case of an xPM project the goal drives the identification of a solution, while in the MPx project the solution drives the identification of a goal. In both projects, the goal and the solution change in tandem with each iteration, and ideally converge toward a deliverable that has business value. The INSPIRE method can be used for both types of projects.

Putting It All Together

We have seen that with some minor reinterpretations, APF can be adapted to xPM projects. The critical difference between APF and xPM is in APF the goal is clear, while in xPM it is not. In APF, therefore, the solution converges to satisfy the goal. In xPM both the goal and the solution converge to alignment. The APF approach can work equally well in an xPM project.

Discussion Questions

The following questions are posed for your use. Use them to test your understanding and potential application of the materials presented in the chapter. If you are using this book for a course you are teaching, the questions will provoke good class discussion.

1. If you have a project that fits the conditions of an xPM project, why might you want to use an APF approach?

2. Are there any differences between the characteristics of an APF team and an xPM team?

Chapter 9

APF Frequently Asked Questions

I like people who can do things. When Edward and I struggled in vain to drag our big calf into the barn, the Irish girl put her finger into the calf's mouth and led her in directly.

—*Ralph Waldo Emerson, American essayist and poet*

Despite my best efforts to make APF intuitive, it doesn't always work. Questions about just understanding the concepts and principles always seem to come up. Sometimes it's my fault, and sometimes just a minor clarification is needed. In practicing APF, the same thing happens: A situation arises that doesn't seem to be covered by the APF guidelines, and it needs an explanation.

APF Is a Work in Process

APF was first used in my consulting practices in 2001, and has been made public only in the last four years. It is still enjoying its formative and maturing years, and in need of more testing and use. Feedback is critical at this point in its maturation. If you are using APF and have some suggestions, by all means pass them to me at rkw@eiicorp.com. I'll make sure your suggestions make it into the public arena.

For now, here are a number of questions that have come up in client engagements and numerous public presentations all over the world.

As clients and colleagues embark on APF projects for the first time, they take a leap of faith. Naturally, questions arise. So far, APF has held up to the promise of 100-percent success all the time. Following are the more significant of the questions I have received. I pass my responses on to you because you will probably have the same questions. If your questions are not answered in this chapter, let me hear from you at rkw@eiicorp.com.

Note

APF is a didactic framework. If you don't continually ask the tough questions and seek out the answers, you will never find a solution.

You Mean I'm Going to Ask My Clients for $1M and One Year, and I Can't Tell Them What They Will Get?

This is by far the most frequently asked question. This bothers senior managers as well as traditional project managers because it flies in the face of conventional thinking. APF requires a whole new mindset—one that stands in stark contrast to the mindset required for Traditional Project Management projects. One may be tempted to believe that this is a major weakness of APF. It isn't, and I'll explain why.

In a TPM project, scoping is defined as part of project initiation, and the client is given an estimate of the time and cost to produce the deliverables as part of that process. That would probably be okay were it not for scope-change requests that come up as clients learn that what they really need is different from what they originally wanted. The final result can be a patchwork of changes and fixes. If that isn't enough trouble, the quality of the final deliverables becomes compromised in order to accommodate the many changes. Much of the cost and time invested in planning and developing the original scope is wasted, as it is redone several times in order to accommodate scope changes. In the end the client is reasonably satisfied at best and the project ends.

Let's look at what would happen if the project were approached as an APF project. First of all, the APF Project Management Life Cycle (PMLC) model is designed for a project that is looking for the solution to a critical but unsolved problem, or for a way to effectively take advantage of an untapped business opportunity. In both cases, the final deliverables cannot be known at the beginning of the project. They can only be discovered during the execution of the project. Yes, it's true that you can't tell exactly what you will deliver at the end of the project; but whatever it is it will be the best that could have been delivered given the collective wisdom of yourself and your client and within the constraints of the time and money invested by the client. You would know this because you and the client would participate in the decisions at every client checkpoint. If there were a better solution and your project did not discover it, the discovery of that solution would have to wait for divine intervention or for someone to come along with insight you and the client do not currently possess. It might be that the solution you deliver wouldn't be all that's expected, but it would be the best that could have been found.

The Nature of an APF Project

Yes, it's true that you can't tell exactly what you will deliver at the end of the project; but whatever it is it will be the best that could have been delivered given the collective wisdom of yourself and your client and within the constraints of the time and money invested by the client.

Second of all, the time spent creating a detailed plan using TPM would not be spent using the APF approach; this time would instead be allocated to development. The only parts of the solution implemented would be parts known to be included in the end result. No reworking of plans means no waste of time and budget on useless or unnecessary development. That time and money would be spent on actual development of final deliverables. What this boils down to is the spending of time and money on the best business value that you and the client, in a collaborative partnership, could identify.

Remember: The project was complex, its solution was not known at the outset, and reaching an acceptable solution was critical to the organization. You didn't have any choice. The project had to be done and done in the best way possible. There really wasn't any alternative other than APF.

It is critical that clients understand this, accept it, and do the very best they can in participating in the hunt for an acceptable solution. Clearly, their meaningful involvement is a critical success factor.

Can the Clients Increase the Budget or Deadline?

Of course they can. APF is such that at any client checkpoint, the progress to date and business justification for the project should be revisited. A decision to change time or cost constraints can then be made based on the best information available. You do not have this luxury in a TPM project, because there is no business-value consideration on which to base such a decision.

In an APF project, time and budget can be increased or decreased, and even project termination is possible. Adding time or money makes sense if the project is converging on a solution deemed to be better than expected, but the time or money previously allocated wasn't sufficient to achieve that solution. The decreasing-resources side of the picture isn't pretty, but it is the part of APF that separates it from every traditional approach and most agile approaches. If the current solution isn't converging on an acceptable end result, the client should pull the plug. Save the unspent money and time for a fresh approach.

Terminating the solution search permanently is not an option when the successful completion of the project is critical to the enterprise. If the current approach isn't showing some results early on, cancel the current project and come at it from a different vantage point. This is not a sign of failure. It is a sign that clear business-value thinking and client focus are the important factors.

What if You Can't Get the Client to Be Meaningfully Involved?

This is a tough situation you are going to have to face. In my earlier days, I might have said I would find some work-around and pursue the project without the meaningful involvement of the client. Now, with several years experience to draw on, I just wouldn't do the project until the client was willing to be meaningfully involved. I've tried both strategies and had a few successes even without strong client involvement, but left a lot of blood on the trail behind me. I often won the battle but lost the war. In general, neither strategy (proceeding without the client, or refusing to proceed at all) met with my satisfaction.

Now that I have a few decades of experience behind me, I tend to follow a more-diplomatic route. The success of the project is critical to the continued operation of the business, and it is beyond your authority to cancel or postpone it. On the assumption that the project will go ahead, what would you, could you, or should you do?

Of prime importance is to find out what barriers to meaningful involvement exist in the mind of the client. There could be many, as the following discussion illustrates.

The Client Is Hesitant to Get Involved in a Project that Is Technical because of Prior Bad Experiences

If this is the problem, the technical professionals have inherited some significant baggage from their grandfathers' time. In those days, the customer wasn't really encouraged to get Involved. The operant approach was to just get the requirements document written and approved, then turn the project over to the development and delivery teams. The prevailing attitude was that the client would only slow the process down. Fortunately, that attitude hasn't survived, but the memory of it persists. Some clients are much more comfortable "minding their own business" and leaving technology to the technical folks. Such clients get involved only when the development and delivery team ask them to. This type of client's attitude is, "That's a technical project and I don't know anything about technology. Just show me the results when you are done."

The burden is on the project team to change this attitude. Depending on the particular circumstances the client is facing, different initiatives on the part of the project team can be employed. Workshops, seminars, site visits, conferences, and other venues have been productive.

The Client Team Doesn't Understand APF

Training, training, and more training are called for here. There are three models I have used, and all have been successful. Which you choose depends on what the client team needs and how best to interact with that team. The three models are as follows.

Commercial Off-the-shelf (COTS) Facilitator-led Training

This option is included here mostly for the sake of completeness, but it has worked on occasion. If the clients tend to be proactive and like to work things out for themselves, this type of training might give them enough of a push to overcome their hesitancy. An outside facilitator is the critical success factor. Having one tends to create safer ground for the client than if an internal facilitator is used. The outside facilitator can offer a fresh perspective that an insider can't. If the facilitator can field questions with specific answers applicable to the attendees' environment, it should work.

Custom-designed Instructor-led Training

This will cost more than COTS training because of the time needed to understand the environment, conduct a needs analysis, and modify the course of training accordingly. It does have the added benefit that the content is to-the-point and not wasteful of attendees' time and money. The majority of my training engagements have been of this type. They tend to have a consulting component as well, and deliver maximum business value for the costs involved.

Real-time Consultant-led Training

This is an interesting variation on training delivery. In this variation, the training is embedded in the execution of the project. The project itself becomes a case study, if you will, in how to conduct an APF project. Internal consultants can be most effective, because they already understand the environment. If an outside consultant is used, this is obviously the most expensive of the three models. Remember, an APF project is complex and its success is critical to the organization. Failure is not an option. I have used this model three times as an outside consultant and twice as an internal consultant, and been successful in all five. This variation is the most expensive of the three, but it is worth the added cost.

The Client Team Isn't Comfortable Suggesting Changes because of Prior Bad Experiences

If the clients' experiences have been mostly with TPM projects, they will have been conditioned to the idea that change is not welcomed. In an APF project the reverse is the case: Change is expected. So some unlearning will have to take place.

I have two suggestions for dealing with this type of situation. The first is to lead by example. Even if your ideas are not the best, they may encourage the client to begin participating. The second, and one that has worked well for me, is to question the client at each checkpoint. Your objective here is to create conversation with the client and ferret out the client's ideas for solution improvement. There will be a positive learning experience here that will benefit this and succeeding APF projects with this client. For this to be successful, clients have to be comfortable, and not feel like they are being given the third degree or being asked to defend their position.

The Client Team Doesn't Understand (or Won't Accept) Its Role

You can always overcome lack of understanding with training. If you have had previous successful experiences with other clients that this client can relate to, try getting testimonials or direct input from those satisfied clients. Having clients accept their role is absolutely essential to every APF project. I strongly advise that you assure yourself of their role acceptance before you embark on an APF project with them.

The Client Team Is Very Passive and Seems Uninvolved in Team Meetings

You have to get to the root cause immediately. Training, workshops, interviews, discussions with satisfied clients, and the use of mediators are all strategies I have used effectively in these situations.

The Client Team Won't Risk Making a Bad Decision

This may be part of the organization's culture. The client needs to understand that you are both in it together, and both will take credit or blame for whatever happens. Assure clients that to the best of your ability you won't let them choose the wrong course of action. You will have done your homework and presented them with only feasible alternatives. Even though they will have the most important responsibilities in the project, you are not hanging them out to dry.

The Project Team Won't Accept the Client's New APF Role

Project teams are accustomed to taking the lead in their projects. That is not what happens in an APF project. There is joint ownership, with the client being the default decision-maker.

How Much Planning Do You Do Up Front for the Contents of the First Few Cycles?

As little as possible. The secret to APF planning is to try *not* to guess the future. You can't know the future, so don't waste any time on it, and certainly don't put any planning effort into it. Stick with the artifacts you know will be in the end result and put your planning effort into those. These will be cycle-length plans (one or two weeks), and should be fairly simple.

As for APF planning tools, I prefer and strongly suggest the use of low-tech tools over high-tech tools. A one- or two-week planning effort doesn't need an automated tool. Using such a tool is like killing mosquitoes with sledgehammers. Whiteboards, marking pens, and sticky notes work just fine. I have successfully managed $5 million, three-year APF projects with nothing more than these tools. And these are long APF projects! Tools like MS Project are terrific and they have their place—but not in APF. I always remind my clients that if you establish a project plan using an automated tool, then you have to maintain that plan as part of managing the project. Ask yourself whether the added overhead is worth it.

What if the Team Is Resistant to APF?

Get a new team! Seriously, introducing APF into a TPM development environment is challenging. As project manager for the development team, you will need to sell APF. Out of many APF projects, I've had only one occasion when such resistance arose. I conducted a high-level workshop before any work was done, and then conducted mini-workshops in parallel with the project. That got the job done, but there were still some laggards on the development team. The architects had the biggest problem adjusting. They were purists, and felt they needed to have all the information up-front so they could get everything done in one pass. They just had to get used to the idea that that doesn't happen in an APF project. Fortunately, I had good credibility with them, and they gave me room to work. Even after this first APF project was completed, I knew it would take a few more projects before I would win them over fully.

Can a Distributed Team Use APF? How?

Agile project management practices strongly encourage having a colocated team, and for good reason: Having the team members within physical sight of one another is the foundation of a creative environment because it fosters immediate feedback and discussion of ideas. Not having that condition can be a major obstacle in your search for that elusive solution or way to exploit an untapped business opportunity.

What if the team can't be colocated, but the project is clearly an APF project? You use APF, of course. This will be as real test of its adaptability and a real test of your ability as a project manager to make APF work. I know APF works in a distributed environment, because one of the early APF projects I managed had a team of 35 technical staff spread out all over the globe. Twelve time zones separated team members from one another. The secret to success here is good and open communications. Here is how we managed communications in this project (the project on which I based the Kamikazi Software Development Company case study):

- Daily project-team meetings were 15-minute teleconferences. All other project meetings had timed agendas with meeting materials distributed ahead of time.

- Meeting times were adjusted to share the scheduling inconveniences as equally as possible.

- All team leaders gave status reports (on schedule, ahead of schedule, behind schedule) only for tasks open for work.

- If a team leader was behind schedule, we discussed when they would get back on schedule and whether they needed help.

- All requests for help or offers of help were discussed outside of the project-team meetings.

- Problem solving or issues resolution were discussed outside of the project-team meetings and involved only the affected parties.

- Clients were routinely invited to all project-team meetings.

- Team leaders posted their status for access by all project-team members.

- No decisions were made or action items scheduled in daily project-team meetings.

As it happens, these same guidelines are used for project-team meetings when the project team is colocated. APF is truly adaptive.

Besides these operational matters, there is the deliverables aspect of an APF project. First of all, the swim lanes, whether they be integrative or probative, should be independent of one another. Time-zone differences can wreak havoc on the project schedule. I have also experienced situations where time zones can be worked to advantage. For example, at 6 p.m. EST, I can e-mail the description of a problem to a team member in Mumbai, where it is 4 a.m. the next day. He can begin working on it at the start of his workday. He can then forward any progress on finding a solution back to me at the end of his workday in Mumbai, which will be about 8 a.m. EST, the start of my next workday.

Can Part of a Project Use APF? How?

Yes. Refer to Chapter 7: Adapting APF for details on how to do this. It is fairly straightforward to integrate an APF component into either a Linear or an Incremental PMLC model.

Do You Have to Worry about Micro-management?

Getting senior management used to the APF creative environment and how they should operate within it will be a challenge. Burn charts and Earned Value Analysis are examples of metrics they are used to seeing in TPM project reports, but these are not APF metrics. APF metrics tend to be trend-type metrics (changes in the number of probative swim lanes compared to the number of integrative swim lanes over the history of the project, for example). Even these metrics have different interpretations depending on the status of the solution and how far you have journeyed into the life cycle of the project. The best management strategy for senior managers is to do whatever they can to facilitate and support the APF project team and trust the team to make the best business decision it can. Beyond that, management should stay out of the way and let the process happen!

How Do You Implement APF in an Organization Heavily Invested in TPM?

There are only three strategies I can recommend. I have had direct experience with or knowledge of all three, and with proper planning and leadership, they work!

Bottom-up Implementation

If you have one or more respected project managers who would fall on their swords for APF, a bottom-up approach can be made to work. I have a colleague who uses this approach, but in a very passive way. She uses APF religiously on every project she is assigned to manage for which APF is appropriate. She does nothing overt to promote APF, but rather depends totally on showing its power by way of example. Her success rate exceeds that of her colleagues by a substantial amount. She says nothing about how she does it. Her success speaks for itself in all reports that compare the performance of the 20 project managers in her Project Management Office. At some point in time her fellow project managers can't resist, and ask her how she is so successful while they aren't. Her answer blows them away! She tells me that others are beginning to adopt some of her suggestions. So she has planted the seeds of APF. In time they will grow.

Another bottom-up strategy is to choose two projects as demonstration projects for APF. Because of the nature of APF projects, this is a high-risk strategy. You want the projects to be unqualified successes, or you will bury any chances for APF in your organization. I would look for these demonstration projects in departments suffering a lot of pain due to their project-failure rates.

Top-down Implementation

If you have a sponsor whose leverage, credibility, sales ability, and power in the organization are without question, then a top-down approach can be made to work. That sponsor could be the CIO, the VP of Product Development, the CFO, or any other C-level executive. The sponsor has to sell APF to the organization and appoint you the project manager for the APF implementation project. This is your chance, and it will come only once. I would not use demonstration projects in this situation. Rather, I would appoint a representative task force staffed by project managers of all skill and experience levels. The task force should include resource managers and key client representatives as well. The members should all have credibility in their business units, because you want the deliverables from their efforts to be widely accepted in the organization.

The CEO Says, "Do It!"

This won't happen very often, so consider yourself blessed if it does. You have been given a lot of power, so don't abuse it. The task-force approach is still my recommendation. Keep the CEO and other C-level executives involved through a strong communications program. As part of that communications program, include frequent open-invitation presentations on APF and your version in particular. Seek broad input, and make sure you provide feedback on all ideas received.

Putting It All Together

I think it is important to keep asking questions. As I wrote earlier, APF is a work-in-progress. I'm still discovering opportunities for improvement, and I built APF. You should experience the same. Ask me, and I'll do my best to answer you.

Chapter 10

Taking Stock

At this writing, APF is less than 10 years old. Its development has been an exciting and challenging journey. The journey continues. The learning and discovery continue. I'm encouraged by the feedback I've received, by my own experiences using APF, and by my clients that have added APF to their Project Management Life Cycle model portfolio. Their testimonials lead me to the conclusion that I am on the right track.

APF is a work-in-process. Designing and building the APF PMLC model is itself an APF project. APF is new. APF is exciting. APF does not waste your time or your money. APF is the approach that will address many of your concerns about project failure, cost overruns, missed schedules, and other events that are impairing the successful conduct of your business activities.

My colleagues had a chance to review APF long before I introduced it to the public, and they felt that at least 70 percent of the projects they encounter today would benefit from using APF instead of either the TPM or xPM approaches. I thank them for their confidence in APF even though it is a work-in-process. As I continue to experience its use with my clients, I will undoubtedly find improvements and enhancements that will provide even more payback to my clients.

Note

APF is a work-in-process. Designing and building the APF PMLC model is itself an APF project.

I am taking a bold step forward, and I know that it is in the right direction. The bottom line is that APF works very well on the project types for which it was designed (process design and improvement and new-product development), and many project types (such as IT systems design and development) for which it was not designed. It completely fills a void left by current agile project management models, which focus almost exclusively on systems-development projects.

Organizational Environment

To successfully incorporate APF into the organization's portfolio of PMLC models requires a cultural change and an open-style management approach. The culture must support a creative environment. The new management style must be facilitative. It must remove every barrier and obstacle possible so teams are free to move in directions that make sense to them rather than being limited by the need for compliance with the organization's processes and procedures. This means that a high level of trust must be placed in project teams. At the same time, the client team and the developer team must be held accountable.

Making Choices

You don't choose APF just because you like it. You choose it because the characteristics of the project, your organizational environment, your human-resource skill and competency profile, your client's willingness to participate, and market conditions all suggest that APF is the best fit, and maybe the only fit, among PMLC models. From my colleagues, I have heard that some companies use agile PMLCs exclusively; in one case, Scrum is the PMLC model of choice for all projects. I'd like to hear the rationale for that exclusivity, because it simply doesn't seem to make any sense. If that organization really does use Scrum for every project, it must have only senior-level developers who are colocated, and every client must be able to step up to the bar and assume the required Product Owner role. I doubt such an organization exists.

Prioritization Rules

The rules for prioritizing will be different for every organization. The more commonly considered factors will be business value, risk, technological complexity, and effort to implement.

Value of the Project Landscape Model

My project-landscape model (see Figure I.4 in the Introduction) is based on two variables, **goal** and **solution;** and two values for those goals, **clear** or **not clear.** I guess my Polish heritage and my drive for simplicity and intuitiveness led me to this model. It works, and that's really all that is important. It is timeless and will continue to work into perpetuity. I am not aware of a more-intuitive or robust way to classify projects when the purpose of the classification is to choose a best-fit PMLC model. The known project-management approaches—linear, incremental, iterative, agile, and extreme—fit this landscape perfectly. The known systems-development models also fit this landscape perfectly. I believe my approach will be proven to provide a logical structure for PMLC model selection where none existed before. That is critical to any attempt to developing an effective project-management discipline.

The Current State of APF

APF has come a long way in its journey to maturity, but there is still a long way to travel.

What Have We Done?

In terms of this book, we've reached the end of this adventure. If you have stayed the course, I want to thank you for your continuing interest. You now have another arrow in your quiver.

APF is a new and refreshing approach to a class of projects that heretofore did not fit very well with the available approaches. The primary reason for the lack of fit was the absence of any process requirement that the client be meaningfully involved with the project from inception. We have discussed the critical importance of that involvement, and you have clearly seen the role of the client throughout the life cycle of the APF project. You have come to appreciate the reasons why in an APF project the client is really the pilot and the project manager the navigator. Together, the client and the project manager form a project-manager "mind meld"—as the co-managers of their APF project, they are of one mind in their expectations, enthusiasm, and commitment to the project. They share equally in success or failure. This may seem idealistic to you, but it is the reality of successful APF projects. If we expect to have a positive impact on project success, we need some outside-the-box thinking. APF is not a silver bullet, but it is a fix for many of the problems that have plagued project teams and their clients.

In looking back over the material we've covered, I want to come back to the six core values of APF, first discussed in Chapter 1:

1. Client-focused
2. Client-driven
3. Incremental Results Early and Often
4. Continuous Questioning and Introspection
5. Change Is Progress to a Better Solution
6. Don't Speculate on the Future

Now that you have an understanding of what APF is all about, it makes sense to look at some details for each of the core values.

1. Client-focused

If business outcomes and business value are what sold upper management on your project, it makes sense to me that we should then evaluate the success or failure of the project on its ability to deliver on those promises. I am amazed at how many projects do not do that. In post-implementation review after post-implementation review, no check is made of whether or not the project delivered on those promises. Some senior managers have even told me: "It doesn't matter. The project is over and I've got other pressing projects that are already behind schedule."

Client focus is pervasive through the entire APF project life cycle. This is most evident in the task of prioritizing functionalities. The client is responsible for those decisions, with the support of the project team. Prioritization decisions will be based on the business value the client assigns to each piece of functionality. It is the responsibility of the project manager to keep the client focused on feasible choices.

2. Client-driven

The client is on the hook for delivering on promised business results, and one way or the other the client is paying for the project. The client must be in charge of the direction the project takes and decisions to continue or abort the project. This calls for much more client involvement than most project managers are used to. They have to view their role as a facilitative one, and to support the client all along the way. Remember, the client is the pilot, and the project manager is the navigator.

3. Incremental Results Early and Often

We already know from our prototyping experiences that once the client has demonstrated interest in the project, we have to show results quickly. Prototyping is a way to provide that quick response, which is why so many tools have been created to make fast response possible. APF supports early results. In an APF project, the early cycles are short cycles. That makes fast response possible, and helps sustain the energy and excitement that we have cultivated in our clients regarding the project.

4. Continuous Questioning and Introspection

The heart and soul of an APF project is the relationship that is established between the project manager and the client. Here is where all of the guards must come down, and the client and the project manager must learn to work as one. So strong a relationship has never been promoted in any other project-management approach I am familiar with, but you now know that it is essential for APF project success. It makes for better decisions. "What," "where," "who," and "when" questions should be courageously asked and candidly answered. This is not the place for playing political games or trying to get "one up" on the other party. Being honest and open is the very essence of the core values of APF.

5. Change Is Progress to a Better Solution

The frequency of change over the life of an APF project is a good indicator of tempo and convergence toward an acceptable solution. It tells us that learning and discovery are taking place, and that the client is meaningfully engaged with the team. It's a good sign in an APF project when change occurs frequently in the early cycles and trends toward less frequency as the project moves further into the cycles. I find it interesting that in a TPM project, change is viewed as the enemy. It sends a signal that the clients really didn't know what they wanted at the beginning of the project and are only now learning what they need. Change in a TPM project upsets the plan, the schedule, and creates havoc with resource managers. In an APF project, on the other hand, change is expected and welcomed. It is considered a sign of a healthy project, one that is converging on an acceptable solution. APF is designed to anticipate change and to accommodate it without incident.

6. Don't Speculate on the Future

If you don't know the future, why plan for it? I first raised that question in Chapter 1. You have learned that APF is designed to minimize the amount of effort spent on non-value-added work. In today's business world, time-to-market is a critical success factor. If we can't figure out how to get a project done faster, our competition will, and we'll lose business. APF departs from TPM in that the Work Breakdown Structure is not developed up-front but rather evolves over time. At the completion of each cycle we expand the WBS to include activities that came into focus as a result of learning and discovery about the solution. The APFist doesn't guess at the contents of the WBS. When activities appear in the WBS, it is because we know that they will be part of the ultimate solution. To do otherwise is to risk spending time planning activities that never contribute to the end result. That wastes time, and APFists don't waste time!

What Do We Still Need to Do?

APF is such a radical departure from what most businesspeople understand project management to be all about that you need some type of orientation program to get executives and business units on board. Anticipating some of the questions they will have, you should include in your orientation program answers to the following.

- What kinds of projects do we have that would benefit from an agile approach?
- What is the Adaptive Project Framework (APF)?
- Why is APF a better approach than the current approaches?
- What is the role of the executive in APF?
- What is the role of the client in APF?
- What should we expect from an APF project?

How Should We Do It?

Training, training, and more training are critical. Initially, the training should come before the first APF project, and it could be at a high (overview) level. During the execution of the project, look for opportunities to include more-detailed training. Use the project as the vehicle for training. This is an excellent way to get the message across that APF is really different, and that every APF project will be different. Share your project experiences across the organization so others will benefit from the learning moments those projects provide. Sharing best (and worst) practices will be valuable, especially early in the history of APF in your organization.

Practice, practice, and more practice are also critical. APF is application-oriented, and only through critically reviewed applications will APF improve over time. Developing APF is an APF project without end! If those of you who use APF will keep me in your experience loop, I will be forever grateful.

The End State of APF

There is no substitute for APF experience. The learning curve can be steep for some people, shallow for others, so be ready to anticipate both. Eventually, the overall experience level of the organization will be fully matured and an APF mindset will prevail!

Having seen the success of APF in actual client practice, I am convinced that it should be the model of choice for every agile project and most extreme projects.

Implementing APF in Your Organization

I recommend selecting one of the following two approaches for implementing APF in your organization.

Top Down

If executive managers recognize the value of having an agile PMLC model in their portfolio of PMLC models and if you have their solid support, then a formal task-force approach is the clear choice.

That approach might go something like the following. We'll use the Kamikazi Software Systems case study to illustrate implementation planning.

Prepare a Project Overview Statement for Executive Endorsement

An example of this type of POS is given in Figure 10.1.

The Problem/Opportunity statement is an obvious statement of the situation. It should be a non-contested statement of the project-management problem Kamikazi is facing. The Goal statement may seem a bit pompous, but it can be defended quite well. Except for APF, all other agile models apply primarily to software-development projects. APF can handle those as

PROJECT OVERVIEW STATEMENT	Project Name APF Implematation		Project No. KSS09-201		Project Manager Harry Kerry PMO Director
Problem/Opportunity					

PROJECT OVERVIEW STATEMENT

Project Name	Project No.	Project Manager
APF Implematation	KSS09-201	Harry Kerry PMO Director

Problem/Opportunity

The frequency of agile and extreme projects of high complexity and uncertainty at Kamikazi Software Systems has been increasing and the current PMLC Model Portfolio does not include an effective approach to such projects. The failure rate of these projects exceeded 70% for the last 50 such projects.

Goal

Design, develop, and deploy the Adaptive Project Framework (APF) as the defacto PMLC Model for all agile and extreme projects.

Objectives

1. Design an APF PMLC Model to accommodate the management needs of all agile and extreme projects.
2. Document the APF PMLC Model.
3. Establish a continuous APF process improvement program.
4. Design, develop, and deploy a training program to accommodate the needs of all executives, project management, business unit managers, and project team members.
5. Deploy APF.

Success Criteria

1. 90% of project managers who use the APF PMLC Model rate it as an improvement over prior PMLC Models they have been using for such projects.
2. Reduce the agile and extreme project failure rate to less than 40% by the end of the first year of implementation for all projects that use the APF PMLC Model.
3. All project managers will have been trained to use the APF PMLC Model as a prerequisite to using the APF PMLC Model.

Assumptions, Risks, Obstacles

1. Executive managers will support a project environment that accommodates the needs of the agile community.
2. Business units will accept their role and become meaningfully involved in agile and extreme projects.
3. Development teams will incorporate the client into the agile project management process.
4. Considering the high risk of agile and extreme projects a 40% maximum project failure rate may not be attainable.

Prepared By	Date	Approved By	Date
Harry Kerry	11-20-2009	Crash dePlane, President	11-23-2009

Figure 10.1
POS for Establishing an APF PMLC Model

well as process design and improvement projects and new product development projects. It is therefore more robust, and can be used as the PMLC model for any type of agile project and most extreme projects. It will serve well as the de facto PMLC model.

The five statements of Objectives are what you would expect. The Success Criteria are quantitative measures that together define successful implementation of APF. The second criterion may not seem too demanding, but consider the fact that agile and extreme projects are very high-risk projects. The Assumptions, Risks, Obstacles statements acknowledge the realities of an agile or extreme environment.

Recruit the APF Task Force

It is critical that the task force be representative of all parties that can affect or will be affected by APF. If there is a Project Management Office, the Director is the best choice for managing the APF implementation project. If you do not have a PMO, the most senior and respected champion of APF—probably a senior-level project manager—would be my recommended choice. Other likely members of the task force are some or all of the following:

- One or two project managers at each position level
- Human-resource managers
- The director of software development
- One or two business analysts at each position level
- A key staff member from each of the major business units

The task force is more of a sounding board for APF than a design and development task force. I see the project as a presentation to the task force of what APF will look like when deployed, along with elicitation of their feedback. There may be several iterations of presentation and feedback before a final APF process is defined and deployed. Even then, there will be further iterations as a result of experience gained in practice. In effect, APF implementation would be approached as an APF project!

Prepare the Project Plan

The Objective statement provides the structure of the plan. It should have five major parts, one for each objective.

Constructing the Work Breakdown Structure (WBS) for Kamikazi Software appeared straightforward, but Harry wasn't willing to assume the WBS was complete. He chose to use a production prototype following one of the Iterative PMLC models. Since most of the solution was known, Harry planned for the first iteration to deliver all that was known about the solution.

Plan and Hold a Kick-off Meeting

The transition from the traditional PMLC model to APF was a big change for the Kamikazi development teams, so Crash and Harry decided to pull out all the stops and make a major event of the APF implementation project launch. They recruited the agile consultant who was the original architect of APF to keynote the kick-off meeting. His objective was to get the company excited about the business value that would follow from the successful application of APF.

Bottom Up

If the organization needs to be convinced of the value of adding an Agile PMLC model to the portfolio of PMLC models, you will have to champion the effort by demonstrating its value through the actual use of APF.

Choose the demonstration project(s) carefully. They should be projects that

- Are critical to the organization
- You feel reasonably comfortable will successfully deliver acceptable business value to the organization
- Will be projects of high risk, but have mitigation plans that will be successful if needed
- Have a sponsor who has the leverage and power in the organization to effectively support and represent the project to executive management; and
- Will have the meaningful involvement of the client

Above all, you don't want a demonstration project to fail!

As I've previously discussed, one of my colleagues is a respected project manager assigned to the PMO. She has adopted a version of the bottom-up approach that is worth commenting on. She simply uses APF on the projects in her portfolio that require an agile approach. Her PMO Director hasn't been too receptive to agile approaches, so my colleague doesn't advertise APF; she just quietly stays under the radar and goes about her business. Fellow project managers note that she is very successful, whereas they are not. Her project failure rate is minimal compared to theirs. They are starting to ask her what she does to achieve such a high success rate. They have effectively opened the door to the spread of APF across the PMO. She is preparing to walk through that door!

Role and Responsibility of Executive Management

Adopting any agile PMLC model in the organization can be a big culture shock for executives who are of the traditional mindset. They are used to supporting well-defined projects with specified deliverables, and must adapt to supporting poorly defined projects with unspecified deliverables. Heavy-handed management approaches will no longer work. Management must be more hands-off in order to give agile project teams the opportunity to be creative. Teams must be trusted to align with the delivery of business value, and to know when a project is not converging on an acceptable solution so must be terminated. This calls for a facilitation approach rather than a compliance approach.

Putting It All Together

APF is a work-in-process. As you know, it was built in the context of recent client engagements, and is not fully baked as of this writing. Even at this early stage of its growth and development, however, APF shows every promise of making a significant mark on contemporary project-management practices.

I welcome any comments. You may reach me at rkw@eiicorp.com.

Discussion Questions

The following questions are posed for your use. Use them to test your understanding and potential application of the materials presented in this chapter. If you are using this book for a course you are teaching, the questions will provoke good class discussion.

1. Discuss how you might incorporate APF under the monitoring and support functions of a PMO.

2. What are the major challenges to implementing APF in an organization that rigidly adheres to TPM approaches?

CareerAgent Overview

CareerAgent is a lifetime career planning, development, and support tool for the on-the-move professional. Professionals first encounter CareerAgent when they are about to enter the workforce. They may have just graduated from college or just completed a tour of duty in the military. Whatever the case, the professional is looking for a first professional position, or for guidance on how to prepare for a first real job.

CareerAgent Functions

CareerAgent is a complete environment for career planning and professional development. It not only helps professionals define their current and target positions, but also identifies training and development needs as they progress along a defined pathway leading from their current to their targeted positions.

CareerAgent provides the following functions.

- Establishes user's current skills profile
- Defines user's target position
- Creates a career path from current to target position
- Establishes a strategy to move to the next position in user's development plan

- Completes on-the-job development activities
- Completes off-the-job development activities
- Updates user's current skills profile
- Revisits user's target position and career path

The Architecture of CareerAgent

CareerAgent consists of a database and an expert system that uses the database to provide the functions listed above.

It is best to think of the CareerAgent data infrastructure in several layers. At the highest level, the level with which the individual interacts directly, is a matrix with six columns (sectors) and five rows (position levels).

Sectors

CareerAgent defines the six professional sectors shown in Table A.1.

Table A.1 Characteristics of the Six Sectors

Sector Label	Characteristics of this Sector
T	These professionals understand technology and can discuss it in great detail. They are not particularly interested in the business applications of the technology, but enjoy working with the technology as an end in itself.
Tb	These technology professionals understand the language of business but they are not able to take proactive positions in solving business problems. They are able to react to requests from the business side for technology solutions.
TB	These technology professionals are equally comfortable discussing technology and business. They can be expected to proactively suggest technological solutions to business problems. They know how to exploit technology for business value.
BT	These business professionals are equally comfortable discussing business and technology. They can be expected to proactively suggest business solutions using technology. They know how to exploit technology for business value.

Table A.1   Characteristics of the Six Sectors (Continued)

Sector Label	Characteristics of this Sector
Bt	These business professionals understand the language of technology but they are not able to take proactive positions in using technology to solve business problems. They are able to react to suggestions from the technology side for solutions to their business problems.
B	These professionals understand the business and can discuss it in great detail. They are not particularly interested in, nor do they understand, technology applications for their businesses.

Position Levels

CareerAgent uses the five position levels shown in Table A.2.

Table A.2   CareerAgent's Five Position Levels and Their Characteristics

Position Level	Essential Characteristics at This Position Level
Individual Contributor	• Operates in a supervised environment with frequent review. • Is familiar with and uses all applicable methods, procedures, and standards. • Demonstrates effective oral and written communication skill. • Is able to learn new technical information as required. • Demonstrates an analytical approach to problem solving. • Has acquired a broad understanding of the discipline. • Is able to plan, schedule, and monitor own work.
Project Manager	• Responsible for substantial technical decision making associated with team leadership and project management. • Thoroughly familiar with the available tools, templates, and processes associated with project management. • Is able to apply selected tools, templates, and processes to meet set targets for scope, cost, time, and quality. • Is able to communicate effectively both formally and informally with all those with whom working interfaces arise. • Shows initiative, ensures that general competencies are current. • Possesses a clear understanding of the relationship of any specialized role (such as business analyst or software developer) to the context in which the work is carried out.

Continues

Table A.2   CareerAgent's Five Position Levels and Their Characteristics (Continued)

Position Level	Essential Characteristics at This Position Level
Manager	• Has defined responsibility and authority for decision making, or an advisory function having direct bearing on the work of a project manager. • Has a technical background of sufficient depth and breadth to be able to recognize and successfully exploit opportunities for effective development or usage of his or her area of expertise and to lead and manage fully experienced reporting project managers. • Demonstrates a high level of presentation skill applicable to all levels of audience. • Plays a senior role in formulating strategy and policy. • Has specific management responsibility for a specialized activity, which normally includes full budgetary and policy implementation authority for a significant overall function or a significant segment of a larger unit (such as program-manager or project-management office).
Director	• Has defined responsibility and authority for decision making, or an advisory function having direct bearing on the work of a business unit or major function (for example, Director of a project-management office). • Has a technical background of sufficient depth and breadth to be able to recognize and successfully exploit opportunities for effective development or usage of her or his area of expertise and to lead and manage fully experienced reporting managers. • Demonstrates a high level of presentation skill applicable to all levels of audience. • Plays a senior role in formulating strategy and policy. • Has specific management responsibility for a specialized activity, which normally includes full budgetary and policy implementation authority for a significant overall function or a significant segment of a larger unit.
Executive	• Has defined responsibility and authority for decision making, or an advisory function having direct bearing on the entire business (for example, Vice President of Projects). • Has a business background of sufficient depth and breadth to be able to recognize and successfully exploit opportunities and lead directors and senior managers. • Demonstrates a high level of presentation skill applicable to all levels of audience, both internal and external. • Takes a leadership role in formulating strategy and policy. • Has full budgetary and policy implementation authority for the business.

The position levels can be adjusted to fit any organization's position families and levels. For example, Project Manager will often be divided into several levels such as Team Leader, Assistant Project Manager, Associate Project Manager, Project Manager, and Senior Project Manager. The larger the organization, the greater the number of levels defined.

Role Levels

Embedded in the cells of the CareerAgent matrix are eleven role levels (0–10), shown in Table A.3.

Table A.3 Role Levels

LEVEL	STAFF	CONSULTANT	MANAGEMENT
0	Trainee		
1	Assistant Technician		
2	Associate Technician		
3	Technician		
4	Senior Technician		
5		Assistant Consultant	Supervisor
6		Associate Consultant	Assistant Manager
7		Consultant	Associate Manager
8		Senior Consultant	Senior Manager
9			Director
10			Executive

Figure A.1 provides a generic chart of this layer of CareerAgent.

From Figure A.1, you can see that CareerAgent defines a dual-ladder career path. At the project level, the individual has two choices for moving forward. One is as an individual contributor following the consultant track. The other is as a manager following the managerial track. This is only a

Figure A.1
Enterprise
Structure Model
Role Structure

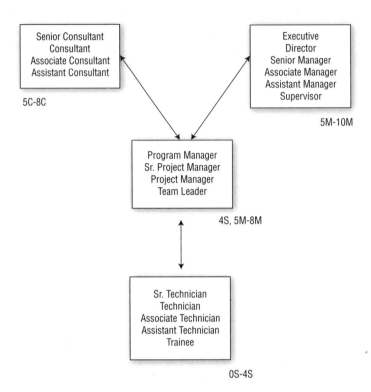

ESM
Generic Role & Role Level Structure

Senior Consultant
Consultant
Associate Consultant
Assistant Consultant

5C-8C

Executive
Director
Senior Manager
Associate Manager
Assistant Manager
Supervisor

5M-10M

Program Manager
Sr. Project Manager
Project Manager
Team Leader

4S, 5M-8M

Sr. Technician
Technician
Associate Technician
Assistant Technician
Trainee

0S-4S

surface-level characterization of CareerAgent. CareerAgent is much deeper and broader, as the next section describes.

The CareerAgent Position Playing Field

The CareerAgent Position Playing Field is the highest-level description of the playing field. At this level, CareerAgent presents the individual with a graphic picture of the position landscape. Figure A.2 depicts this level.

Every position that exists or will ever exist can be mapped into a single cell within this landscape. This graphic is used to map the individual's current position and target position, and the pathway that will be followed to reach the target position.

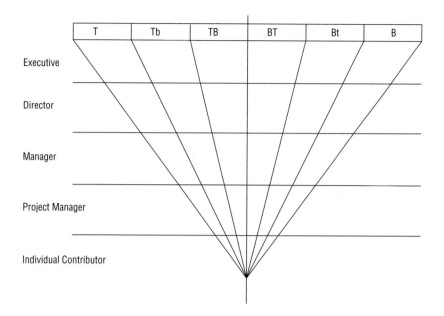

Figure A.2
Career Agent
Landscape

Index

C

CareerAgent
  architecture of, 336
  functions, 335–336
  position levels of, 337–339
  Position Playing Field, 340–341
  professional sectors defined, 336–337
  role levels of, 339–340
case scenarios (requirements elicitation), 120
case studies
  Kamikazi Software Systems. *See* Kamikazi Software Systems study
  overview of, 20–24
  PDQ prioritized Scope Triangle. *See* PDQ prioritized Scope Triangle study
  Snacks Fifth Avenue kiosk design. *See* Snacks Fifth Avenue kiosk design study
  Try & Buy Department Stores. *See* Try & Buy Department Stores study
change
  for better solutions (APF value), 71–72
  change-management process in extreme projects, 288
  encouraged in APF, 80
  as progress (APF core value), 328
Chaos Report 2007, 105, 152
clear/not clear goals, 325
Client Checkpoint phase (APF)
  in APF life cycle, 79–80, 131
  APF project reviews, 246
  artifacts of, 237
  continuing project to next cycle, 241–242
  COS and POS reviews, 246
  cumulative deliverables meeting expectations, 240–241
  decision-making styles, 243–244
  determining deliverables for next cycle, 242
  identifying next cycle swim lane contents, 237–238
  inputs to, 220
  inputs to next cycle planning activity, 234–237
  learning and discovery results, 221
  next cycle, 245
  next cycle length, 239–240
  overview, 217–220
  in PDQ study, 247–250
  planned vs. actual functions/features added, 220–221
  priority of remaining functionalities, 242
  probative swim lane results, 228–229
  questions to be answered, 229–233
  reprioritized list of functionality/features for solution integration, 239
  reprioritized list of probative swim lane ideas, 239
  restarting projects, 243
  Scope Bank overview, 221–223
  Scope Bank status reporting, 223–227
  for testing feasibility, 214
  updating RBS, 227–228
client teams
  defined, 31–32
  evaluating use of APF by, 261
  evaluating workings of, 233
  meaningful involvement with APF projects, 262–263
  profile of, 17
clients
  budget/deadline changes by (APF), 312
  client-driven value (APF), 69–70, 327
  client-facing approach, 218
  client-focused value (APF), 68–69, 326–327
  defined, 31
  meaningful involvement of, 313–316
  role in APF, 63–64
  wants vs. needs of, 3–4

I

iconic prototyping probative swim
  lanes, 157
Idea Generation phase (DSDM),
  55–56
ideas
    evaluating/prioritizing (Couger
      model), 199–202
    generating, 199
    Idea Proposed (Scrum flow), 53
Implementation phase (DSDM), 57
improvement opportunities (Post-
  version Review), 261–263
Inception phase (RUP), 48
incremental models, TPM, 40–43
incremental results (APF core value),
  327
Incubate phase (INSPIRE), 301–303
in-depth discussion probative swim
  lanes, 157
information-gathering probative swim
  lanes, 157
INitiate phase (INSPIRE), 292–296
inputs
    to Client Checkpoint phase, 220
    to next cycle planning activity,
      234–237
INSPIRE
  (INitiate/SPeculate/Incubate/
  REview)
    defined, 285
    Incubate phase, 301–303
    INitiate phase, 292–296
    process, 89
    REview phase, 303–305
    SPeculate phase, 296–300
integrative swim lanes
    basics of, 157–160
    Cycle Build phase, 208–209
    defined, 33
    for next cycle, 245
    tracking size of, 225–227
interdependent variables affecting
  project management, 7–8
interviews (requirements elicitation),
  119
inventory management subsystem
  (PDQ study), 115–116, 187

IRACIS (Increased Revenue or
  Avoided Costs or Improved
  Services), 20, 127
Iron Triangle, PMBOK, 84
issue tracking/resolution (APF cycles),
  177–178
Issues Log, 178, 195–197, 236
iterative models (APM), 44–48

J

Java™ Modeling in Color with UML
  (Prentice Hall), 42–43
just-in-time planning (APF), 61

K

Kamikazi Software Systems study
    documenting SDPM process,
      266–267
    overview, 22–23
    POS for, 112
    prototype documentation system,
      215
    SDPM improvement, 88
kick-off meetings (APF), 141–142,
  332–333
kiosk design. *See* Snacks Fifth Avenue
  study

L

Late Finish Dates/Late Start Dates,
  276
Learn phase (ASD), 50
learning and discovery results (Client
  Checkpoint phase), 221
Life Cycle, APF project management,
  95, 218
linear models, TPM, 38–40
locator subsystem (PDQ study), 114
logistics subsystem (PDQ), 115,
  185–186
Logs
    Issues Log, 178, 195–197
    Risk Log, 178

FREE Online Edition

Your purchase of **Adaptive Project Framework** includes access to a free online edition for 45 days through the Safari Books Online subscription service. Nearly every Addison-Wesley Professional book is available online through Safari Books Online, along with more than 5,000 other technical books and videos from publishers such as Cisco Press, Exam Cram, IBM Press, O'Reilly, Prentice Hall, Que, and Sams.

SAFARI BOOKS ONLINE allows you to search for a specific answer, cut and paste code, download chapters, and stay current with emerging technologies.

Activate your FREE Online Edition at www.informit.com/safarifree

> **STEP 1:** Enter the coupon code: YHURSZG.

> **STEP 2:** New Safari users, complete the brief registration form. Safari subscribers, just log in.

If you have difficulty registering on Safari or accessing the online edition, please e-mail customer-service@safaribooksonline.com